Improving
School-to-Work
Transitions

David Neumark
Editor

Russell Sage Foundation • New York

The Russell Sage Foundation

The Russell Sage Foundation, one of the oldest of America's general purpose foundations, was established in 1907 by Mrs. Margaret Olivia Sage for "the improvement of social and living conditions in the United States." The Foundation seeks to fulfill this mandate by fostering the development and dissemination of knowledge about the country's political, social, and economic problems. While the Foundation endeavors to assure the accuracy and objectivity of each book it publishes, the conclusions and interpretations in Russell Sage Foundation publications are those of the authors and not of the Foundation, its Trustees, or its staff. Publication by Russell Sage, therefore, does not imply Foundation endorsement.

Library of Congress Cataloging-in-Publication Data

Improving school-to-work transitions / David Neumark, editor.
    p. cm.
  ISBN-13: 978-0-87154-642-5
  ISBN-10: 0-87154-642-6
  1. Career education—United States. 2. School-to-work transition—United States. I. Neumark, David.
  LC1037.5.I477 2007
  370.11'3—dc22

                            2006027801

The paper used in this publication meets the minimum requirements of American National Standard for Information Sciences—Permanence of Paper for Printed Library Materials. ANSI Z39.48-1992.

Text design by Suzanne Nichols.

RUSSELL SAGE FOUNDATION
112 East 64th Street, New York, New York 10021
10 9 8 7 6 5 4 3 2 1

Contents

Contributors

David Neumark is professor of economics at the University of California, Irvine, senior fellow at the Public Policy Institute of California, research associate at the NBER, and research fellow at IZA.

Oscar A. Aliaga is research associate at the National Research Center for Career and Technical Education at the University of Minnesota.

Thomas Bailey is director of the Institute on Education and the Economy and the Community College Research Center and is George and Abby O'Neill Professor of Economics and Education in the Department of International and Transcultural Studies at Teachers College, Columbia University.

Charles Dayton is director of the Career Academy Support Network at the University of California, Berkeley.

Laura E. Hill is a research fellow at the Public Policy Institute of California.

Katherine L. Hughes is assistant director for work and education reform research at the Institute on Education and the Economy and the Community College Research Center, Teachers College, Columbia University.

Christopher Jepsen is associate director of the Center for Business and Economic Research at the University of Kentucky.

Melinda Mechur Karp is senior research associate at the Institute on Education and the Economy and the Community College Research Center, Teachers College, Columbia University.

Gregory S. Kienzl is research analyst at the American Institutes for Research.

Andrew Maul is a Ph.D. student at the Graduate School of Education, University of California, Berkeley.

Nan L. Maxwell is professor and chair of the Department of Economics and director of the Human Investment Research and Education (HIRE) Center at California State University, East Bay.

Margaret Terry Orr is on the faculty of Bank Street College in the Department of Educational Leadership.

Ann E. Person is a doctoral candidate in Human Development and Social Policy at Northwestern University.

Deborah Reed is director of the population program at the Public Policy Institute of California.

James E. Rosenbaum is professor of sociology, education, and social policy at the Institute for Policy Research at Northwestern University.

Donna Rothstein is research economist at the U.S. Bureau of Labor Statistics.

David Stern is professor of education at the University of California, Berkeley.

James R. Stone III is professor of work and human resource education in the College of Education and Human Development at the University of Minnesota, and director of the National Research Center for Career and Technical Education.

Christopher Wu is a consultant and data integration lead for the Edusoft Assessment Management System.

Chapter 1

Improving School-to-Work Transitions: Introduction

David Neumark

An array of programs, policies, and institutions in the United States attempts to improve the transitions of youths from school to work. These components of the educational system have taken a back seat in the past decade to educational reform focused on measurable academic outcomes, as reflected in the No Child Left Behind Act of 2001 (NCLB). However, a key criterion for assessing educational quality is whether education enhances labor-market success. Although there is a link between test scores and socioeconomic success, it is doubtful that a focus on testing and academic preparation encompasses all of what schools do to prepare students for the world of work. Most notably, perhaps, many students will not attend four-year postsecondary institutions or even attain any postsecondary education, and the implicit or explicit focus on college preparation that is encouraged by a strong emphasis on testing may serve these students particularly poorly. Despite the shift toward test-based reforms, there are still many extant programs, policies, and institutions that seek more directly to improve school-to-work transitions. This book aims to provide up-to-date, high-quality evidence on the effectiveness of these efforts, whom they help, and how they might be improved.

THE SCHOOL-TO-WORK TRANSITION

The school-to-work transition, as reflected in both research and policy discussions, encompasses two segments of the life cycle of young

1

people. The first is the segment during which students make decisions that shape the links between their schooling and their future
career, including both the content of their education and its duration.
The second is the segment in which young people leave school and
begin to work in the types of jobs that begin to mark the course of
their future careers, in contrast to the part-time or part-year jobs in
which they sometimes work while in school. These two segments of
the life cycle can overlap, and their chronology over the life cycle
can vary from person to person.

The school-to-work transition is to a large extent a phenomenon
of modern economies in societies with mass schooling in which
youths spend many years in general academic education before
entering the workplace; the question then arises of how to connect
schooling and work. This is not the place for a historical inquiry
as to why the school-to-work transition has taken on this particular form. But as documented, for example, in Claudia Goldin and
Lawrence Katz (2003), secondary school enrollment rates soared
in the first half of the twentieth century (from about 18 percent in
1910 to 71 percent in 1940).[1] Some scholars (for example, Kett 1982)
argue that part of the driver for the rise of mass schooling was rapid
industrial change at the end of the nineteenth century, which dimin-
ished the role of crafts and therefore weakened apprenticeship as
an institution for acquiring workplace skills. At the same time, continuing technological change also made it impossible for apprenticeship, even if it had evolved, to provide the numbers of skilled
workers needed. It is perhaps not coincidental, then, that the first
federal efforts supporting vocational education, the Smith-Hughes
Act of 1917, originated in this period.

THE SCHOOL-TO-WORK "PROBLEM"

Despite these earlier developments, however, the identification of
the school-to-work transition as a major "problem" to be addressed
by policy did not arise until the latter part of the twentieth century.
Jacob A. Klerman and Lynn A. Karoly (1995) discuss perspectives
aired during the 1980s and 1990s emphasizing the failures occur-
ring in the transition from high school to work (see, for example,
Rosenbaum et al. 1990). Government reports described school-

to-work transitions as "chaotic," entailing unnecessary periods of joblessness and excessive job instability (U.S. General Accounting Office 1990).

These concerns with youths' unstable attachment to the labor market receive some support from research in labor economics. Drawing on both theory and evidence regarding the human-capital model, this research emphasizes the higher productivity and wages that derive from labor-market experience and job tenure, highlighting the potential costs of time spent churning between many jobs and of repeated spells of nonemployment during the school-to-work transition, as well as the cost of leaving school prematurely (see, for example, Becker 1993; Mincer 1974).

At the same time, the view of school-to-work transitions in this period as problematic can be questioned on two grounds. First, labor economists have noted the potential gains from job search, especially early in the career (Topel and Ward 1992)—a search that may entail moving from job to job and likely experiencing intervening periods of joblessness. Second, Klerman and Karoly (1995) note that the empirical descriptions on which assessments of failure in school-to-work transitions were based may not be accurate. Earlier, Paul Osterman (1980) presented a more nuanced view, suggesting that many youths, prior to settling into quality jobs, initially experience a period of relatively unstable attachment accompanied by many other activities of youths,[2] although some do fail to make a successful transition.[3] Later, though, Osterman and Maria Iannozzi (1993) suggested that the problem of settling down into quality jobs had become more severe for the non-college-bound. Klerman and Karoly's quantitative work confirms the heterogeneity of school-to-work transitions, while documenting that many youths manage to settle into relatively stable jobs. At the same time, their work also shows that a sizable number of youths do not settle into stable jobs—youths more concentrated among high school dropouts than high school graduates. In chapter 2 of this volume, Deborah Reed, Christopher Jepsen, and Laura E. Hill provide up-to-date evidence on school-to-work transitions and on some of the particular issues that arise in the current context, such as school-to-work transitions among immigrant youth.

The issue of the quality of the job into which an individual settles is an important one—highlighted by growing wage inequality, and reminding us that the stability or instability of early labor-market attachment is not the sole barometer of the success of school-to-work transitions. The quality of this job may be influenced by the stability of early labor-market experience, as well as the quality and quantity of education and the links between education and the job. Recent research that tries to estimate the consequences of early job stability from exogenous sources of variation in this stability points to net negative effects from job changing early in the career (Neumark 2002), suggesting that even if most individuals do settle into stable jobs, there are costs to the early instability experienced by youths. Educational research has focused more on the links between education and jobs, emphasizing the school-to-work problem from the perspective of weak links between secondary education and the labor market that reduce students' engagement in school and inhibit transitions into higher-paying (as well as more stable) jobs (see, for example, Hamilton and Hamilton 1999; Hughes, Bailey, and Mechur 2001; Stern et al. 1995).

PROGRAMS, POLICIES, AND INSTITUTIONS ADDRESSING THE SCHOOL-TO-WORK TRANSITION

Policies addressing the school-to-work transition have a long history. As noted earlier, vocational education (later christened "career and technical education") has been supported by the federal government since the Smith-Hughes Act of 1917.[4] For decades, vocational education was distinguished by its isolation from more comprehensive high school curricula (Hayward and Benson 1993), sometimes reflecting the perspective that vocational education programs served students "better suited to applied than academic learning" (Donahoe and Tienda 1999). In the 1980s and early 1990s, however—concurrent with the emergence of concern over the school-to-work "problem"—dissatisfaction with vocational education crested. As argued by Marie Cohen and Douglas J. Besharov (2002), the dissatisfaction with vocational education was spurred in part by concern over the academic skills of the American workforce—as argued in *A Nation at Risk* (U.S. Department of Education 1983)—and perceptions that vocational education had become an "educational backwater" for the disadvantaged and the disabled (U.S. Department of Education 1994).

As a result, the focus of vocational education began to shift toward efforts that integrate academic and vocational skills. A major effort in this direction was the development of an approach called Tech Prep (Ryan 2001), in which some vocational education is introduced into comprehensive high school curricula while vocational education is sequenced during high school with two years of further related study at postsecondary institutions. Tech Prep received a major impetus from the reauthorization, in 1990, of the Carl D. Perkins Applied Technology and Vocational Education Act. In chapter 3, James R. Stone III and Oscar A. Aliaga provide additional information on these policy developments, and present descriptive information on contemporaneous participation in these various types of vocational education (and in school-to-work programs, discussed later).

The second major effort toward integrating academic and vocational skills was the development of "career academies," "schools within schools" that integrate academics with general job readiness and preparation in a particular career field. Chapter 5, by David Stern, Christopher Wu, Charles Dayton, and Andrew Maul, and chapter 6, by Margaret Terry Orr, Thomas Bailey, Katherine L. Hughes, Gregory S. Kienzl, and Melinda Mechur Karp, provide more information on the development of career academies and present evidence on their effectiveness; these chapters also discuss, in different ways, issues arising in the implementation of the career-academy model in schools.

Where Tech Prep was a specific response to the perception that academic skills had to be bolstered for career- and technical-education students, during the early and mid-1990s a perspective coalesced around more general concerns with school-to-work transitions in the United States, stemming from a lack of connections between school and work for the much larger set of students pursuing comprehensive curricula. Government reports described the existing school-to-work system as producing youths who were "unmotivated in school and spend years bouncing from one low-paying job to another" (U.S. Congress, Office of Technology Assessment 1995, 3). Researchers and others advocated that the United States adopt a more orderly school-to-work system, like that of the German apprenticeship system or the informal contracts between Japanese schools and employers (Commission on the Skills of the American Workforce 1990; Hamilton 1990; Lerman and Pouncy 1990; Glazer 1993; and other work reviewed in Heckman 1993).

These perspectives provided much of the impetus for the School-to-Work Opportunities Act (STWOA), passed in 1994. This act sought to create an integrated system of youth education, job training, and labor-market information, to provide a faster and more successful transition from school to stable employment. As described in the act,[5] Congress passed the STWOA in response to three areas of particular concern for public education: (1) a lack of connection between school and work that led many youths to be unmotivated in school and to experience subsequent difficulty moving out of low-wage jobs; (2) youths completing school with insufficient skills needed for the labor market; and (3) increasing labor-market demands for complex thinking, close teamwork, and the ability to learn on the job. The STWOA encouraged the development of programs aimed at helping young people develop the skills needed in the workforce and make better connections to careers through school-to-work transition systems.

The STWOA provided $1.5 billion of federal funding to support the development of school-to-work initiatives by the states. The federal funding was intended to serve as seed money to establish school-to-work transition systems that included formal partnerships among secondary and postsecondary institutions and employers. Research has established that in many states the legislation did spur the development of such systems (see, for instance, Hershey, Silverberg, and Haimson 1999; Neumark and Allen 2003; Neumark 2006). For example, a national evaluation by Mathematica Policy Research, a non-partisan research firm, of the implementation of the STWOA (Hershey, Silverberg, and Haimson 1999) documented that by 1997 more than 83 percent of secondary school districts in states with federal STWOA grants had established school-to-work partnerships.[6] However, this evaluation also offered some cautions regarding implementation, and characterized overall progress on the STWOA agenda as "modest" because school-to-work implementation was not seen as "at the core of states' high-priority education reforms" (1). Moreover, after its initial five years the STWOA was not reauthorized. As a result, funding for school-to-work activities has in some cases been cut drastically, although many states stepped into the breach with limited funding.[7] The reduced funding has legitimated concerns expressed in the Mathematica evaluation regarding whether states or local partners would continue to fund partnerships if and when federal funding ended.

Although the STWOA has been described as stemming from more general concerns about school-to-work transitions than those addressed by Tech Prep, the school-to-work programs envisioned under the STWOA can in fact be viewed in two ways: as the logical extension of efforts to integrate academic and vocational education for the traditional target audience of those bound for at most two-year degrees; and alternatively as a substantial expansion of the integration of vocational and academic education calling for school-to-work programs for all students. As Cohen and Besharov (2002) point out, both of these themes can be found in the STWOA.

Certainly the STWOA was based in part on concerns about disadvantaged and non-college-bound youths and their problems in achieving a successful school-to-work transition. And school-to-work practitioners and advocates commonly argue that school-to-work programs like those encouraged by the STWOA are especially helpful for the "forgotten half"—the non-college-bound among whom the less-advantaged are concentrated.[8] But the broader target population is reflected in the fact that the STWOA was less restricted to pathways that lead through community or technical colleges, instead making school-to-work available to all students and including paths that lead to four-year colleges and universities. And the STWOA was less explicitly geared toward "underserved populations" such as minorities, women, and the economically disadvantaged. Finally, Cohen and Besharov also note the findings from the national evaluation of the STWOA (Hershey, Silverberg, and Haimson 1999) that, in its implementation, programs targeting the non-college-bound were less common. The chapter I wrote with Donna Rothstein assesses evidence as to whether the types of programs encouraged by the STWOA in fact tend to deliver greater benefits to this "forgotten half."

Finally, it is important to emphasize that although much of the action surrounding school-to-work occurs in high schools, community colleges and occupational colleges play an important role. (In the case of Tech Prep, of course, the role is explicit and integrated with high school education.) But as pointed out by W. Norton Grubb (2001), among others, community colleges now play an important role in the workplace preparation of lower-skilled adults, and this is true of occupational colleges in particular. Thus, a comprehensive look at programs, policies, and institutions that address the school-to-work transition should also cover these post-secondary institutions. Chapter 7, by Ann E. Person and James E. Rosenbaum, looks explicitly at what community and occupational colleges do (or should do) to enhance their students' transitions to the workplace.

TERMINOLOGY

It is useful at this point to clarify terminology. My choice of the generic if somewhat circumlocutory phrase "programs, policies, and institutions that address school-to-work transitions" is intentional. I deliberately do not lump all of these under the heading "school-to-work programs." Not until the STWOA was passed did the phrase "school-to-work program" came into popular use. For example, *The Forgotten Half,* a report issued in 1988, although clearly concerned with issues of transitions from school to work, did not refer to school-to-work programs, but the 1998 report *The Forgotten Half Revisited* uses this phrase in discussing the STWOA (William T. Grant Foundation 1988, 1998). Thus, "school-to-work programs" is too narrow. It does not include career and technical education, and certainly not the community and occupational college efforts at labor-market linkages. In this book, "school-to-work programs" is used to refer to the types of programs encouraged by the STWOA, such as mentoring, internships, apprenticeships, and so forth. The classification of Tech Prep is more ambiguous. It sometimes comes under the label of "school-to-work programs," because of its classi-fication in government surveys as well as qualitative evidence about what STWOA grantees did,[9] but Tech Prep could also be viewed as distinct, at least from a policy perspective, because it is attributable to the Perkins legislation.[10] Regardless, as the preceding discussion makes clear, efforts to improve school-to-work transitions are broader and include career and technical education more generally as well as the efforts of postsecondary institutions—hence the use of the more encompassing term to refer to programs, policies, and institutions. The phrase "school-to-work efforts" is sometimes used as shorthand.

In addition, school-to-work efforts sometimes involve encouraging students to get more education prior to entering the workforce. Tech Prep is a prime example of this. Thus, some programs and policies might be thought of as "school-to-school-to-work." Alternatively, given that the broader goal is to improve youths' career decision-making, which may often entail further education, some states adopted the label "school-to-career." In this book "school-to-work" is used as a general term to refer to the entire process of transitioning from school to work, recognizing that there may be multiple schooling "stops" along the way.

OVERVIEW AND CHAPTER CONTENTS

The chapters of this book contribute to our knowledge about programs, policies, and institutions in the United States that seek to improve school-to-work transitions. The book begins with descriptive evidence on school-to-work transitions in recent years, emphasizing differences across demographic and immigrant groups that now represent a large share of the youth population—differences that condition how school-to-work policy efforts might best target different groups. Next, it turns to descriptive evidence on participation of high school students in the various types of programs or curricula that aim to improve school-to-work transitions, to provide a snapshot of this participation after a period of school-to-work-related policy reform in the 1990s.

Chapters 4, 5, and 6 present new research on the effectiveness of the programs that aim to improve school-to-work transitions, how these effects are distributed, and how school-to-work efforts might be improved. These chapters all share a common conceptual framework of estimating the treatment effects of school-to-work programs, although each chapter considers a different angle. Chapter 4 explores whether—as is often asserted—school-to-work programs are particularly effective for the non-college-bound. Chapters 5 and 6 examine the efforts of career academies. Chapter 5 focuses on incorporating information on implementation of the career-academy model into estimates of the model's effects and on the potentially symbiotic relationship between studying the impacts of career academies and monitoring and improving their effectiveness. Chapter 6 presents a detailed analysis of the effectiveness of a well-implemented career-academy model.

Chapters 7 and 8 turn to the role of institutions and possible institutional changes that can enhance school-to-work transitions. Chapter 7 moves beyond high school to study community and occupational colleges. It emphasizes labor-market linkages at these institutions—both how these institutions develop such linkages and how they help students. Chapter 8 looks at survey data for one particular labor market, to try to link information on the skills employers are demanding in a local labor market to information on the skills students are supplying, and to find out how students' skills influence school-to-work transitions. The goal is to highlight, in this particular case, what skills are valued in the labor market, and explore how schools might become better attuned to the skills demanded by employers and do more to provide students with these skills. A common theme in the final two chapters is the importance of information about labor markets in efforts to improve school-to-work transitions, and the implications of this for educational institutions. More detailed summaries of the chapters follow.

Descriptive Evidence
on School-to-Work Transitions

Deborah Reed, Christopher Jepsen, and Laura Hill document differences in school-to-work transitions across demographic groups and between immigrants and nonimmigrants, which is important given the increased diversity and higher immigrant share among the youth population, and the imperative to think about what types of programs best address the needs of different groups. Their analysis is based on data from the U.S. Census of Population and the National Educational Longitudinal Study (NELS).

Between 1980 and 2000, the share of the population aged thirteen to twenty-four that is native-born white declined from 75 to 61 percent; it is projected to decline to 55 percent by 2020. The African American share has remained fairly constant, but the Hispanic share rose sharply since 1980 to 16 percent in 2000, and is projected to increase to 22 percent by 2020. The authors document a wide variety of dimensions along which several nonwhite native-born groups have school-to-work transitions that may be viewed as less successful: a higher likelihood of single motherhood or a teen birth (for women); lower likelihood of high school completion; less college education and lower earnings; and a higher share neither working nor in school. The authors also document similar patterns of less successful school-to-work transitions for immigrants from Mexico, and more successful transitions for Asian immigrants.

Reed, Jepsen, and Hill find that differences in family and school characteristics account for many of the racial and ethnic differences in educational attainment and teen fertility, although not as much for successful transitions to work (for those who do not obtain a bachelor's degree). In the case of Mexican immigrants, some of the differences in schooling attainment are attributable to these immigrants coming as teenagers and not enrolling in school in the United States. This evidence suggests that it is important that those who design and evaluate school-to-work programs consider the programs' potentially different impacts on different demographic groups, and perhaps target some groups of minorities as a way of improving later labor-market outcomes for them. This chapter also raises the possibility that for immigrant groups, such as Mexicans, who come for employment but have low school enrollment rates, school-to-work policies might consider focusing on programs to attract youths into schools rather than targeting those already in school. In addition, the large share of Mexican immigrants among youths points to the potential value of including language training in school-to-work efforts.

Participation in Career and Technical Education and School-to-Work Programs

Chapter 3, by James Stone III and Oscar Aliaga, in which they use data from the new 1997 National Longitudinal Survey of Youth (NLSY97), provides a rich description of participation in secondary education programs with a career focus. The chapter examines not only school-to-work programs but also career and technical education, which is often viewed as narrower than school-to-work. Career and technical education is typically defined as course work in a specific occupational or vocational program, whereas school-to-work encompasses a broader set of programs covering career majors, Tech Prep, and a set of school-to-work activities that Stone and Aliaga characterize as "work based," including job shadowing, cooperative education, workplace mentoring, school-based enterprise programs, and internships and apprenticeships. The authors place the types of activities and concentrations that they study within the broader context of the history of educational policy relating to vocational education, Tech Prep, and school-to-work, elaborating on some of the history outlined earlier. They then use the NLSY97 to provide a picture at the end of a decade of school-to-work-related policy reform of who participates in these various types of programs or curricula.

On the basis of self-reported curriculum concentration, the authors find rather low participation in career and technical education, with about 12.5 percent of high school students identifying themselves as either career and technical education (CTE) concentrators or dual-career (CTE and academic) concentrators, as opposed to academic or general concentrators. In contrast, 32.7 percent of high school students report participation in career majors, and just under one-half report participation in at least one of the specific school-to-work activities just listed, with the largest share in job shadowing. The authors also study the overlap between career and technical education and dual concentration and participation in school-to-work programs, and find that these concentrators are significantly more likely to participate in school-to-work than are general or academic concentrators. Stone and Aliaga document the socioeconomic and demographic differences between those who do and do not participate in the different programs and concentrations, finding that CTE and general concentrators come from lower socioeconomic backgrounds, are more likely to be minorities, and are less well prepared academically. Finally, they note that although the number of CTE concentrators is small, many students take CTE courses, and the number of such courses taken does not differ that much between CTE and other concentrators. Thus, they conclude that CTE has become an important part of the high school experience and raise the concern that the No Child

Left Behind policy's emphasis on academic course work is likely to come at the expense of school-to-work and CTE.

School-to-Work and the "Forgotten Half"

School-to-work advocates and practitioners commonly argue that school-to-work programs are particularly helpful for less-advantaged youths, or the broader group of those who in the absence of any intervention are unlikely to attend college—often termed the "forgotten half." As noted earlier, this perspective was reflected in the STWOA, which referred specifically to the problems that disadvantaged and minority youths face in making the school-to-work transition. The main goal of chapter 4 is to use the information on school-to-work programs in the NLSY97, described in chapter 3, to examine evidence of the absolute and relative effectiveness of school-to-work programs for the forgotten half—those less likely to attend college. We use an estimated model of college attendance to classify those in the NLSY97 in terms of whether they were more or less likely to attend college, and then to estimate models for the effects of participation in a variety of school-to-work programs on education- and employment-related outcomes, testing for differences in program effects for those less likely to attend college.

The data provide some evidence that school-to-work program participation is particularly advantageous for men in the forgotten half, with respect to both schooling and work-related outcomes. Mentoring and co-op programs increase these men's postsecondary education, and co-op, school enterprise, and internship and apprenticeship programs boost their employment and decrease idleness after leaving high school.[11] In contrast, there is less evidence of such beneficial effects of these measures for other men, especially on schooling. The evidence that school-to-work programs are particularly beneficial for women in the forgotten half is more limited to work-related outcomes, especially the finding that internship and apprenticeship programs lead to positive earnings effects for these women, measured early in the life cycle. Overall, the evidence suggests that there may be substantial benefits from school-to-work efforts targeted at male high school students whose characteristics and backgrounds make them less likely to attend college, and there may also be labor-market benefits for women in this group.

Career Academies

Chapters 5 and 6 look at career academies, a type of school-to-work program that has had a quite high profile. Career academies are high school programs directed toward a particular broad career area and provide context for some of the academic instruction. They also have work-based components such as internships and other career exploration activities. David Stern, Christopher Wu, Charles Dayton, and Andrew Maul in chapter 5 present two types of analysis. First, they report on how the Career Academy Support Network (CASN) uses transcript data to monitor implementation of career academies and describe some standard evaluation-type results on the effects of these academies. In the more innovative part of the chapter the authors construct measures of career-academy implementation and then try to establish whether the measures are associated with more effective career academies. This is an important effort because there may be a gulf between simply establishing a program and actually implementing an effective one, and in many cases researchers have little or no knowledge about implementation. In addition, of course, understanding how implementation influences the effectiveness of career academies (or other programs) is invaluable to practitioners.

The strongest evidence of the effects of career academies is that participants are more likely to remain in their high schools, although the authors do not know whether those who do not remain in their high school drop out or simply move elsewhere. They also find that academy students have increased attendance, but they find no evidence of improvement in terms of credits earned or reduced disciplinary problems, and they find even a hint of lower grades. The authors are quite frank, however, in pointing to the limitations of these estimates as causal effects, and speculate that the greater "holding power" of academies may depress the observed achievements of academy students, because the academies are more likely to retain poor performers. When the authors try to ask whether implementation is associated with stronger program effects, the answer appears to be no, although they caution that for this analysis the cohort of students in an academy is the unit of observation, effectively, and they have only twenty-two of these in their data set. There is no question that more research along these lines would be extremely useful, and ultimately the contribution of this chapter is likely to be the impetus for further research incorporating implementation measures into studies of program effectiveness, although this places high demands on researchers.

In chapter 6, Terry Orr, Thomas Bailey, Katherine Hughes, Gregory Kienzl, and Melinda Mechur Karp study the National Academy Foundation's (NAF) Career Academies. The NAF sponsors hundreds of academies, with funding from industry to support academies in travel and tourism, finance, and information technology. The authors use a sample of career-academy participants in nine programs and a comparison group of nonacademy students from the same schools. This chapter builds nicely on the previous chapter's concern with implementation of the career-academy model, because the authors focus on academies judged to have fully implemented the NAF career-academy model. In a sense, then, it presents results from what might be considered career academies using "best practices." The data used in this chapter are from students still in high school; hence the authors can only focus on issues of the high school experiences that are results of the programs, the programs' effects on students' engagement and achievement while they are in high school, and their college and career aspirations and plans. This is a limitation because in some sense the litmus test for school-to-work programs is what they deliver in terms of career development.

The evidence indicates, perhaps not surprisingly, that the career academies created a distinct high school experience grounded in career-related courses, summer internships, college-level courses, courses in computer technology, and career-planning activities. More important, participation is associated with participants' greater engagement with education and the school, such as enjoying school and feeling as though they belong, and their reports that other students encourage them to work hard and do well, although there was no significant effect of participation on attendance or high school grade point average. Finally, career-academy participation is associated with a higher likelihood of planning to go to and being accepted at a four-year college. In relation to the issue of implementation raised in chapter 5 by Stern, Wu, Dayton, and Maul, chapter 6 presents evidence that suggests that a well-implemented career academy can have beneficial effects, although the authors of both chapters point to the value of research that tries to pin down variation in career-academy implementation and the effects of this variation on outcomes. As Orr, Bailey, Hughes, Kienzl, and Karp suggest, this variation in implementation may help to explain differences in results across various studies of the effects of career academies—something we would clearly like to better understand.

Two-Year Colleges

All of the work to this point, and much of the existing research literature, focuses on high schools. As Ann E. Person and James E. Rosenbaum point out in chapter 7, however, linkages between high schools and labor markets are largely regarded as weak, and many students enter postsecondary education instead of entering the labor market directly, nearly half of them at community colleges. Moreover, two-year colleges—especially those that are occupational (that is, they offer accredited associate's degrees in a range of occupational fields such as health technicians, business, etc.)—face the same challenges as high schools in trying to create effective transitions from school to work. Thus, extending the analysis of school-to-work to postsecondary institutions is of critical importance, as is considering what high schools might learn from the experiences of postsecondary institutions. To this end, Person and Rosenbaum in chapter 7 provide a mixed qualitative and quantitative study of labor-market linkages among faculty at two-year colleges in which they compare seven public community colleges and seven private occupational colleges. The latter are hardly representative, and may instead provide examples of "best practices" at such schools.

The qualitative evidence from interviews with program chairs points to a number of dimensions along which labor-market linkages are taken more seriously at the private occupational colleges than at community colleges, even though the latter take formal responsibilities for labor-market linkages. The authors also conducted a survey of over four thousand students at these colleges by means of which they tried to examine quantitatively whether the teachers' or the institutions' labor-market linkages as perceived by students appeared to increase students' effort or reduce the likelihood of their considering dropping out. They find evidence of these beneficial effects. The quantitative evidence points to the potential benefits of these linkages, and the qualitative evidence indicates perhaps more than anything else how to strengthen these linkages. Among some of the factors identified by interviewees as aiding in labor-market linkages are part-time and adjunct faculty who have better connections to the field (although this also has some costs), advisory committees with links to local labor markets, and the participation of faculty in professional associations.

From School to Work: Skills in Entry-Level Jobs

Nan Maxwell, in chapter 8, uses a unique survey of San Francisco Bay Area workers and employers involved in entry-level jobs to study the extent to which particular sets of skills ease transitions into the labor market by securing both employment and higher wages. She finds that academic skills such as reading and writing, math, and communications are associated with considerably higher employment rates. She also finds that workers with particular skills that are in relatively short supply in this labor market earn higher wages. Of course the latter result is not surprising, but the use of data on both skills supplied by workers and skills demanded by employers provides a unique look at this question.

The research does not address school-to-work programs per se. But it does provide some indirect evidence that building skills among workers who enter the labor market after high school is associated with better school-to-work outcomes, and in particular suggests that it can be quite important to figure out ways to tie the skills that are emphasized in school-to-work programs to those that are in relatively high demand in local labor markets. Interestingly, though, this chapter points to the value of what might be considered a rather general set of skills, encompassing academic skills such as English and math, as well as what some researchers have labeled the "new basic skills" such as communication, problem solving, and the ability to carry out simple tasks on a computer. Of course, this may reflect the fact that this study focuses on what is in some respects the low end of the labor market, requiring no more than a high school education. Nonetheless, it seems to suggest that policy interventions targeting individuals in this group may have the potential to improve their labor-market transitions by encouraging formation of these skills. And it seems likely—although such an assertion is beyond the scope of this chapter—that as workers accumulate more labor market experience the better starts afforded by possession of these skills translate into further gains.

CONCLUSIONS

The conclusions that arise from the combined research presented here should be of interest to researchers, policymakers, and practitioners involved with the programs, policies, and institutions that aim to improve school-to-work transitions in the United States. The key conclusions are as follows:

- Black and Hispanic natives have less successful school-to-work transitions than native whites. There is evidence that school-to-work programs appear to deliver more benefits to the less-advantaged, especially among men, which may also help to explain why students concentrating in career and technical education (CTE) and participating in school-to-work programs are disproportionately members of minorities. These findings suggest that it may be particularly important to target school-to-work efforts toward blacks and Hispanics, but we need to be careful not to foreclose academically oriented educational pathways for these groups.
- Mexican immigrants also have less successful school-to-work transitions than native whites, and many young Mexican immigrants never enroll in school. Together, these results point to the value of trying to deliver school-to-work programs to Mexican immigrants, using venues other than or at least in addition to high schools, and to the potential value of including language training in school-to-work efforts.
- About half of U.S. students participate in school-to-work programs, and many take at least some CTE courses. Consequently, for many students increases in academic course requirements are likely to entail reductions in CTE courses, possibly echoing the overall deemphasis of school-to-work efforts associated with test-based educational reforms.
- Career academies appear to have some beneficial effects on the high school experience, including increased engagement, better attendance, less dropping out, and a higher likelihood of going to a four-year college. There is variation in the implementation of the career academy model across schools, although as-yet-crude measurements of implementation do not seem to be associated with the effects of career academies. On the other hand,

the evidence of beneficial effects on the high school experience and higher education plans comes from academies that appear to have strong implementation.

- Linkages between faculty and the labor market at two-year colleges increase the effort reported by students and decrease consideration of dropping out of educational programs. Private occupational colleges may be particularly good at encouraging and developing these linkages, in part via labor-market contacts among faculty members. Community colleges could likely provide a benefit to their students by emulating these efforts.

- Survey evidence on a key target audience of school-to-work efforts, those entering the labor market immediately after high school, points to the importance of skills for securing employment and a higher wage. That said, the most important skills appear to be "new basic skills" such as communication, problem solving, and the ability to carry out simple tasks on a computer, rather than specific workplace skills. Although these skills are relatively general, the academic emphasis of high school curricula may not emphasize these skills sufficiently. More generally, institutional efforts to create a flow of information to high schools about the skills needed in the labor market their students are likely to enter would most likely parallel the evidence from private occupational colleges and enhance the effectiveness of school-to-work programs.

All in all, these conclusions point to some potential benefits of programs, policies, and institutions aimed at improving school-to-work transitions of youths in the United States, and suggest that we should be cautious about educational policies that focus exclusively on test scores and academic preparation. At the same time, these conclusions point to some continuing and some new challenges, including adapting school-to-work efforts to help young immigrants; using school-to-work efforts to boost socioeconomic outcomes among minorities and the less-advantaged more generally, while avoiding the creation of a dual system of education that discourages the pursuit of academic pathways among qualified members of these groups; ensuring that programs that are implemented with public or private support and effort are strong and effective; and, perhaps most important, ensuring a flow of information between school-to-work programs and institutions and the labor markets their participants will transition into.

I hope that the research described in this book provides researchers with food for thought to investigate these issues further, informs policymakers about the potential benefits from school-to-work efforts but also about challenges and shortcomings that need to be addressed on an ongoing basis, and helps practitioners figure out how their programs, policies, and institutions can do more to improve school-to-work transitions for our nation's youths.

The views expressed are those of the authors and do not reflect the views of the Public Policy Institute of California.

NOTES

1. They note that child labor laws, compulsory schooling laws, and requirements for "continuation school" (part-time schooling for those working but below the maximum age for compulsory schooling) tightened considerably in the same period, but discount these laws as a major factor in rising enrollment rates.

2. Osterman characterizes this period as one "in which adventure seeking, sex, and peer group activities are all more important than work" (16). An economic perspective on this is that because the wage is low early in the career, young individuals choose to consume more leisure.

3. Joseph F. Kett (1982) notes similar arguments made in the much earlier debate over vocational education around the time of the Smith-Hughes Act.

4. Interesting questions have been raised about the extent to which vocational education prepares one for a "career," conceptualized as a sequence of jobs entailing increasing responsibility and earnings, or just for one's first job. The same question could be asked of all programs, policies, and institutions that seek to improve school-to-work transitions. It is important to bear this point in mind when one considers evaluations of these programs, policies, and institutions, which—in the event that they have data on labor-market outcomes, which is itself rare—typically have information only on very early outcomes. (See, for example, Kemple and Scott-Clayton 2004, and chapter 4 of this volume, by Neumark and Rothstein.)

5. For the text of the Act, see http://www.fessler.com/SBE/act.htm (accessed August 7, 2006).
6. More detail on a variety of school-to-work programs—not necessarily attributable to the STWOA—is provided in Thomas Bailey and Donna Merritt (1996).
7. See, for example, Tracy Schmidt (2000).
8. See, for example, Debra Donahoe and Marta Tienda (1999) and William T. Grant Foundation (1988).
9. See Mary Joyce and Neumark (2001) and Neumark (2006).
10. In chapter 3, Stone and Aliaga draw the distinction between Tech Prep and these other school-to-work activities by referring to the latter as "work-based" school-to-work activities.
11. Because these results for the effects of school-to-work programs on idleness are present mainly among men, we doubt that they reflect substitution of time between work in the labor market and time spent parenting.

REFERENCES

Bailey, Thomas, and Donna Merritt. 1996. *School-to-Work for the College-Bound*. New York: Institute on Education and the Economy.

Becker, Gary S. 1993. *Human Capital: A Theoretical and Empirical Analysis, with Special Reference to Education*. 3rd edition. Chicago: University of Chicago Press.

Cohen, Marie, and Douglas J. Besharov. 2002. "The Role of Career and Technical Education: Implications for the Federal Government." Unpublished paper. U.S. Department of Education, Office of Vocational and Adult Education.

Commission on the Skills of the American Workforce. 1990. *America's Choice: High Skills or Low Wages*. Rochester, N.Y.: National Center on Education and the Economy.

Donahoe, Debra, and Marta Tienda. 1999. "Human Asset Development and the Transition from School to Work: Policy Lessons for the 21st Century." Unpublished paper. Princeton University, Office of Population Research.

Glazer, Nathan. 1993. "A Human Capital Policy for the Cities." *The Public Interest* 112(Summer): 27–49.

Goldin, Claudia, and Lawrence Katz. 2003. "Mass Secondary Schooling and the State: The Role of State Compulsion in the High School Movement." NBER Working Paper No. 10075. Cambridge, Mass.: National Bureau of Economic Research (November).

Grubb, W. Norton. 2001. "Second Chances in Changing Times: The Roles of Community Colleges in Advancing Low Wage Workers." In *Low Wage*

Workers in the New Economy, edited by Richard Kazis and Marc Miller. Washington, D.C.: Urban Institute Press.

Hamilton, Stephen F. 1990. *Apprenticeship for Adulthood.* New York: Free Press.

Hamilton, Stephen F., and Mary A. Hamilton. 1999. *Building Strong School to Work Systems: Illustrations of Key Components.* Washington, D.C.: National School-to-Work Office.

Hayward, G. C., and C. S. Benson. 1993. "The Changing Role of Vocational-Technical Education in the United States." *CenterWork* 4(2). Berkeley: National Center for Research on Vocational Education, University of California, Berkeley.

Heckman, James. 1993. "Assessing Clinton's Program on Job Training, Workfare, and Education in the Workplace." NBER Working Paper No. 4428. Washington, D.C.: National Bureau of Economic Research (August).

Hershey, Alan M., Marsha K. Silverberg, and Joshua Haimson. 1999. *Expanding Options for Students: Report to Congress on the National Evaluation of School-to-Work Implementation.* Princeton, N.J.: Mathematica Policy Research, Inc.

Hughes, Katherine L., Thomas R. Bailey, and Melinda J. Mechur. 2001. *School-to-Work: Making a Difference in Education.* New York: Columbia University, Teachers College, Institute on Education and the Economy.

Joyce, Mary, and David Neumark. 2001. "School-to-Work Programs: Information from Two Surveys." *Monthly Labor Review* 124(8): 38–50.

Kemple, James J., and Judith Scott-Clayton. 2004. *Career Academies: Impacts on Labor Market Outcomes.* New York: Manpower Demonstration Research Corporation.

Kett, Joseph F. 1982. "The Adolescence of Vocational Education." In *Work, Youth, and Schooling: Historical Perspectives on Vocationalism in American Education,* edited by Harvey Kantor and David B. Tyack. Palo Alto: Stanford University Press.

Klerman, Jacob A., and Lynn A. Karoly. 1995. *The Transition to Stable Employment: The Experience of U.S. Youth in Their Early Labor Market Career.* Santa Monica: RAND Corporation.

Lerman, Robert I., and Hilliard Pouncy. 1990. "The Compelling Case for Youth Apprenticeship." *The Public Interest* 101(Fall): 62–77.

Mincer, Jacob. 1974. *Schooling, Experience, and Earnings.* New York: National Bureau of Economic Research.

Neumark, David. 2002. "Youth Labor Markets in the U.S.: Shopping Around vs. Staying Put." *Review of Economics and Statistics* 84(3): 462–82.

———. 2006. "Evaluating Program Effectiveness: A Case Study of the School-to-Work Opportunities Act in California." *Economics of Education Review* 25(3): 315–26.

Neumark, David, and Ann Allen. 2003. "What Do We Know About the Effects of School-to-Work? A Case Study of Michigan." *Journal of Vocational Education Research* 28(1): 59–84.

Osterman, Paul. 1980. *Getting Started: The Youth Labor Market.* Cambridge, Mass.: MIT Press.

Osterman, Paul, and Maria Iannozzi. 1993. "Youth Apprenticeships and School-to-Work Transitions: Current Knowledge and Legislative Strategy." National Center on the Educational Quality of the Workforce Working Paper No. 14. Philadelphia: National Center on the Educational Quality of the Workforce, University of Pennsylvania.

Rosenbaum, James E., Takehiko Kariya, Rick Settersten, and Tony Maier. 1990. "Market and Network Theories of the Transition from High School to Work: Their Application to Industrial Societies." *Annual Review of Sociology* 16: 263–99.

Ryan, Paul. 2001. "The School-to-Work Transition: A Cross-National Perspective." *Journal of Economic Literature* 39(1): 34–92.

Schmidt, Tracy. 2000. *A Survey of School-to-Work Actions: The 2000 State Legislative Sessions.* Washington, D.C.: National Conference of State Legislators.

Stern, David, Neal Finkelstein, James R. Stone, John Latting, and Carolyn Dornsife. 1995. *School to Work: Research on Programs in the United States.* London and Washington, D.C.: Taylor & Francis/Falmer Press.

Topel, Robert H., and Michael P. Ward. 1992. "Job Mobility and the Careers of Young Men." *Quarterly Journal of Economics* 107(2): 439–80.

U.S. Congress, Office of Technology Assessment. 1995. *Learning to Work: Making the Transition from School to Work.* OTA-HER 637. Washington: U.S. Government Printing Office.

U.S. Department of Education. 1983. *A Nation at Risk: The Imperative for Educational Reform.* Washington: U.S. Government Printing Office.

———. 1994. *National Assessment of Vocational Education: Final Report to Congress.* Washington: U.S. Government Printing Office.

U.S. General Accounting Office. 1990. *Preparing Noncollege Youth for Employment in the U.S. and Foreign Countries.* Washington: U.S. Government Printing Office.

William T. Grant Foundation. 1988. *The Forgotten Half: Pathways to Success for America's Youth and Young Families.* New York: William T. Grant Foundation.

———. 1998. *The Forgotten Half Revisited.* New York: William T. Grant Foundation.

— Chapter 2 —

Transitions to Work
for Racial, Ethnic,
and Immigrant Groups

Deborah Reed, Christopher Jepsen,
and Laura E. Hill

THE YOUTH POPULATION of the United States is becoming increasingly diverse in terms of race, ethnicity, and nativity. Although U.S.-born, non-Hispanic whites remain the majority group, their share fell from 75 to 61 percent between 1980 and 2000 and is expected to fall to 55 percent by 2020. More than 10 percent of youths are immigrants and nearly one in four has a foreign-born parent.[1]

The diversity of the youth population is of tremendous importance in designing and evaluating school-to-work programs, policies, and institutions that focus on improving work transitions and outcomes, such as those formerly funded under the federal School-to-Work Opportunities Act (STWOA) of 1994. Youths from different racial, ethnic, and immigrant backgrounds tend to have different patterns of experiences in the transition from school age to working age in terms of the timing and likelihood of completing high school, attending college, achieving success in employment, and beginning a family. Differences in patterns in the transition from school to work suggest the potential need for different program services, such as English language or basic skills training as well as the need for different design features such as implementation in the workplace instead of in schools or the inclusion of childcare.

The growing diversity of our population combined with differing patterns of transition also points to the importance of evaluating whether specific school-to-work efforts are effective for youths from different racial and ethnic backgrounds. For school-to-work efforts to be successful, they must meet the needs of increasingly diverse youth populations. In particular, youths with early labor-market difficulties are strongly concentrated among racial and ethnic minorities. Similarly, the target population of programs for youths who will not be completing high school and moving on to college on schedule is to an increasing degree nonwhite. To the extent that school-to-work efforts can be used to raise the prospects of youths who would otherwise likely have low educational attainment and low earnings, these programs increasingly need to be effective for minority populations. If successful for minorities, these programs could also operate to reduce the substantial educational and labor-market divides between racial and ethnic groups.[2]

Understanding transitions to work for Hispanic youths is of particular importance because, at 16 percent of the youth population, they constitute the largest minority group and their share is expected to grow the fastest, to 22 percent in 2020. Among Hispanics, growth in the Mexican and Mexican American population has been particularly strong, from 5 percent to 10 percent of the youth population. The share of Asians has also grown substantially, from 2 percent to 4 percent, and is expected to grow to 7 percent by 2020. In contrast, the share of U.S.-born blacks has been fairly steady and is expected to remain at roughly 13 percent.

This chapter is primarily a descriptive piece, seeking to provide a fuller picture of the diverse youth population and the relationships among race, ethnicity, nativity, socioeconomic status, and youth transitions to work. What is clear from this analysis is that school-to-work and related programs, to be successful, must effectively engage and support disadvantaged minority youth, especially blacks and increasingly Hispanics, both immigrant and U.S.-born.

PATTERNS OF TRANSITION TO WORK FOR U.S.-BORN YOUTHS BY RACE AND ETHNICITY

We explore patterns in the transition to work by comparing activities and outcomes across racial and ethnic groups for U.S.-born youths.[3] In order to provide a fuller sense of the transition patterns as opposed to focusing only on outcomes, we investigate three age groups that span the period of transition from when youths are mostly at school (ages sixteen and seventeen) to when about half of youths are in school (nineteen to twenty-one) to when the majority are not in school and are working (twenty-three to twenty-five).[4] For each age group we consider activities in the areas of school, work, and family formation. We limit our analysis to a few key measures in order to emphasize elements of transition across age groups and differences by demographic group. Notably missing is information on involvement with the criminal justice system; this information is not covered in the census. Other research suggests that this may be a major element for young black men (Holzer, Offner, and Sorensen 2004).[5]

Patterns of school and work activities suggest some similarities across racial and ethnic groups (figure 2.1). The share of youths in school falls steadily from about 90 percent or more at ages sixteen to seventeen to roughly 20 percent at ages twenty-three to twenty-five for most groups (with the exception of Asians, for whom school enrollment remains high—40 percent—in this age group). The proportion of youths who combine school and work is substantial for all groups.

The patterns differ across racial and ethnic groups in several important ways, particularly in the proportion enrolled in school in the late teens and early twenties. For youths at these ages who are not in school, work is the dominant activity, but the share of these youths who are neither in school nor working is particularly high for some groups. Among black and Native American men, the share neither working nor in school is between 30 and 35 percent. The share is also very high among Puerto Rican men (over 25 percent) and among Mexican American and other Hispanic men (over 20 percent).[6] Among women, these same groups also have very high shares—roughly 30 percent—of youths aged nineteen to twenty-one and twenty-three to twenty-five who are neither working nor in school (figure 2.1, lower panel).[7]

The high shares of youths neither in school nor working are indicative of worse outcomes in the school-to-work transition. This conclusion is reinforced by examination of young-adult school and work outcomes. These same groups have particularly low rates of high school completion, college attendance, and college completion (table 2.1).[8] Young adults in these groups, plus Southeast Asians, are also more likely to have low earnings than are other groups.

FIGURE 2.1 **School and Work Activities of U.S.-Born Youths, by Race and Ethnicity, as of 2000**

Men

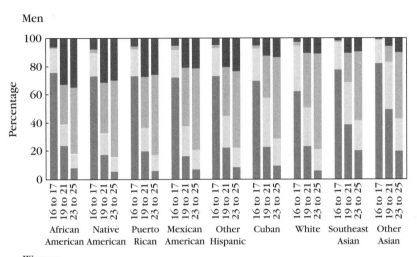

Women

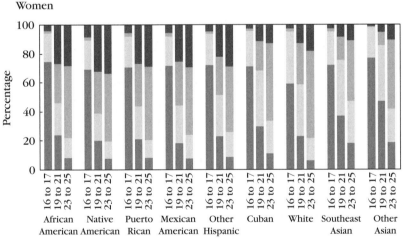

■ Neither School nor Work   ▧ Work Only   ░ School and Work   ■ School Only

Source: Authors' calculations from Census 2000 (PUMS, 5 percent).
Notes: Ages in year 2000.
U.S.-born Puerto Ricans do not include those born in Puerto Rico. Statistics do not include non-Hispanics identifying more than one race or "some other race." The full sample has over 1.3 million observations (combining men and women across the three age groups). The smallest subsample, Southeast Asian women ages twenty-three to twenty-five, has 189 observations. All differences with whites of more than 3 percentage points are statistically significant at the 10-percent level.

TABLE 2.1   Youth Outcomes, U.S.-Born Men and Women, as of 2000 (Percentage of Population)

	Black	Native American	Puerto Rican	Mexican	Other Hispanic	Cuban	White	Southeast Asian	Other Asian
Men, aged sixteen to seventeen									
Has child	2*	2*	2*	2*	2*	1	1	1	1
Men, aged nineteen to twenty-one									
High school diploma	65*	66*	63*	65*	67*	82	84	80*	93*
Some college	30*	27*	28*	29*	36*	52	50	51	71*
Earnings less than $15,000	72*	70*	63*	64*	65*	54*	58	62*	65*
Married, no child	10*	8	6*	9*	11*	8	8	9	9*
Married, has child	2*	4*	4*	5*	4*	2*	3	1*	1*
Single, has child	3*	4*	3*	4*	3*	1	1	0*	0*
Men, aged twenty-three to twenty-five									
High school diploma	74*	75*	72*	70*	74*	89	89	84	96*
Some college	38*	38*	38*	39*	43*	69*	60	63	83*
Bachelor's degree	9*	6*	8*	7*	10*	26	23	25	48*
Earnings less than $15,000	45*	44*	36*	37*	37*	28	26	42*	27
Married, no child	13*	12*	11*	16*	16*	15	15	14	9*
Married, has child	10*	16*	15	19*	15*	12	14	4*	3*
Single, has child	5*	7*	5*	5*	5*	2	3	0*	1*

	5*	4*	4*	5*	4*	2	2	1	1*
Women, aged sixteen to seventeen									
Has child	5*	4*	4*	5*	4*	2	2	1	1*
Women, aged nineteen to twenty-one									
High school diploma	76*	73*	72*	73*	77*	89	88	86*	95*
Some college	42*	37*	39*	39*	45*	64*	60	60	77*
Earnings less than $15,000	77*	80	70*	76*	75*	63*	72	60*	65*
Married, no child	6*	8*	7*	9*	9*	8*	10	9	10
Married, has child	3*	10*	7	12*	9*	5*	7	3*	1*
Single, has child	19*	13*	14*	9*	9*	3*	5	2*	1*
Women, aged twenty-three to twenty-five									
High school diploma	81*	80*	76*	77*	81*	92	92	94*	97*
Some college	51*	47*	47*	48*	54*	76*	68	78*	89*
Bachelor's degree	15*	10*	12*	11*	16*	36*	31	38	59*
Earnings less than $15,000	53*	63*	46*	51*	49*	28*	41	33*	28*
Married, no child	6*	11*	8*	12*	12*	15	17	10*	10*
Married, has child	13*	25*	19*	29*	24*	13*	22	7*	5*
Single, has child	35*	20*	27*	15*	16*	9	9	5*	2*
Population share, aged sixteen to twenty-five	13	<1	1	6	2	<1	61	<1	2

Source: Authors' calculations from Census 2000 (PUMS, 5 percent).

*Indicates that the difference with whites is statistically significant at the 10-percent level. The share earning less than $15,000 is calculated among those with earnings in the past year who were not enrolled in school. Presence of children is based on coresidence with biological child, adopted child, or stepchild. See notes to figure 2.1.

In summary, these patterns show that blacks and Native Americans and Mexican Americans, Puerto Ricans, and other Hispanics are more likely to have adverse outcomes in the transition from school to work, including lower educational attainment, lower earnings, and larger shares of these groups neither working nor in school. Minorities constitute a particularly large share of youths with early labor-market difficulties. Hispanics make up 28 percent of youths in the twenty-three-to-twenty-five age group who are neither in school nor working (not shown in table 2.1). Blacks make up another 20 percent. Among youths who are working with low earnings at ages twenty-three to twenty-five, 22 percent are Hispanic and 16 percent are black. Thus, school-to-work efforts that focus on improving outcomes for youths who are likely to have early labor-market difficulties need to find effective strategies for Hispanic and black youths.

Notably, Mexican Americans and other Hispanics—the latter comprising mainly Central Americans—are among the fastest-growing ethnic groups, and their proportion of the population is expected to grow substantially in the next twenty years.[9] Thus, the need for effective programs will likely grow in the coming decades. Because Mexican Americans are more likely than other groups to be raising children as young adults (table 2.1), the growing numbers of Mexican American youths suggest that in the future, school-to-work programs may need to be more family-oriented, perhaps by offering youths more opportunities to earn income while in school and by promoting work opportunities that provide enough income to support a family.

FAMILY RESOURCES AND OUTCOMES FOR THE U.S.-BORN

For U.S.-born youths, we explore the relationship between family resources such as parental education and income and the school, work, and fertility outcomes of young adults. The results not only help us understand factors that contribute to racial and ethnic differences in attainments, but also may suggest that family characteristics observed early in the life course can help programs target youths most at risk of low educational attainment. Our findings are consistent with previous research, which shows that family factors can explain much of the lower educational attainment and higher teen fertility of black and Hispanic youth. We extend this research to consider the importance of family factors for early work success among youths who do not go on to college.

We use the National Education Longitudinal Study (NELS) to study the importance of family factors.[10] The NELS is a nationally representative sample of eighth-graders who were first surveyed in the spring of 1988. Follow-up surveys were conducted in 1990, 1992, 1994, and 2000. The NELS is a valuable data source for this study because we observe characteristics such as family income at early ages that can then be related to outcomes at later ages. In addition, the NELS covers enough years that we can observe young-adult outcomes, which is why we chose not to use more recent longitudinal surveys such as the National Longitudinal Survey of Youth from 1997 or the Adolescent Health Survey. The NELS data also include important information on schools, including course offerings and enrollment. However, these school characteristics are generally endogenous to schooling and work decisions. For example, students who are planning on going directly into a bachelor's program may be less likely to take vocational educational courses in high school. Schools where most students generally go on to college may be less likely to offer vocational courses. Thus, including these measures will bias the results. For this reason, we limit our investigation to the role of family factors.[11]

Outcome measures from the NELS are not defined exactly the same as those used in the previous section, based on Census 2000. In general, the NELS has more detailed information for the specific cohort. For example, to measure high school completion in the NELS we use high school diploma received by 1994 (recall, the sample is based on eighth-graders in 1988). By comparison, using Census 2000 we measured high school diploma or GED received for youths aged nineteen to twenty-one (some of whom were enrolled in high school at the time of the census). The NELS measures all forms of post-secondary enrollment in addition to college and displays much higher enrollment than census data. For teen births, NELS has information on age at first birth. In Census 2000 we examined the presence of a coresident child. Therefore, the magnitudes of unadjusted group differences as measured in NELS are not directly comparable to those shown in the previous sections, which are based on the census. We do not examine outcomes for Hispanics other than for Mexican Americans nor for Native Americans or Southeast Asians because the sample sizes were too small.

In order to explore differences in outcomes across groups, we use a linear probability model to model the probability of achieving an outcome such as high school completion.[12] We use whites as our reference group, but we present the results in a format that allows for comparisons between any groups. Estimated coefficients on indicator variables for each of the three other groups (blacks, Mexican Americans, and Asians) describe whether the outcome is more common or less common for that group relative to whites. To provide a baseline, our first "model" includes only the racial and ethnic indicator variables. The purpose of this model is to estimate the size of racial and ethnic gaps in the NELS data for direct comparison to the results from our next model, which includes controls for maternal education. The third model adds controls for family resources: family income in the eighth grade; being raised by a single parent; number of siblings; and family size.

The coefficient estimates for our control variables were generally as expected (see appendix tables A-1 and A-2 for model results).[13] We find that family income and maternal education are generally positively associated with good outcomes for youths. Being raised by a single parent and having many siblings tend to be associated with worse outcomes. Interestingly, youths who were raised in families in which English was not spoken in the home tended to have higher educational attainment, controlling for other factors. In a separate analysis, we found that for Mexicans, whites, and Asians, the children of immigrants tended to have higher educational attainment than the children of the U.S.-born, controlling for other factors. This may reflect selectivity of immigrants. For example, although Mexican immigrants tend to have low maternal education and low family income, those who choose to raise their young children in the United States may place a higher value on education than do similar U.S.-born.

Previous research has shown that after accounting for family-background differences, educational attainments of Hispanic and black youths were similar or better than those of white youths during the 1970s and 1980s (Cameron and Heckman 2001; Hauser

1993). Our findings on youths during the 1990s are consistent with this research, with the exception of results for black men. We find that after adjusting for family background, there are no statistically significant differences between Mexican American and white men for high school completion, college attendance, or college completion (figure 2.2). Results are similar for Mexican American women compared to white women, with the exception that Mexican American women are somewhat less likely to complete college, even when compared to white women with similar backgrounds. For black women, we find that family background can account for all of the differences relative to white women. For black men, family background is an important factor, but their educational attainments are below those of white men even after taking these differences into account. The results for black men differ from research based on earlier periods and may reflect a real change during the 1990s. Sandra E. Black and Amir Sufi (2002) find that during the 1990s blacks (men and women combined) were less likely to attend college, even when compared to white youths from similar backgrounds. Asian American women's higher education relative to whites is partially explained by family background, but family factors do not explain much of Asian American men's higher education attainment relative to white men.

We examine teen fertility because young women who have children as teens typically face a difficult transition from school age to working age. Teen mothers are less likely than women who delay childbearing to finish high school and to enroll in college. Teen mothers also have elevated poverty rates and are less likely than other female teens to form a stable, two-parent family.[14] After adjusting for family background, we find that young Mexican American women are not more likely than white women to have a child during the high school years, but that family background only explains part of the higher teen fertility among black women (figure 2.3).[15] We also find that family background only explains part of the lower teen fertility among Asian American women.

Our results as well as previous research demonstrate the importance of family factors as determinants of educational outcomes and teen fertility. But do these factors also determine successful work transitions? In particular, we are interested in whether family resources help explain early workforce success for youths who do

FIGURE 2.2 **Educational Attainment of Ethnic Groups Relative To Whites (Percentage-Point Differential with Whites)**

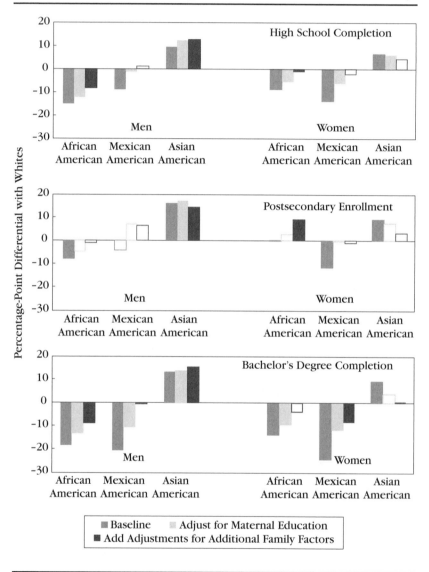

Source: Authors' calculations from NELS.
Notes: High school completion defined as diploma by 1994 (six years after eighth grade). Postsecondary enrollment and bachelor's completion measured in 2000 (respondents were roughly age twenty-six). White-filled bars signify difference with whites is not statistically significant at the 10-percent level.

FIGURE 2.3 **Fertility of Female Teens Relative to Whites**

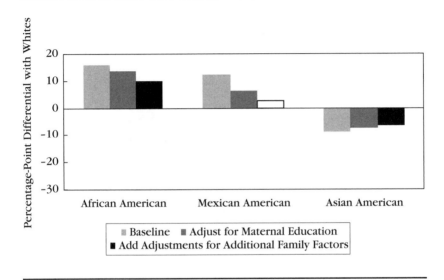

Source: Authors' calculations from NELS.
Note: See notes to figure 2.2.

not enter four-year colleges after high school. Our criterion for a successful transition to work is consistent workforce participation since high school and substantial earnings at age twenty-five for youths who have less than two years of college education. More specific criteria for a successful transition are that a person has worked at least some in the two years after high school (1992 to 1994), worked full-time for at least six months during 1997, 1998, and 1999, and had annual earnings in the top two-thirds of workers in 1999 ($21,000 and higher for men and $14,000 and higher for women). On the basis of this definition of successful transition, almost 60 percent of men and almost 50 percent of women were successful. Because we include in our study group only youths with less than two years of postsecondary education, the results are affected by sample-selection bias; those not going on to postsecondary education are likely to have low levels of unobserved skills; for groups where postsecondary education is fairly common, such as Asian Americans, the degree of selection bias may be particularly strong. In contrast, the sample selection is not likely to be greater for blacks and Mexican Americans than for whites, because whites are more likely than these minorities to have enrolled in two years of post-secondary education.

Blacks, Mexican American, and Asian American men all are substantially less likely than white men to successfully transition to work, and less than one-third of this achievement gap can be explained by family factors (figure 2.4).[16] In general, the family characteristics in our models do not explain very much of the variation in the successful transition to work between or within racial and ethnic groups. Whereas the adjusted R-squared in the college completion model was 22 percent, it was only 10 percent in the successful-transition-to-work model. The results suggest that early work outcomes for youths not going on to pursue a bachelor's degree are not determined primarily by the socioeconomic conditions of families that are observed in our data.[17] The factors that explain these gaps remain unknown but could include measures

FIGURE 2.4 **Successful Transition to Work of Men Relative to Whites**

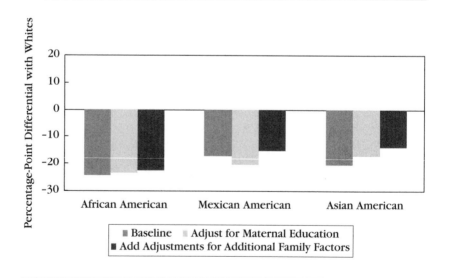

Source: Authors' calculations from NELS.
Note: See notes to figure 2.2. Figure includes young adults who have less than two years of postsecondary education. See text for definition of "successful transition."

of school quality, local economic conditions, social networks, or discrimination. Among women, there were no substantial gaps in successful transitions to work between whites, Mexican Americans, blacks, and Asian Americans.[18]

In sum, we find that family resources help explain the lower educational attainment and higher teen fertility of black and Hispanic youths relative to white youths. Youths with low maternal education and low family income can be identified early and enrolled in programs to promote educational attainment and reduce teen fertility. If successful, such programs would reduce racial and ethnic gaps in these outcomes. In addition, the strong connection between family resources and youth outcomes means that improving critical outcomes for these youths will likely pay off for their children, the next generation of minority youths. On the other hand, we find that among youths who do not go on to a bachelor's degree soon after high school, family resources do not explain much of the lower levels of early work success of Hispanic and black men (we found no race-ethnic differences in levels of early work success among women). Thus, among youths not pursuing a bachelor's degree after high school, targeting those with low maternal education and low family income does not appear to be an effective means of identifying individuals who are less likely to have successful early work outcomes.

UNDERSTANDING IMMIGRANT OUTCOMES

We examine the transition to work separately for immigrant youths because their patterns of transition differ from those of U.S.-born from the same ethnic group. Furthermore, to understand immigrant transitions we must consider an additional factor: their age when they arrived in the United States (Hill 2004; Portes and Rumbaut 1996). We focus on the two largest immigrant youth groups: Mexicans, who account for 38 percent of immigrant youth ages thirteen to twenty-four; and Asians, accounting for 15 percent of immigrant youths.[19]

Analysis by age of arrival is important because school and work activities differ by age of arrival, especially for Mexican immigrants. Among Mexican youths who arrived by the age of twenty-four,

FIGURE 2.5 **School Enrollment Among Foreign-Born Mexicans and Asians by Age of Arrival, as of 2000**

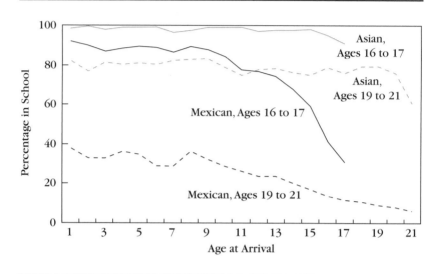

Source: Authors' calculations from Census 2000 (PUMS, 5 percent).
Notes: For youth aged sixteen and seventeen, the share enrolled includes those who have not finished high school. For those aged nineteen to twenty-one, the share includes those who have not finished a bachelor's degree.

only about one-fourth arrived by age fourteen. The share who arrived at each age increased steeply from age fifteen to seventeen: by about 8 percent for each single year of age from seventeen through twenty-four.[20] Among Mexican immigrants who arrived before the age of ten, school enrollment was similar to that of U.S.-born Mexican Americans: roughly 90 percent for youths aged sixteen and seventeen and about 35 percent for those aged nineteen to twenty-one (figure 2.5). For those arriving after age ten, school enrollment declines steadily with age at arrival.

For Asian youths, arriving before the age of fourteen is more common than for Mexican youths, 37 percent of Asian youths arrived by the age of fourteen. The share of Asian youths that arrived at each age increases moderately after age fifteen and increases steeply from age twenty (about 5 percent) to age twenty-four (about 10 percent). Among Asian immigrants ages sixteen and seventeen, school enrollment was similar to that of U.S.-born Asians, at just under 100 percent for those arriving by age fifteen (figure 2.5). A small drop for those arriving at ages sixteen and seventeen may reflect difficulty enrolling in school upon arrival. For Asian immigrants ages nineteen to twenty-one, school enrollment was just over 80 percent for those arriving before age ten and just under 80 percent for those arriving after age ten. For U.S.-born Asians, school enrollment at ages nineteen to twenty-one was slightly higher, about 85 percent.

We examine the transition from school age to working age for immigrants by age of arrival in four groups:

1. Those arriving by the age of five
2. Those arriving between ages twelve and fourteen (inclusive)
3. Those arriving between ages sixteen and eighteen
4. Those arriving between ages nineteen and twenty-two

Within each group we interpret changes that are linked with age as representing transitions. For immigrants, however, the cohort analysis is more problematic than for U.S.-born because of selective return migration. For example, if unsuccessful youths are more likely to return to their country of origin, then aggregate outcomes would appear to improve as the cohort ages. In addition, selection into migration or return migration may differ by historical time period. For example, immigrants who arrived in different time periods may have different levels of skills.[21]

Mexican immigrants who arrive at early ages have school and work activity patterns similar to those of Mexican Americans (figure 2.6).[22] For immigrant men arriving at older ages, the lower share enrolled in school was matched by a higher share in work, so that the share neither in school nor working was about the same for the U.S.-born and immigrants, roughly 20 percent, regardless of age at arrival. Mexican women follow a markedly different pattern: of those arriving at older ages, lower shares were both in school and working (figure 2.6, lower panel): at ages nineteen to twenty-one, about half of those who had arrived in their teens were neither in school nor working. Most of these young women had already formed a family. About half of Mexican women who had arrived in their teens were married or raising a child by the age of nineteen

FIGURE 2.6 **School and Work Activities Among Mexican Youths by Age of Arrival, as of 2000**

Men

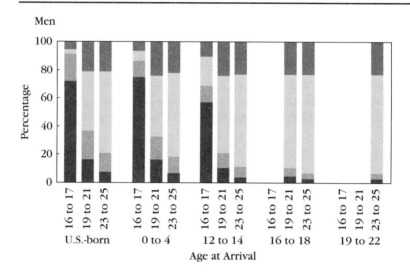

Women

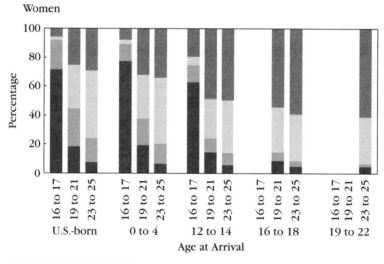

■ Neither School nor Work   ▨ Work Only   ▨ School and Work   ■ School Only

Source: Authors' calculations from Census 2000 (PUMS, 5 percent).
Notes: Ages in year 2000.
The full sample has over 51,000 Mexican immigrant observations (combining men and women across the three age groups). The smallest subsample, Mexican women ages sixteen and seventeen who arrived before age five, has 804 observations. Differences with U.S.-born of more than three percentage points are statistically significant at the 10-percent level.

to twenty-one (table 2.2). Mexican immigrants were substantially less likely than Mexican Americans to attain a high school diploma or attend college.

Similar to U.S.-born Asians, Asian immigrant youths have relatively high levels of school enrollment (figure 2.7). Nevertheless, Asian immigrants arriving in their teen years had substantially lower educational attainment than did U.S.-born Asians (table 2.3). Asian women arriving in their teenage years were more likely to be neither in school nor working (about 20 percent) than were U.S.-born Asian women (just over 10 percent). They were also much more likely to have formed a family; over 30 percent had a family by age twenty-three to twenty-five, compared to only 17 percent of U.S.-born Asians (table 2.3).

We cannot model the family and other factors associated with young-adult outcomes for immigrants because large data sets with substantial numbers of immigrants, such as the census and the Current Population Survey, do not have information on childhood family income or parental education. However, for children who are coresident with their parents, we can examine the family resources that we found to be associated with good educational outcomes for natives: high maternal education level; high family income; having been raised by married parents; and having few siblings. Mexican immigrants are less likely than Mexican Americans to have a mother who has completed high school and they are less likely to be in families living above the poverty line (table 2.4). These factors likely contribute to the lower educational attainment of Mexican immigrants relative to Mexican Americans. U.S.-born Asians and Asian immigrants have much greater family resources than do Mexican natives and immigrants. Among Asians who arrived as young children, family resources nearly match those of Asian Americans, which is consistent with the similar educational outcomes between these two groups (table 2.4). Family resources were slightly lower for Asian immigrants who arrived in their early teens, and these youths' educational outcomes were also lower.

In sum, we find that many immigrant youths from Mexico arrive after the age of fifteen and a large share do not appear to enroll in school in the United States. Their educational attainment is therefore quite low and is strongly related to experiences (such as education)

TABLE 2.2 Outcomes for Mexican Youths, by Age at Arrival, as of 2000 (Percentage of Population)

	U.S.-Born	0 to 4 Years	12 to 14 Years	16 to 18 Years	19 to 22 Years
Men, aged sixteen to seventeen					
Has child	2	2	2		
Men, aged nineteen to twenty-one					
High school diploma	65	54*	38*	24*	
Some college	29	20*	10*	5*	
Earnings less than $15,000	64	62	59*	60*	
Married, no child	9	11*	13*	14*	
Married, has child	5	6	8*	8*	
Single, has child	4	3	3*	2*	
Men, aged twenty-three to twenty-five					
High school diploma	70	61*	42*	27*	29*
Some college	39	30*	16*	8*	9*
Bachelor's degree	7	6*	2*	1*	2*
Earnings less than $15,000	37	37	43*	45*	50*
Married, no child	16	15	20*	20*	20*
Married, has child	19	23*	23*	29*	22*
Single, has child	5	5	6	5*	3*
Women, aged sixteen to seventeen					
Has child	5	6	6*	5*	3*

Women, aged nineteen to twenty-one				
High school diploma	73	64*	44*	28*
Some college	39	31*	16*	7*
Earnings less than $15,000	76	76	78*	80*
Married, no child	9	12*	15*	20*
Married, has child	12	16*	23*	28*
Single, has child	9	6*	7*	4*
Women, aged twenty-three to twenty-five				
High school diploma	77	67*	46*	28*
Some college	48	40*	21*	8*
Bachelor's degree	11	8*	3*	1*
Earnings less than $15,000	51	52	69*	72*
Married, no child	12	15*	14*	13*
Married, has child	29	36*	39*	53*
Single, has child	15	12*	11*	7*

Source: Authors' calculations from Census 2000 (PUMS, 5 percent).
*Indicates the difference with U.S.-born Mexicans is statistically significant at the 10-percent level. See notes to table 2.1.

FIGURE 2.7 **School and Work Activities Among Asian Youth by Age of Arrival, as of 2000**

Men

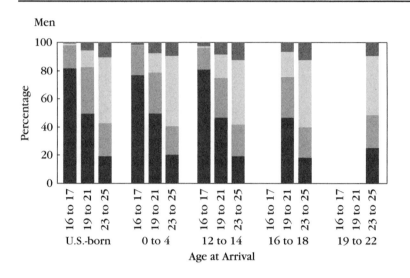

Women

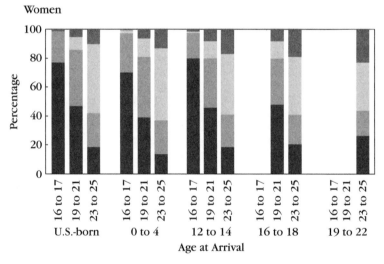

■ Neither School nor Work   ▨ Work Only   ▨ School and Work   ■ School Only

Source: Authors' calculations from Census 2000 (PUMS, 5 percent).
Notes: Ages in year 2000.
The full sample has almost 16,500 Asian immigrant observations (combining men and women across the three age groups). The smallest subsample, Asian women ages sixteen and seventeen who arrived at ages twelve to fourteen, has 439 observations. Differences with U.S.-born of more than three percentage points are statistically significant at the 10 percent level.

in the origin country and the determinants of migration to this country. To increase educational attainment among Mexican immigrants in the United States, youth policies may need to promote "dropping in" to school as opposed to reducing "dropping out" of school. To reach these youths with work-related programs we may need to focus on targeting them at their workplaces rather than schools and neighborhoods.

IMPLICATIONS FOR SCHOOL-TO-WORK PROGRAMS, POLICIES, AND INSTITUTIONS

For school-to-work efforts to be successful, they must meet the needs of an increasingly diverse youth population. Patterns of activities during the transition from school age to working age suggest that racial and ethnic groups may differ in their need for and ability to use different types of approaches to improving school-to-work transitions. In particular, growth in the number of Hispanic youths and in the size of their share of the total youth population will likely be associated with growth in the number of young adults who are neither at work nor in school, a target population for programs working to improve success in the transition from school to work. Relative to black men, Mexican American men have lower rates of high school completion and higher levels of work activity and a greater proportion of those under twenty-five are raising children. School-to-work efforts to meet the needs of this group may have to focus more on high school completion and to operate with flexible schedules and earnings opportunities that allow participants to meet work and family responsibilities. Many Mexican immigrants arrive after the age of fifteen and a large share do not appear to enroll in school in the United States. Education and work-related programs for Mexican immigrants may need to target the workplace rather than schools.

The analysis points to the value of evaluating whether specific school-to-work efforts are effective for disadvantaged and minority youths, especially blacks and, increasingly, Hispanics. More broadly, which specific public investments are more likely to have strong positive impacts on the future lives of disadvantaged minority youths?

TABLE 2.3 Outcomes for Asian Youths by Age at Arrival, as of 2000 (Percentage of Population)

	U.S.-Born	Arrived 0 to 4	Arrived 12 to 14	Arrived 16 to 18	Arrived 19 to 22
Men, aged sixteen to seventeen					
Has child	1	1	1		
Men, aged nineteen to twenty-one					
High school diploma	93	93	85*	82*	
Some college	71	66*	56*	51*	
Earnings less than $15,000	65	66	55*	60*	
Married, no child	9	3*	6*	6*	
Married, has child	1	0	0	1	
Single, has child	0	0	1	1	
Men, aged twenty-three to twenty-five					
High school diploma	96	97*	91*	88*	92*
Some college	83	85	75*	70*	78*
Bachelor's degree	48	51	37*	36*	44*
Earnings less than $15,000	27	28	26	32*	28
Married, no child	9	7	10	16*	13*
Married, has child	3	3	3	4	2*
Single, has child	1	1*	1	1	1*

Women, aged sixteen to seventeen					
Has child	1		1	1	
Women, aged nineteen to twenty-one					
High school diploma	95	95	93*	84*	
Some college	77	75	63*	58*	
Earnings less than $15,000	65	66	66	62	
Married, no child	10	7*	9	10	
Married, has child	1	1	3*	3*	
Single, has child	1	1	2	1	
Women, aged twenty-three to twenty-five					
High school diploma	97	97	95*	92*	92*
Some college	89	87	81*	75*	77*
Bachelor's degree	59	54	43*	40*	42*
Earnings less than $15,000	28	32*	28	34*	44*
Married, no child	10	15*	16*	18*	24*
Married, has child	5	7*	12*	12*	17*
Single, has child	2	4	3	1*	2*

Source: Authors' calculations from Census 2000 (PUMS, 5 percent).
*Indicates that the difference with U.S.-born Asians is statistically significant at the 10-percent level. See notes to table 2.1.

TABLE 2.4   **Family Resources Among Mexican and Asian Immigrant Youths, Aged Thirteen to Eighteen, as of 2000 (Percentage of Population)**

	Mother Has High School Diploma	Mother Has Bachelor's Degree	Family Income Above Poverty	Parents Married	Has Two or Fewer Siblings
Mexican American	51	6	77	64	84
Arrived aged 0 to 4	20*	3*	70*	74*	71*
Arrived aged 12 to 14	18*	3*	65*	59*	82*
Asian American	86	47	92	81	95
Arrived aged 0 to 4	87	46	91	83*	94*
Arrived aged 12 to 14	75*	36*	79*	80	94*

Source: Authors' calculations from Census 2000 (PUMS, 5 percent).
*Indicates that the difference with U.S.-born children of the same ethnicity is statistically significant at the 10-percent level. To limit selectivity of the sample (which requires coresidence with parents), the sample includes only youths under age eighteen and, among immigrants, only those who arrived before age fifteen.

Family resources, such as maternal education and family income, are strong predictors of young-adult success, and limited family resources help explain the lower educational attainment and higher teen fertility of black and Hispanic youths. On the other hand, among all youths who do not pursue postsecondary education, family resources are not strong determinants of early workforce success. Thus, youths at risk of teen fertility and low educational attainment can be identified from family conditions observed early in the life course, but family conditions other than race and ethnicity are not strong predictors of early workforce problems. Programs targeted toward low-resource families, if successful, will likely reduce racial and ethnic gaps in education and teen fertility, but would not be as effective in reducing gaps in early work success for youths not going on to college. Additionally, the strong connection between family resources and educational attainment means that improving educational outcomes for these future parents will likely pay off for the next generation of minority youths.

TABLE A-1 Linear Probability Models for Educational Attainment

	Females			Males		
	High School	Postsecondary Enrollment	Bachelor's Completion	High School	Postsecondary Enrollment	Bachelor's Completion
Black	-0.008	0.089**	-0.040	-0.080**	-0.013	-0.087**
	(0.029)	(0.024)	(0.031)	(0.032)	(0.036)	(0.022)
Mexican	-0.020	-0.011	-0.080**	0.012	0.064	-0.004
	(0.033)	(0.043)	(0.034)	(0.040)	(0.045)	(0.031)
Asian	0.049	0.029	0.006	0.127**	0.144**	0.158**
	(0.039)	(0.042)	(0.053)	(0.028)	(0.037)	(0.049)
Mother is high school graduate	0.137**	0.163**	0.095**	0.126**	0.137**	0.039**
	(0.024)	(0.031)	(0.020)	(0.039)	(0.042)	(0.019)
Mother has some college	0.119**	0.249**	0.204**	0.201**	0.279**	0.125**
	(0.027)	(0.029)	(0.021)	(0.037)	(0.036)	(0.021)
Mother is college graduate	0.157**	0.282**	0.432**	0.208**	0.342**	0.411**
	(0.027)	(0.030)	(0.029)	(0.040)	(0.036)	(0.030)
English not spoken at home	-0.026	0.086**	0.045	0.049	0.059*	-0.069**
	(0.030)	(0.034)	(0.032)	(0.030)	(0.032)	(0.031)
Family income	0.003**	0.005**	0.005**	0.003**	0.006**	0.004**
	(0.000)	(0.001)	(0.001)	(0.001)	(0.001)	(0.001)
Family income squared	-0.001**	-0.001**	-0.001**	-0.001**	-0.002**	-0.001**
	(0.000)	(0.000)	(0.000)	(0.000)	(0.000)	(0.000)
Raised in single-parent home	-0.036	-0.021	-0.011	-0.056**	0.043	-0.071**
	(0.027)	(0.020)	(0.024)	(0.028)	(0.031)	(0.020)
Number of siblings	-0.013*	-0.015**	-0.026**	-0.012*	-0.020**	-0.023**
	(0.007)	(0.006)	(0.006)	(0.007)	(0.008)	(0.005)

(continued)

49

TABLE A-1 *Continued*

	Females			Males		
	High School	Postsecondary Enrollment	Bachelor's Completion	High School	Postsecondary Enrollment	Bachelor's Completion
Family size	0.007	−0.012*	0.000	−0.004	0.005	−0.003
	(0.009)	(0.007)	(0.007)	(0.009)	(0.009)	(0.006)
Observations	6,440	5,433	5,433	6,863	5,288	5,288
Adjusted R-squared	0.10	0.15	0.20	0.10	0.14	0.22

Source: Authors' calculations from the National Education Longitudinal Study (1994–2000).
Notes: Bootstrapped standard errors are in parentheses. Models contain additional controls for region as well as dummy variables for missing control variables (such as family income).
*Denotes coefficients that are statistically significant from zero at the 10-percent (two-tailed test).
**Denotes coefficients that are statistically different from zero at the 5-percent (two-tailed test).

TABLE A-2   **Linear Probability Models for Teenage Motherhood and Successful Transition to Work**

	Teenage Motherhood	Successful Work Transition	
	Females	Females	Males
Black	0.101**	0.042	−0.324**
	(0.027)	(0.058)	(0.054)
Mexican	0.028	0.016	−0.151**
	(0.027)	(0.074)	(0.070)
Asian	−0.064**	−0.033	−0.137*
	(0.022)	(0.100)	(0.077)
Mother is high school graduate	−0.085**	−0.010	−0.014
	(0.026)	(0.049)	(0.050)
Mother has some college	−0.104**	0.012	−0.062
	(0.025)	(0.048)	(0.049)
Mother is college graduate	−0.135**	0.042	−0.165**
	(0.027)	(0.070)	(0.065)
English not spoken at home	0.030	0.057	−0.084
	(0.025)	(0.065)	(0.060)
Family income	−0.003**	0.004	0.002*
	(0.000)	(0.002)	(0.001)
Family income squared	0.001**	−0.001	−0.001
	(0.000)	(0.001)	(0.000)
Raised in single-parent home	0.006	0.099	−0.022
	(0.025)	(0.044)	(0.049)
Number of siblings	0.023**	−0.018	0.004
	(0.007)	(0.012)	(0.010)
Family size	−0.010	0.003	−0.003
	(0.010)	(0.015)	(0.014)
Observations	6,430	2,260	2,515
Adjusted R-squared	0.10	0.03	0.10

Source: Authors' calculations from the National Education Longitudinal Study (1994–2000).
Notes: Bootstrapped standard errors are in parentheses. Models contain additional controls for region as well as dummy variables for missing control variables (such as family income).
*Denotes coefficients that are statistically significant from zero at the 10-percent (two-tailed test).
**Denotes coefficients that are statistically different from zero at the 5-percent (two-tailed test).

Partial funding for this project was generously provided by the William and Flora Hewlett Foundation. We thank Frank Furstenberg, Magnus Lofstrom, David Neumark, and two anonymous reviewers for helpful comments on early drafts of this paper. Pedro Cerdan and Shelley De Alth provided valuable research assistance.

NOTES

1. Diversity statistics are based on authors' calculations from the U.S. Census for 1980 and 2000 and the March Current Population Survey for 2003. Projections are from the U.S. Bureau of the Census (2000).
2. See James P. Smith (2001) for a summary of recent trends in labor-market conditions for blacks, whites, and Hispanics.
3. See Debra Donahoe and Marta Tienda (1999) and papers cited therein. Elizabeth Fussell and Frank Furstenberg (2003) document historical patterns in the transition to adulthood by race, nativity, and gender.
4. We analyze activities and outcomes across cohorts of youths and interpret higher educational attainment and more work activities at older ages as reflecting educational progress and the transition to work. We note that the data are cross-sectional, and differences by age could reflect cohort differences. However, the temporal differences between the cohorts are fairly small, because the sample includes those born between 1974 and 1984.
5. Over 8 percent of black men in their twenties were in prison in 1999, and some estimates put the share of African American males involved in the criminal justice system through jail, probation, or parole at 30 percent (Blumstein 2001).
6. Paul Offner and Harry J. Holzer (2002) find that among young men aged sixteen to twenty-four who are out of school and who have not attended college, black men have much lower employment than do white men, whereas Hispanic men's employment is similar to that of white men. Similarly, we find that among those not in school, Hispanic men have higher employment than black men but lower employment than white men. The difference is due in part to our focus on U.S.-born Hispanics (young foreign-born Hispanic men have higher employment levels) and in part to our inclusion of men who have a higher education level than a high school diploma. In addition, we note that Hispanic men are much more likely than white men to be in the "neither school nor work" group. At ages nineteen

to twenty-one, much of this difference with white men is related to lower school attendance among Hispanic men relative to white men. At ages twenty-three to twenty-five, much of the difference is related to the lower employment of Hispanic men.

7. Our focus on patterns in 2000 overlooks the substantial changes for blacks during the 1990s. Employment declined for young black men with less than a high school diploma. Harry J. Holzer, Paul Offner, and Elaine Sorensen (2004) find that this employment decline for black men can be partially explained by increased incarceration and lowered incentive to work due to increased withholding of earnings for child support obligations. Employment improved for young black women, much of which Bruce D. Meyer and Dan T. Rosenbaum (1999) attribute to the expansion of the Earned Income Tax Credit with a smaller role for welfare benefit reductions, changes in training programs, and expansions of child-care subsidies.

8. Young adults' high school completion as measured by the census includes those who complete high school after dropping out as well as those who obtain general equivalency diplomas. High school dropout rates show similar patterns to those shown in table 2.1, but higher rates of incompletion (Swanson 2003).

9. More than 15 percent of Hispanics did not identify a specific ethnicity in the 2000 census. The Census has substantially fewer Central Americans than the American Community Survey, suggesting that in the 2000 census a large share of Hispanics who did not identify a subgroup are Central American. For this reason, in our analysis of the 2000 census, we group Central Americans and all others, noting that this group is mainly Central Americans.

10. We cannot replicate this analysis for a representative sample of the foreign-born, because foreign-born youths who did not attend eighth grade in the United States are not represented in the NELS. For the NELS sample, we actually include in our analysis all U.S.-raised youths, that is, immigrants who arrived before the age of five years. In other work (Reed et al. 2005), we examine the representativeness of the NELS relative to the Current Population Survey (see also Grogger and Trejo 2002). We conclude that the NELS is reasonably representative of U.S.-born and "near-native" (those arriving before age five) whites, blacks, Mexican Americans, and Asians. However, for whites and Asians, the samples were not representative when separated in terms of second- versus third-generation immigrants.

11. See William Carbonaro (2004) for a NELS analysis exploring racial and ethnic differences in high school courses and experiences and their effects on college graduation. See Joshua Haimson and Jeanne

Bellotti (2004) for a discussion of participation in work-based learning activities during high school, including participation rates for blacks, Hispanics, and whites.

12. The use of a linear probability model avoids the distributional assumptions associated with a logit or probit model (Wooldridge 2002). We used a bootstrap method for calculating standard errors in all linear probability models. We also estimated the models using a logit specification. In general, we found the coefficients in the linear model to be of similar magnitude to the marginal effects of the logit model, but the logit model resulted in lower standard errors (more statistical significance) in some cases.

13. See Robert Haveman and Barbara Wolfe (1995) for a review of the literature on the determinants of youth outcomes.

14. Researchers have questioned the degree to which teen fertility causes poor outcomes, suggesting instead that teenage women who have children were likely to have poor outcomes even in the absence of early childbearing (Bronars and Grogger 1994; Geronimus and Korenman 1992; Hotz et al. 1999). Other researchers have suggested the relationship is causal (Hoffman 1999; Hoffman et al. 1993; and Klepinger et al. 1995, 1999). However, the causality question is not central to our goals of examining the determinants of racial and ethnic differences in teen fertility and of identifying whether family characteristics can be used to identify women at risk for a teen birth.

15. Avner Ahituv and Marta Tienda (2004) have similar findings.

16. Pedro Carneiro, James J. Heckman, and Dimitriv V. Masterov (2005) find that AFQT scores explain a large portion of the wage gaps for Hispanics and blacks and that family factors help explain AFQT scores. Their findings, similar to our results, suggest a partial role for family factors. Family factors play a somewhat larger role in their models, probably because they have more measures of family conditions and because they consider the entire wage spectrum, whereas we consider successful transitions only among those who complete less than two years of college.

17. This result is perhaps surprising because family resources help determine education, and education is an important factor in early workforce success. The importance of family resources for workforce success is likely biased downward because we limit the sample to youths who have less than two years of college education. In particular, among youths with high maternal education and high family income, those who do not obtain a bachelor's degree may be strongly selected to be those who are less able or less motivated. Our interest here is not in determining the causal impact of family resources on

workforce success but in determining whether low family resources are indicative of a lower likelihood of success among youths who do not earn a bachelor's degree.

18. In other words, for women the unadjusted gaps with whites were small and not statistically significant.

19. Youth outcomes vary across Asian subgroups. The largest distinctions are between youths from Southeast Asian refugee-sending countries and other Asian youths. For brevity, we do not investigate outcomes for Southeast Asian immigrant youths. In other work we find that although Southeast Asian immigrant youths tend to have lower family resources, their school enrollment and work patterns are similar to other Asians' (Reed et al. 2005).

20. Age-at-arrival patterns are based on authors' calculations from the 2000 census for age cohorts nineteen to twenty-one, twenty-three to twenty-five, and thirty to thirty-three.

21. George J. Borjas (1995) bases his suggestion that immigrant selection changed on the finding that the entry wage of immigrants arriving prior to 1980 was higher than that of immigrants arriving in the 1980s. Kristin F. Butcher and John DiNardo (2002) demonstrate the importance of the U.S. wage structure and the minimum wage (and not merely immigrant selection) in explaining immigrant wages in different periods.

22. For brevity, we do not separate U.S. natives by second and third generation. In other work (Reed et al. 2005) we show that educational outcomes for second-generation Mexican Americans and Asian Americans are higher than for third-generation youths of the same background. However, when compared with the education of their own parents, third-generation Mexican Americans and Asian Americans made substantial progress.

REFERENCES

Ahituv, Avner, and Marta Tienda. 2004. "Employment, Motherhood, and School Continuation Decisions of Young White, Black, and Hispanic Women." *Journal of Labor Economics* 22(1): 115–58.

Black, Sandra E., and Amir Sufi. 2002. "Who Goes to College? Differential Enrollment by Race and Family Background." Unpublished paper (mimeographed). University of California, Los Angeles.

Blumstein, Alfred. 2001. "Race and Criminal Justice." *America Becoming: Racial Trends and Their Consequences,* volume 2, edited by Neil J. Smelser, William Julius Wilson, and Faith Mitchell. Washington, D.C.: National Academies Press.

Borjas, George J. 1995. "Assimilation and Changes in Cohort Quality Revisited: What Happened to Immigrant Earnings in the 1980s?" *Journal of Labor Economics* 13(2): 201–45.

Bronars, Stephen, and Jeff Grogger. 1994. "The Economic Consequences of Unwed Motherhood: Using Twin Births as a Natural Experiment." *American Economic Review* 84(4): 1141–56.

Butcher, Kristin F., and John DiNardo. 2002. "The Immigrant and Native-Born Wage Distributions: Evidence from United States Censuses." *Industrial and Labor Relations Review* 56(1): 97–121.

Cameron, Stephen J., and James J. Heckman. 2001. "The Dynamics of Educational Attainment for Black, Hispanic, and White Males." *Journal of Political Economy* 109(31): 455–99.

Carbonaro, William. 2004. "Racial and Ethnic Differences in College Graduation: The Lasting Effects of Students' High School Experiences." Unpublished paper (mimeographed). Department of Sociology, University of Notre Dame.

Carneiro, Pedro, James J. Heckman, and Dimitriv V. Masterov. 2005. "Labor Market Discrimination and Racial Differences in Premarket Factors." Discussion Paper Series, No. 1453. Bonn, Germany: Institute for the Study of Labor (IZA).

Donahoe, Debra, and Marta Tienda. 1999. "Human Asset Development and the Transition from School to Work: Policy Lessons for the 21st Century." Unpublished paper. Princeton University, Office of Population Research.

Fussell, Elizabeth, and Frank Furstenberg. 2003. "The Transition to Adulthood During the 20th Century: Race, Nativity, and Gender Differences." Unpublished paper. Tulane University and University of Pennsylvania.

Geronimus, Arline T., and Sanders Korenman. 1992. "The Socioeconomic Consequences of Teen Childbearing Reconsidered." *Quarterly Journal of Economics* 107(November): 1187–1214.

Grogger, Jeffrey, and Stephen J. Trejo. 2002. *Falling Behind or Moving Up? The Intergenerational Progress of Mexican Americans.* San Francisco: Public Policy Institute of California.

Haimson, Joshua, and Jeanne Bellotti. 2004. "Student Participation in the Use of Work-Based Learning." In *Working Knowledge: Work-Based Learning and Education Reform,* edited by Thomas R. Bailey, Katherine L. Hughes, and David Thornton Moore. New York: Routledge/Falmer.

Hauser, Robert M. 1993. "Trends in College Entry Among Whites, Blacks, and Hispanics." In *Studies of Supply and Demand in Higher Education: A National Bureau of Economic Research Project Report,* edited by Charles T. Clotfelter and Michael Rothschild. Chicago and London: University of Chicago Press.

Haveman, Robert, and Barbara Wolfe. 1995. "The Determinants of Children's Attainments: A Review of Methods and Findings." *Journal of Economic Literature* 33(4): 1829–78.

Hill, Laura E. 2004. *The Socioeconomic Well-Being of California's Immigrant Youth*. San Francisco: Public Policy Institute of California.

Hoffman, Saul D. 1999. "Teenage Childbearing Is Not So Bad After All . . . Or Is It? A Review of the New Literature." *Family Planning Perspectives* 30(5): 236–39, 243.

Hoffman, Saul D., E. Michael Foster, and Frank F. Furstenberg Jr. 1993. "Reevaluating the Costs of Teenage Childbearing." *Demography* 30(2): 291–96.

Holzer, Harry J., Paul Offner, and Elaine Sorensen. 2004. "Declining Employment Among Young Black Less-Educated Men: The Role of Incarceration and Child Support." Unpublished paper (mimeographed). Georgetown University, Washington, D.C.

Hotz, V. Joseph, Susan Williams McElroy, and Seth Sanders. 1999. "Teenage Childbearing and Its Life Cycle Consequences: Exploiting a Natural Experiment." NBER Working Paper No. 7397. Washington, D.C.: National Bureau of Economic Research.

Klepinger, Daniel, Shelly Lundberg, and Robert Plotnick. 1995. "Adolescent Fertility and the Educational Attainment of Young Women." *Family Planning Perspectives* 27(1): 23–28.

———. 1999. "How Does Adolescent Fertility Affect the Human Capital and Wages of Young Women?" *Journal of Human Resources* 34(3): 421–48.

Meyer, Bruce D., and Dan T. Rosenbaum. 1999. "Welfare, the Earned Income Tax Credit, and the Labor Supply of Single Mothers," NBER Working Paper No. W7363, Cambridge, Mass.: National Bureau of Economic Research.

Offner, Paul, and Harry J. Holzer. 2002. "Left Behind in the Labor Market: Recent Employment Trends Among Young Black Men." Center on Urban and Metropolitan Policy, Survey Series. Washington, D.C.: Brookings Institution.

Portes, Alejandro, and Ruben Rumbaut. 1996. *Immigrant America: A Portrait*. Los Angeles: University of California Press.

Reed, Deborah, Laura E. Hill, Christopher Jepsen, and Hans P. Johnson. 2005. *Educational Progress Across Immigrant Generations in California*. San Francisco: Public Policy Institute of California.

Smith, James P. 2001. "Race and Ethnicity in the Labor Market: Trends over the Short and Long Term." *America Becoming: Racial Trends and Their Consequences,* volume 2, edited by Neil J. Smelser, William Julius Wilson, and Faith Mitchell. Washington, D.C.: National Academies Press.

Swanson, Christopher B. 2003. *Who Graduates? Who Doesn't? A Statistical Portrait of Public High School Graduation, Class of 2001.* Washington, D.C.: Urban Institute, Education Policy Center.

U.S. Bureau of the Census, Population Division, Population Projections Branch. 2000. *Population Projections of the United States by Age, Sex, Race, Hispanic Origin, and Nativity: 1999–2100.* Washington: U.S. Bureau of the Census.

Wooldridge, Jeffrey W. 2002. *Econometric Analysis of Cross Section and Panel Data.* Cambridge, Mass.: MIT Press.

—— Chapter 3 ——

Participation in Career and Technical Education and School-to-Work in American High Schools

James R. Stone III and Oscar A. Aliaga

D URING THE LATE 1970s and early 1980s, at a time when the U.S. economy was seen as not competitive with respect to other major industrial countries, concerns were voiced about the quality of the public education system. Critics of public education linked the quality of public schools to the perceived economic problems of the day and argued that improving the quality of schools was critical to future economic competitiveness. Spurred by reports such as *A Nation at Risk* (Gardner 1983), states and federal legislators then sought to fix what was perceived to be a poorly performing education system. Different educational reforms have focused on increasing the number of rigorous academic courses required for graduation and introducing changes in work-related education. This presumed relationship between educational quality and national economic performance has since been challenged (see National Research Council 1999), but many education reformers continue to make this case.

Those reforms included measures to increase participation of high school students in career and technical education (CTE), to better prepare students for the world of work, and to ensure that students were well prepared for educational and economic attainment. Toward this end the federal government initiated in the early 1990s

59

a wave of CTE reforms that set forth national guidelines and provided funding for program and systems change with the general purpose of improving the quality of high school preparation for careers. We are now at a time when the federal government is proposing a substantial change in CTE legislation, changes premised in part on assumptions about the lack of progress made under previous legislation.

In this chapter we report on the extent to which, at the end of the twentieth century, students in this country were enrolled in career and technical education and in school-to-work (STW) activities of various kinds: career-major (CM), Tech Prep (TP), and specific work-based STW activities, including cooperative education, job shadowing, mentoring, school-based enterprise, and apprenticeships or internships. We also examine the extent to which career majors, Tech Prep, and specific work-based learning STW activities have become a part of the schooling of all adolescents.

PURPOSE AND GENERAL APPROACH

The purpose of this study is to examine participation in CTE and in STW activities at the end of the twentieth century. We do so from the perspective that social origins affect school achievement. Studies in the sociology of education tradition have explored the impact of social factors on educational achievement. Specifically, they have focused on sets of factors that influence how students do in school. One such factor is family background (Dauber, Alexander, and Entwisle 1996; Ensminger and Slusarcick 1992; Roscigno and Ainsworth-Darnell 1999), which comprises socioeconomic status, race, and family structure characteristics. In particular, research studies during the twentieth century have focused on the differences in educational achievement arising from social inequalities (Gamoran 2001). It has been well documented that race and ethnic differences in achievement reflect not only the quality of schooling, but also conditions outside school, since "what students bring to school from home greatly influences how they perform" (Peng, Wright, and Hill 1995, 20). But they are also related to educational processes such as course-taking patterns, students' aspirations, and tracking. Other factors are the effects of school behavior and community characteristics (Dauber, Alexander, and Entwisle 1996; Stull 2002), in particular prior academic achievement at the pre–high school level and family values and expectations (Ensminger and Slusarcick 1992).

We therefore examine the direct effects of a set of social factors on CTE participation and participation in school-to-work activities: students' family background characteristics such as gender, race, and ethnicity; family socioeconomic status such as father's and mother's education; school performance and achievement (eighth-grade GPA); and community characteristics (for example, community location).

FEDERAL CTE REFORM OF THE 1990s

Federal involvement in CTE extends back to 1917, to the passage of the Smith-Hughes Act, and historically has been geared toward supporting general occupational preparation, family and consumer sciences, and specific areas of labor-market preparation assumed to require less than a baccalaureate degree. With the passage of the Carl D. Perkins Vocational and Applied Technology Education Act in 1990 (also known as Perkins II), however, the policy focus changed and in the early 1990s began to target specific programs less and education reform more. The Carl D. Perkins Vocational and Technical Education Act of 1998 (Perkins III) continued this direction, while strengthening the requirements for accountability. Between the Perkins II and Perkins III amendments, the federal government, in 1994, also sought to influence the creation of more transparent and viable systems of workforce development through the passage of the School-to-Work Opportunities Act (STWOA), which was considered an overall attempt to foster change within state education systems. The purpose of these three laws was to improve the academic and technical competence of students emerging from the nation's high schools and consequently improve the transition from school to careers. All three laws affected high school students graduating in the latter part of the decade of the nineties.

Perkins II

The strategy embodied in Perkins II for improving the quality of the labor force was to upgrade secondary and two-year college education programs in order to more fully develop the academic and occupational skills of all segments of the population, not just those presumed to be heading for early labor-market entry. This shift recognized the need for all students to prepare for the workforce of the future.

Perkins II included three unique components. First, Congress created a national program called Tech Prep. In the mid-1980s, Dale Parnell (1985), among others, had argued that students were leaving high school unprepared for either work or further education, thus limiting their ability to succeed beyond secondary school. This lack of preparation was most acute in the areas of mathematics, science, technology, and communication skills (Craig 1999). Parnell's proposed solution was a four-year program of study that comprised the last two years of high school and two years of post–high school education and training and had a heavy emphasis on math and science. This "two plus two" model became part of Perkins II.

Second, Perkins II focused on curriculum integration, a notion that goes back almost a full century to John Dewey (1916). Perkins II failed to define curriculum integration beyond stating that it was a set of coherent course sequences designed to lead to student achievement of academic and CTE competencies, as opposed to random course work. By the mid-1990s when employers were beginning to voice concerns about academic deficiencies in their newly hired workers that were most acute in high-performance workplaces, curriculum integration was seen as a possible answer (Hayward and Benson 1993).

Third, Perkins II emphasized accountability. Before Perkins II, little accountability was required of states beyond reporting enrollment numbers and policy compliance (Hoachlander 1995). Now, states were told to develop performance measures, to determine standards for those measures, and to base student and program evaluations on those standards.

The School-to-Work Opportunities Act

The STWOA was passed in 1994 and was designed to encourage states to create more coherent systems to bridge the gap between education and work for all students, not just the select few who aspired to a narrow range of professional careers that offered transparent pathways (Hamilton 1990), providing funds for this purpose. Unlike Perkins II, which revamped existing CTE education programs, the STWOA established a national framework for the development of new systems to help youth make the transition from school to the workplace by forming coalitions of post-secondary institutions, employers, labor organizations, government, community groups, parents, and students. Building on the belief that students learn best by doing and then applying what they learn in school to the workplace, STWOA funded school-employer partnerships to design and support new work-based learning programs as defined in the act (Levesque et al. 2000). Although the STWOA expired in October 2001, some states continue to support school-to-work activities because the federal funds were only intended to be seed money (Cutshall 2001; Halperin 1994). The STWOA also encouraged alternative school-based structures such as career majors or pathways, career academies, and Tech Prep, as well as specific work-based learning pedagogies, such as cooperative education and job shadowing, designed to connect youth to the workplace.

Perkins III

The stated aim of Perkins III was to place CTE in the broader framework of education reform. It eliminated the "set-asides" for special targeted populations but offered states more flexibility to allow for experimentation and new program development. Perkins III also sought (Bailey and Kienzl 1999) to further CTE by focusing federal investment on programs that

- Integrated academic and CTE education
- Involved parents and employers
- Provided strong connections between secondary and post-secondary education
- Developed, improved, and expanded the use of technology
- Provided professional development for teachers, counselors, and administrators

But the most important change that came with Perkins III was an increased emphasis on accountability.

CTE AND THE HIGH SCHOOL EXPERIENCE

Adolescents enter high school with different home and neighborhood backgrounds, different levels of academic preparation, varying degrees of commitment to education, and a wide range of goals and aspirations for their post–high school years. Which concentration or curriculum pattern a student follows depends on both individual choice and the sorting and tracking mechanisms used in schools (Garet and DeLany 1988). Since building the workforce skills and increasing the academic performance of high school students was viewed as vital for the health of the domestic economy (Bozick and MacAllum 2002), the federal Perkins reform legislation aimed to provide both workforce skills and improved academic performance to all students. This approach was a departure from traditional vocational education perceptions, policies, and practices, which had focused mostly on the disadvantaged (Halperin 1994) or those considered non-college-bound.

The goal of these CTE-focused school reforms was perceived as an effort to blur the boundaries between curriculum concentrations. The idea of emphasizing the improvement of work and academic skills for all students was based on the positive associations found between work-based learning and students' educational outcomes (Wanacott 2002). Early research indicates that CTE and school-to-work can help decrease dropout rates and increase college enrollment, as well as improve attendance and grades, although there are no studies available about the impact on test scores (Hughes, Bailey, and Mechur 2001). Other studies have reported the positive, yet limited, impact of CTE and school-to-work on at-risk youth (Castellano, Stringfield, and Stone 2003).

Despite the intent of federal legislation to increase the availability of work-related education for all students, high schools tend to have their own internal logic. Even after years of reform efforts, most high schools still have one recognized academic concentration and another concentration for students thought to be headed for early entry into the labor market. The rest of the students are left to wander haphazardly through their high school years, mostly under the umbrella or influence of a pseudo-academic concentration, a problem that has been recognized for more than a decade (Hallinan 1994; Hughes, Bailey, and Mechur 2001; Oakes 1994;

Oakes et al. 1992). Those students represent a third, or "general," concentration.

One result of the several CTE reform efforts is the emergence of a fourth concentration offered to students who follow both a rigorous academic sequence of courses and a rigorous sequence of CTE courses. These "dual concentrators," although their numbers are small, may represent the culmination of the reform efforts by combining the two long-standing philosophical traditions and curricula prevalent in high schools since the early 1900s. This group has generated considerable interest among policymakers and practitioners. Some evidence suggests these students, unlike traditional CTE concentrators, perform as well on traditional measures of achievement as academic concentrators (Plank 2001; Silverberg et al. 2004).

CTE ENROLLMENT PRIOR TO THE SCHOOL REFORM OF THE 1990s

The application of the school reform legislation brought changes in programs and systems, but it also provided new policy areas to be explored. One often-debated issue concerns defining and measuring CTE participation. How one makes these distinctions have a profound effect on the examined outcomes. Thus, in order to understand CTE and school-to-work participation patterns in the late 1990s, we first examined research that described participation patterns for the 1980s and early 1990s. While this analysis would appear to be straightforward, it is not.

Researchers use two main approaches to describe CTE and school-to-work participation, and each yields different findings. "Transcript analysis" involves defining CTE participants post hoc by imposing a template on their transcripts. On the other hand, "self-classification" is based on the assumption that students are in the best position to define their curricular concentration.

CTE Participation: Transcript Analysis

Stephen Roey and his colleagues (2001) illustrated how high school students are sorted into curriculum patterns. Imposing a template over transcript data so as to organize curricula into concentrations, they found that the percentage of high school graduates from both public and nonpublic institutions who were CTE concentrators has progressively decreased from 23.2 percent in 1982 to 4.4 percent in 1998. At the same time, academic concentrators followed the opposite trend—increasing from 42.5 percent in 1982 to 71 percent in 1998. The authors also tracked a group that combines academic and CTE course work, or dual concentrators; this group grew from 9 percent in 1982 to 19.3 percent in 1998.

John Tuma (1996) found similar declining trends in CTE concentration. Basing his analysis on the U.S. Department of Education's (USDE) High School Transcript Study and the National Educational Longitudinal Study of 1988 (NELS88), he reported that in 1982, 33.7 percent of public high school graduates were CTE concentrators, but that number fell to 24.4 percent in 1992. Stephen Plank (2001), also using the NELS88 data, calculated that 18.9 percent of 1992 graduates were CTE concentrators and 36.3 percent were academic concentrators. Both Roey et al.'s (2001) and Plank's (2001) analyses were guided by the classification scheme described in the National Center for Education Statistics' (NCES) guidelines on course classification (Alt and Bradby 1999; Bradby and Hoachlander 1999).

Karen Levesque and her colleagues (2000) tracked enrollments and found that CTE concentrators constituted 33.1 percent of all students in 1982 and fell to 21 percent by 1994. The 2004 National Assessment of Vocational Education (NAVE) concluded that although the most commonly used measure of participation indicates that the decline through the decade of the 1980s appears to have leveled off, the share of occupational concentrators fell substantially between 1982 and 1992 and has been fairly steady since then, at about one-quarter of all high school graduates (Silverberg et al. 2004). These sometimes contradictory findings suggest that using researcher-imposed templates on transcripts does not guarantee consistent findings.

CTE Participation: Self-Classification Analyses

Other researchers have used a self-classification approach to measure CTE participation among high school students, provided through student surveys. Where transcript analyses follow course-taking patterns, self-classification data are more likely to show student intent rather

TABLE 3.1   **Curriculum Concentration Participation, All Youths in Survey, All Years (Percentages and Weighted Estimates)**

Concentration[a]	Description	Percentage	Population Estimate
General	General program	52.2	10,026,963
Academic	College preparatory, academic, or specialized academic program	34.6	6,641,333
CTE	CTE, business, and career program	6.6	1,270,071
Dual	Combination academic and CTE program	5.9	1,126,828
Total		99.3[b]	19,197,151
Sample N		8,765	

Source: National Longitudinal Survey of Youth (1997).
[a]Last reported for years 1997 through 2001.
[b]Does not add up to 100 percent because others did not report participation in these concentrations.

than student placement by counselors or others. For example, the almost 35 percent of youth who self-classified as academic concentrators is a proportion more closely aligned with current estimates of college enrollment (see Rosenbaum 2002) than are estimates derived from transcript analysis. Similarly, we might assume that the true number of CTE concentrators is much lower than that identified through transcript analysis, as noted by Richard Arum and Yossi Shavit (1995) in their analysis exploring the differences between self-classification and transcripts. (For an extended discussion of the different participation estimates, see Stone and Aliaga 2003.)

Results for our current analysis of the NLSY97 data that sum students' experiences over their high school years show that 6.6 percent of youth self-identified as CTE concentrators and 34.6 percent as academic concentrators (see table 3.1). The differences in the results using transcript data versus self-classification are critical to understanding how curriculum concentration relates to educational and economic outcomes of interest.

The preceding review highlights the lack of current knowledge about who participated in CTE and STW at the end of the 1990s. This gap is the focus of the present study. This study will also provide data and analysis covering other topics for which little or no data and information have been reported for the late 1980s or early 1990s. For example, research on CTE prior to the mid-1990s does not report on career majors and reports only on a limited basis for Tech Prep as these are recent innovations. The concept of STW is similarly absent or lightly addressed in the literature (Boesel, Rahn, and Deich 1994; Levesque et al. 1995; Milne 1998). Thus, the analysis provided in this chapter can be considered a benchmark analysis for student participation in CTE, STW and STW-related activities in the 1990s.

RESEARCH QUESTIONS

In these analyses, we examine data from a series of questions asked of a nationally representative sample of adolescents enrolled in school between 1997 and 2001. This study asks:

1. What characteristics define participants in the different curricula offered in American high schools? We are especially interested in the extent to which youths who concentrate in CTE or dual concentrations differ from youths in other curricular concentrations as a function of characteristics they bring with them when they enter ninth grade.
2. What characteristics define participants in school-to-work activities in American high schools?
3. To what extent have the programmatic and pedagogic strategies supported by the STWOA become embedded in the high school curriculum concentrations? To what extent do non-CTE youth participate in school-to-work and school-to-work-related activities?

DATA

We analyzed data from the first five rounds of interviews of the National Longitudinal Survey of Youth (NLSY97), to answer the three questions posed by the study. The NLSY97—described by the U.S. Department of Labor's Bureau of Labor Statistics (2002) as a database consisting of a nationally representative sample of approximately nine thousand youth twelve to sixteen years old as of December 31, 1996—was designed to document the transition from school to work and into adulthood. The survey was administered through personal interviews with the youths and gathered extensive information on their education and training, among other variables. Youths who had attended the ninth grade or higher were asked a number of questions about their participation in school programs, including what curriculum concentration they believed best described their high school experience and the extent to which they participated in CTE, career majors, Tech Prep, and work-based school-to-work activities. We analyze each research question with descriptive data, and then we explore the probabilities of participation in CTE and STW activities using logistic regression analyses.

To understand what the NLSY97 data can tell us about the study questions, it is important to note that the sample members began graduating from high school in 1998, so their secondary schooling was influenced by Perkins II and the STWOA. Perkins III (Carl D. Perkins Vocational and Technical Education Act of 1998)—which further encouraged many of these same initiatives—had just been enacted at the time the early wave of this cohort was leaving high school.

Demographic data used in these analyses come primarily from the round 1 of interviews. Race is a variable created from a question in the survey that can be answered by checking four racial categories (white, black, native American, and Asian or Pacific Islander), as well as other. For the analyses reported here, we used only the first two and largest groups—white and black. Other possible racial groups (for example, Asian) were too small to provide a meaningful basis for analysis. Ethnicity is derived from a different question in the survey that asked whether the respondent was Hispanic or not.

For the purpose of comparing youth according to their socioeconomic status, we used parent education as a proxy for income, as suggested by Adam Gamoran (2001). The parent education information also comes from round 1 of interviews because we wanted to obtain a more uniform picture about socioeconomic status at the start of the study, when respondents were generally living at home with their families when the study began. Subsequent data for those categories may have changed over time as respondents left their homes or communities and became more difficult to track. Also, having measures of key socioeconomic variables at the point they entered high school will more accurately reflect the effect of those variables on their high school trajectory and outcomes (Peng, Wright, and Hill 1995). Data for concentration participation reflect the last concentration reported.

RESULTS

We present results in two sections. The first relates to participation in the CTE curriculum. The second is for participation in the STW activities.

Curriculum Participation in U.S. High Schools

An estimated 6.6 percent of youth identified themselves as CTE concentrators, that is, they follow a specific sequence of courses in an occupational area (see table 3.1). This figure is far lower than current NCES reports of 20.9 percent, which are based on transcript analyses for public high schools (Hudson and Hurst 1999; Levesque et al. 2000). Estimates for dual concentrators, who follow a college prep sequence and a CTE concentration simultaneously, show more similarities with those of the other studies. Although these percentages appear to be small, when participation is measured in other ways CTE is shown to engage a large number of students across the nation. According to the most recent NAVE report, vocational education has become a large component of school course taking (Silverberg et al. 2004); it indicates that more than 98 percent of students have taken at least one CTE class during their high school experience, and about 43 percent of high school students took at least three occupational credits.

In describing the characteristics of youth who participate in the four curricular options, we included characteristics when they entered ninth grade, including self-reports of gender, race and ethnicity, parents' education, community location, and their eighth-grade GPA (see table 3.2). For this part of our study we analyzed four separate logistic regression models, with self-report of curriculum concentration coded 1 and the others coded 0 as the reference

TABLE 3.2 Variable Descriptive Statistics, by Curriculum Concentration

Independent Variable	All Students	Curriculum Concentration[b]				Minimum and Maximum
		General	Academic	CTE	Dual	
Personal characteristics						
Gender (Female)	0.49	0.47	0.54	0.41	0.42	0 to 1
	(0.50)	(0.50)	(0.50)	(0.49)	(0.49)	
Race (Black)	0.18	0.18	0.14	0.29	0.22	0 to 1
	(0.38)	(0.38)	(0.35)	(0.45)	(0.41)	
Ethnicity (Hispanic)	0.13	0.16	0.09	0.12	0.09	0 to 1
	(0.33)	(0.36)	(0.29)	(0.33)	(0.29)	
Parent Education[a]	13.03	12.56	14.04	12.08	12.49	1 to 20
	(3.03)	(3.01)	(2.97)	(2.50)	(2.65)	
Community location						
Urban	0.26	0.28	0.21	0.30	0.29	0 to 1
	(0.44)	(0.45)	(0.41)	(0.46)	(0.45)	
Rural	0.21	0.21	0.19	0.28	0.23	0 to 1
	(0.41)	(0.41)	(0.39)	(0.45)	(0.42)	
Suburban	0.53	0.50	0.60	0.43	0.48	0 to 1
	(0.50)	(0.50)	(0.49)	(0.49)	(0.50)	
Eighth-grade GPA	2.91	2.69	3.35	2.56	2.73	0.5 to 4.0
	(0.84)	(0.84)	(0.66)	(0.78)	(0.81)	

Source: National Longitudinal Survey of Youth (1997).
Notes: Data for the independent variables are for 1997.
Overall, N = 8,984. However, N for specific analyses varies.
[a]Number of years of the father's education if the respondent lives with two parents. Otherwise defined as the education of the parent or nonparent adult with whom the respondent lived. Standard deviation in parentheses.
[b]Last curriculum concentration is reported.

TABLE 3.3   **Logistic Regression Probabilities (Odds Ratios)
for Curriculum Concentration Participation**

Independent Variable (Omitted)	Curriculum Concentration (Dependent Variable)			
	General	Academic	CTE	Dual
Gender				
Female	1.009	1.138*	0.893	0.719*
(Male)				
Race				
Black	0.710*	1.174*	1.694*	1.277*
(White)				
Ethnicity				
Hispanic	1.280*	1.101	0.391*	0.615*
(Non-Hispanic)				
Parent education	0.936*	1.134*	0.895*	0.947*
Community location				
Urban	1.308*	0.644*	1.284*	1.081
Rural	1.001	0.844*	1.442*	1.160
(Suburban)				
Eighth-grade GPA	0.508*	2.826*	0.723*	0.916
N	6,934	6,934	6,934	6,934
−2 log likelihood	8930.68	7528.23	3580.31	3186.46

Source: National Longitudinal Survey of Youth (1997).
Note: Last curriculum concentration is reported. Data for the independent variables are for 1997.
*Statistically significant at $p < .05$. General, academic, CTE, and dual models were significant at $p < .05$.

category. The models of curriculum participation are displayed in table 3.3.

One predictor that is significant across all four models for curriculum concentration is parents' education, our proxy for family socioeconomic status. The odds that youth would report participating in the academic concentration increased by 13 percent with each one-year increase in parents' education. Parent education served as a predictor for participation in the other three concentrations but in a negative direction: as parents' education levels increased, students were less likely to report participating in the general, CTE, or dual concentrations.

Females were more likely to identify themselves as academic concentrators than were males. Urban and rural youth were less likely then suburban youth to self-identify as taking the academic concentration. Academic ability is, not surprisingly, a predictor of participation in this concentration. That is, for every unit increase in (self-reported) eighth-grade GPA, the odds that youths will identify as academic concentrators increased by a factor of 2.8.

Five background characteristics predicted participation in the CTE concentration. Blacks were more likely than whites to identify with this concentration, and Hispanics were less likely than non-Hispanics. Like their general-concentration counterparts, CTE youth entered high school with lower academic ability than other youth. And it follows that as parent education increased, the odds that a youth would identify as a CTE concentrator decreased; this is another characteristic CTE concentrators share with general concentrators as they enter high school. Like general concentrators, CTE concentrators are more likely to live in urban communities than suburban. These data suggest that CTE and general concentrators bring similar academic preparation, share similar socioeconomic backgrounds, and come from similar communities, but follow divergent pathways once in high school.

General concentrators can be identified by five background characteristics—race, ethnicity, GPA, community location, and parent education—as follows. The odds that black youth were general concentrators were 71 percent those of white youth, and the odds that Hispanic youth identified with the general concentration were 28 percent greater than non-Hispanic youth. As eighth-grade GPA increased, the odds that a youth identified with the general concentration significantly decreased. Urban youth were 31 percent more likely than suburban youth to indicate they were in the general concentration.

Dual concentrators tend to be most like other students in terms of academic ability entering high school as well as the kind of community in which they live. However, females are less likely then males to identify with this curriculum, and blacks are 28 percent more likely than whites to identify with this curriculum concentration. As with their CTE and general concentration counterparts, as parent education increases youths are less likely to identify as dual concentrators. These data suggest that social class and community, race, ethnicity, and ability are still key defining characteristics when youths enter high school and choose or are placed in particular curriculum concentrations.

TABLE 3.4   **High School Participation in Career Major, Tech Prep, and Specific School-to-Work Activities (Percentages and Population Estimates)**

STW Activities and Programs	Percentage[a]	Estimated Population
Career major	32.7	6,136,522
Tech Prep	13.4	2,519,751
Participation in specific STW activities		
Cooperative education	14.6	2,741,117
Job shadowing	21.6	4,052,771
Mentoring	9.2	1,717,738
School-based enterprise	12.2	2,284,360
Internship or Apprenticeship	9.5	1,776,621
No participation in Tech Prep or any STW activities in all years while in high school	51.4	9,637,027
Total estimated population		18,759,677
Sample N		8,498

Source: National Longitudinal Survey of Youth (1997).
Notes: "No Participation in Tech Prep or STW" data refer to students who did not participate in *all* high school years.
Percentage sums to more than 100 because of multiple options to respond.
[a]Analyses for 1997 to 2001 are performed for participation in CTE-related activities at any point during high school.

Participation Patterns in Career Majors, Tech Prep, and Specific STW Activities

The second question the study seeks to examine is the extent to which youths participated in the reforms at the heart of the STWOA. To get answers we examined participation in those activities at any point during high school. We also examined how background characteristics combined with curriculum concentration to characterize youths who participated in the career majors, Tech Prep, and the work-based school-to-work activities identified in this data base (cooperative education, job shadowing, mentoring, school-sponsored enterprise, and apprenticeships and internships).

Our estimates show that only a modest proportion of youths reported participation in any one of the STW activities at any time during their high school careers (see table 3.4). The majority of youths reported not participating in any of these activities at all while in high school.

About a third of students indicated they were career major participants at some point in their high school career. This percentage is considerably higher than the combined percentage of CTE and dual concentrators. As well, nearly a third of academic students reported participating in a career major (see table 3.5). The explanation for these apparent discrepancies lies in the definition of concentrator and career major. CTE and dual concentrators enroll in three or more sequential, specific labor-market or occupational preparation courses in a particular occupational program—for example, carpentry and auto technology. Career majors are more loosely defined but typically refer to career academies or career pathways. These are curriculum organization strategies, not program definitions. For example, it is possible to be in a health academy and take only one or two specific occupational courses. Career majors are designed to include all students, including academic and general concentrators.

Over a fifth of high school youths participated in job shadowing. A substantial proportion of youths, approximately 25 percent, participated in cooperative vocational education or apprenticeships or internships, both arguably intensive work-based learning activities. These are perhaps surprisingly high participation rates coming after nearly two decades of increasing academic requirements.

Descriptive statistics on the youth who participated in school-to-work activities, presented in table 3.5, allow us to explore the relationship between curriculum concentration and participation in career majors, Tech Prep, and work-based STW, and the extent to which the STWOA has influenced the infusion of career-focused learning in American high schools for all students. As discussed earlier, the STWOA supported high school structural reforms such as career majors (career pathways, career academies, and career clusters are variants on this theme), along with support for existing structural (Tech Prep) and career-focused pedagogic activities such as job shadowing.

We find that whereas more than half of CTE and dual concentrators participated in a career major, only 30 percent of general and academic concentrators did so. Given the wide implementation of career clusters; the number of states, such as Washington, that have mandated career pathways; and the growing number of career academies that have emerged during the 1990s, one could argue that these student reports provide evidence that the STWOA was not

TABLE 3.5 Variable Descriptive Statistics, by STW Activity

				STW Activity				
					Specific School-to-Work Activity			
	All Students	Career Major	Tech Prep	Cooperative Education	Job Shadowing	Mentoring	School-Based Enterprise	Internship or Apprenticeship
Gender (female)	0.49	0.48	0.42	0.49	0.53	0.56	0.55	0.50
	(0.50)	(0.50)	(0.49)	(0.50)	(0.50)	(0.50)	(0.50)	(0.50)
Race (black)	0.18	0.22	0.23	0.23	0.17	0.24	0.20	0.20
	(0.38)	(0.42)	(0.42)	(0.42)	(0.38)	(0.43)	(0.40)	(0.40)
Ethnicity (Hispanic)	0.13	0.13	0.13	0.12	0.10	0.11	0.10	0.14
	(0.33)	(0.33)	(0.34)	(0.33)	(0.30)	(0.31)	(0.30)	(0.34)
Parent education[a]	13.03	12.79	12.63	12.67	13.25	13.26	13.18	13.02
	(3.03)	(2.72)	(2.58)	(2.77)	(2.98)	(2.80)	(2.76)	(2.89)
Community location								
Urban	0.26	0.26	0.24	0.27	0.24	0.29	0.29	0.29
	(0.44)	(0.44)	(0.43)	(0.44)	(0.42)	(0.45)	(0.45)	(0.45)
Rural	0.21	0.22	0.22	0.20	0.24	0.19	0.18	0.16
	(0.41)	(0.41)	(0.41)	(0.40)	(0.43)	(0.40)	(0.39)	(0.37)

	(1)	(2)	(3)	(4)	(5)	(6)	(7)	(8)
Suburban	0.53	0.52	0.53	0.53	0.53	0.52	0.53	0.55
	(0.50)	(0.50)	(0.50)	(0.50)	(0.50)	(0.50)	(0.50)	(0.50)
Eighth-grade GPA	2.91	2.87	2.80	2.89	2.98	2.99	3.01	2.92
	(0.84)	(0.82)	(0.82)	(0.79)	(0.82)	(0.82)	(0.83)	(0.83)
Curriculum concentration								
General	0.53	0.29	0.12	0.12	0.20	0.08	0.11	0.08
	(0.50)	(0.45)	(0.32)	(0.33)	(0.40)	(0.27)	(0.31)	(0.27)
Academic	0.35	0.31	0.10	0.12	0.23	0.10	0.14	0.10
	(0.48)	(0.46)	(0.31)	(0.33)	(0.42)	(0.30)	(0.34)	(0.30)
CTE	0.07	0.56	0.31	0.30	0.24	0.11	0.15	0.14
	(0.25)	(0.50)	(0.46)	(0.46)	(0.42)	(0.32)	(0.36)	(0.35)
Dual	0.06	0.52	0.29	0.31	0.21	0.13	0.14	0.14
	(0.24)	(0.50)	(0.45)	(0.46)	(0.41)	(0.34)	(0.34)	(0.35)

Source: National Longitudinal Survey of Youth (1997).

Note: Standard deviation in parentheses. Data for the independent variables are for 1997. Data on participation in STW activities indicate participation at any point during high school. Overall N = 8,984. N for specific analyses varies.

[a]Number of years.

successful. There are two other possible explanations for these find-ings, however. We know from the NLSY97 school administrators survey that less than one-fourth of all schools report offering a career major concentration (see Stone, Kowske, and Alfeld 2004), a statistic that suggests the limited impact of the STWOA. This obviously limits the opportunity for non-CTE students to participate in career-related education. The findings for Tech Prep and the work-based STW activities are similar except for reports of participation in job shad-owing, mentoring, and school-based enterprise. The percentages of youth who reported participation in these three school-to-work activ-ities, while low, are approximately the same across all concentrations, suggesting a more balanced diffusion within high schools.

We employed the same model used to analyze curriculum con-centration to determine the characteristics of youths who participated in career majors, Tech Prep, or work-based STW activities (table 3.6). In this case, we explored a model that adds curriculum concentration to examine the relationship between curriculum, especially CTE, and STW participation. Each of the dependent variables were analyzed separately, with participation coded 1 and nonparticipation coded 0.

We found that race is a defining characteristic of STW partici-pation. Black youth were significantly more likely than white youth to participate in all but job shadowing. Gender, too, is a defining characteristic in Tech Prep, job shadowing, mentoring, and school-based enterprise: females were significantly more likely to participate in the latter three activities and less likely to participate in Tech Prep. The odds that a Hispanic student would participate in Tech Prep, job shadowing, and school-based enterprise were significantly lower than for non-Hispanics. Hispanics did not differ in their likelihood of participating in a career major or any of the other STW activities.

As the education level of students' parents increased, youth were significantly less likely to participate in a career major, Tech Prep, or cooperative education. However eighth-grade GPA had limited predictive power in defining STW participation, with the exception of cooperative education and school-based enterprise. Each unit increase in eighth-grade GPA increased the odds of par-ticipation in cooperative education and school-based enterprise by 11 percent and 19 percent, respectively.

There were significant relationships between curriculum concen-tration and various elements of STW. As noted earlier, the career

TABLE 3.6 Logistic Regression Probabilities (Odds Ratios) for High School Participation in STW Activities and School Experience Indicators

| | | | | STW Activity | | | |
| | | | | | Specific School-to-Work Activity | | |
Independent Variable (Omitted)	Career Major	Tech Prep	Cooperative Education	Job Shadowing	Mentoring	School-Based Enterprise	Internship or Apprenticeship
Gender							
Female (male)	1.012	0.913*	1.015	1.116*	1.194*	1.129*	1.037
Race							
Black (white)	1.202*	1.168*	1.194*	0.999	1.267*	1.143*	1.144*
Ethnicity							
Hispanic (non-Hispanic)	0.949	0.925	0.992	0.837*	1.056	0.843*	1.054
Parent education	0.966*	0.962*	0.970*	1.018	1.028	1.002	0.996
Community location							
Urban	1.031	0.949	1.025	0.941	1.114	1.079	1.171*
Rural	1.023	1.045	0.974	1.161*	0.956	0.927	0.798*
(Suburban)							
Eighth-grade GPA	0.974	0.975	1.112*	1.015	1.047	1.185*	1.060
Curriculum concentration							
General	0.577*	0.559*	0.608*	0.894*	0.793*	0.826*	0.694*
CTE	1.528*	1.857*	1.736*	1.102	1.039	1.125	1.180
Dual	1.573*	1.653*	1.551*	0.982	1.172	1.133	1.379*
(Academic)							
N	6,735	6,732	6,732	6,732	6,732	6,732	6,732
−2 log likelihood	8290.15	5255.96	5524.52	6926.22	4052.60	4841.57	4058.84

Source: National Longitudinal Survey of Youth (1997).

Notes: Data for CTE-related activities are for participation at any point during the high school experience. Eighth-grade GPA is last reported for 1997 to 2001. The STW activity models are all significant at p < .05.

*Statistically significant at p < .05.

majors or career pathway was one of the important school reform structures introduced in the STWOA with the aim of involving all students. We find, however, that the odds that CTE and dual concentrators participated in a career major were more than 50 percent greater than for their academic counterparts and that the odds of general concentrators were half that of academic youths. In fact, general concentrators, compared to academic concentrators, were less likely to participate in any STW activity.

CTE and dual concentrators were, respectively, 1.9 and 1.7 times more likely than academic concentrators to participate in Tech Prep. Given that Tech Prep was built largely on articulation agreements between two-year colleges and CTE courses, this relationship is not surprising. Similarly, our finding that the odds of a CTE or dual concentrator participating in cooperative education are significantly greater than an academic concentrator is not unexpected. Like Tech Prep, cooperative education is part of the traditional CTE curriculum.

In three of the STW activities—job shadowing, school-based enterprise, and mentoring—we find no difference in participation between the CTE, dual, and academic concentrators. The odds that a CTE or academic concentrator would participate in an internship or apprenticeship were similar, but dual concentrators were significantly more likely and general concentrators significantly less likely than academic concentrators to engage in this STW activity. This finding may be explained in part by the fact that many apprenticeships are connected to community colleges, as are some internships, and are often predicated on participation in high school CTE. Thus, youths who work through a community college will likely self identify as dual concentrators because they are combining a two-year college experience with their high school CTE.

The profiles that emerge for the career majors, Tech Prep, and cooperative education students are quite similar in that curriculum concentration, race, and parents' education are significant predictors of participation. We did not find such consistent patterns in the profiles of youth who participated in work-based-learning STW activities except that general concentrators were significantly less likely than academic concentrators to participate in any form of STW.

As we noted at the beginning of this report, there are no benchmarks for participation measures on most of these activities, and the NLSY97 was one of the first efforts to document them. What these data show is a mixed picture of the extent to which STW was a part of the high school experience for all high school students at the end of the twentieth century. Over half of students indicated they did not participate in any of the STW activities at all. Of those who did, curriculum concentration was not predictive of participation in three specific STW work-based learning activities but was predictive for two important structural reforms, TP and career majors, and two of the more intensive work-based learning pedagogies, cooperative education and internships and apprenticeships.

DISCUSSION

In this chapter we have explored questions regarding career and technical education following more than a decade of CTE-focused and general-education reform. We used youth self-report data from the NLSY97 database to explore these questions. Although these data have many strengths, especially for questions related to labor-market activity, there are some shortcomings when the questions turn to educational experience and education-related outcomes. For our analyses, the principal shortcoming is the limited set of definitions of CTE. The options presented to the youth in the interviews do not align with the U.S. Department of Education Secondary School Taxonomy or other curriculum frameworks. Similarly, the definitions of school-to-work are limited, and although some structural reforms are identified (for example, career majors), others are not (career academies). Omitted are questions related to what the STWOA referred to as connecting activities, such as career guidance.

Some of these shortcomings—especially in the identification of specific course-taking patterns—will be addressed through NLSY97 transcript analyses (see Plank, DeLuca, and Estacion 2005). Unfortunately, career majors, career academies, and most of the work-based learning activities (such as internships) are not transcripted, so student self-reports will still be the principal means of measuring participation.

Nonetheless, evidence from the NLSY97 allows us to create a portrait of student participation in career-related education and pedagogies in the late 1990s. We find in our analyses that the average number of CTE courses taken by all students is only slightly lower than that taken by CTE concentrators. Given that CTE concentrators are a very small proportion of all students, these data suggest that many youths are investing in CTE. This is consistent with the recent NAVE report (Silverberg et al. 2004). Despite continuing demands on school schedules for inclusion of more academic courses, CTE remains a large part of the high school experience.

The percentage of youth who self-identify as CTE concentrators is considerably smaller than reported elsewhere. We suggest that this difference may reflect not only the difference between self-report and transcript data but also different student motivation—namely, fear of stigma attached to CTE concentration—when self-reporting. CTE may be a matter of conscious choice for some youth but for others it may be a matter of tracking. The disparity in CTE participation between self-reporting and transcripts may also be explained by the percentage of general concentrators who self-report taking many CTE courses. It is likely that many of these students have been placed in these courses by school counselors. It may also be true that many of these students elect to take CTE courses but do not see themselves as CTE concentrators because they believe, like most youth, that they are going to college and view CTE as a place for the non-college-bound. Regardless of how youth come to identify with a particular curriculum concentration, we find that race, gender, ethnicity, and social class play an important role in such assignments.

CTE and general concentrators come from households in lower socioeconomic groups and enter high school less well prepared academically than other students. This may suggest racial and class distinctions in how high schools counsel, encourage, or perhaps track youths into various curricular alternatives. The use of vocational education as a tracking system is a concept that has been described previously (Oakes, Gamoran, and Page 1992).

The CTE and school-to-work legislation of the 1990s was intended to improve the transition of youth to careers by increasing their contact with and study of the workplace and by improving the academic rigor of the high school experience. In the post–No Child Left Behind era many states are increasing the amount of traditional academic course work required for graduation—for example, requiring four years of mathematics. Such an increase in required course work clearly reduces the time available for elective course work, including CTE. As political leaders seek simple solutions to the complex problems confronting public education, we expect the trend toward mandating more academic course work to continue, and this can be expected to reduce the levels of participation in CTE and school-to-work reported here.

The work reported here was supported under the National Research Center for Career and Technical Education Program, PR/Award No. VO51A990006, administered by the Office of Vocational and Adult Education, U.S. Department of Education. However, the contents do not necessarily represent the positions or policies of the Office of Vocational and Adult Education nor the U.S. Department of Education, and endorsement of our results by the federal government should not be assumed.

REFERENCES

Alt, Martha N., and Denise Bradby. 1999. *Procedures Guide for Transcript Studies.* NCES Working Paper No. 1999-05. Washington, D.C.: National Center for Education Statistics.

Arum, Richard, and Yossi Shavit. 1995. "Secondary Vocational Education and the Transition from School to Work." *Sociology of Education* 68(3): 187–204.

Bailey, Thomas R., and Gregory Kienzl. 1999. "What Can We Learn About Postsecondary Vocational Education from Existing Data?" Paper presented at the National Assessment of Vocational Education Independent Advisory Panel Meeting, Washington, D.C. (May 6–7).

Boesel, David, Mikala Rahn, and Sharon Deich. 1994. *National Assessment of Vocational Education: Final report to Congress.* Washington: U.S. Department of Education.

Bozick, Robert, and Keith MacAllum. 2002. *Does Participation in School-to-Career Limit Students' Educational and Career Opportunities? Findings from the LAMP Longitudinal Study.* Washington, D.C.: Academy for Educational Development.

Bradby, Denise, and Gary Hoachlander. 1999. *1998 Revision of the Secondary School Taxonomy.* NCES Working Paper No. 1999-06. Washington, D.C.: National Center for Education Statistics.

Carl D. Perkins Vocational and Applied Technology Education Act of 1990. 1990. Public Law 101-392. U.S. Code 20 (1990).

Carl D. Perkins Vocational and Technical Education Act of 1998. 1998. Public Law 105-332. U.S. Code 20 (1998).

Castellano, Marisa, Sam Stringfield, and James R. Stone III. 2003. "Secondary Career and Technical Education and Comprehensive School Reform: Implications for Research and Practice." *Review of Educational Research* 73(2): 231–72.

Craig, Jon D. 1999. "The Tech-Prep Associate Degree Program." In *Workforce Education: Issues for the New Century,* edited by A. J. Paultner. Ann Arbor, Mich.: Prakken.

Cutshall, Sandy. 2001. "School-to-Work: Has It Worked?" *Techniques: Connecting Education and Careers* 76(1): 18–22.

Dauber, Susan L., Karl L. Alexander, and Doris R. Entwisle. 1996. "Tracking and Transitions Through the Middle Grades: Channeling Educational Trajectories." *Sociology of Education* 69(4): 290–307.

Dewey, John. 1916. *Democracy and Education.* New York: Macmillan.

Ensminger, Margaret E., and Anita L. Slusarcick. 1992. "Paths to High School Graduation or Dropout: A Longitudinal Study of a First-Grade Cohort." *Sociology of Education* 65(2): 95–113.

Gamoran, Adam. 2001. *American Schooling and Educational Inequality: A Forecast for the 21st Century. Sociology of Education* 74(extra issue): 135–53.

Gardner, David P. 1983. *A Nation at Risk: The Imperative for Educational Reform. An Open Letter to the American People. A Report to the Nation and the Secretary of Education.* Washington: U.S. Department of Education.

Garet, Michael S., and Brian DeLany. 1988. "Students, Courses, and Stratification." *Sociology of Education* 61(2): 61–77.

Hallinan, Maureen T. 1994. "Tracking: From Theory to Practice." *Sociology of Education* 67(2): 79–84.

Halperin, Samuel. 1994. *School-to-Work: A Larger Vision.* Washington, D.C.: American Policy Forum.

Hamilton, Stephen F. 1990. *Apprenticeship for Adulthood.* New York: Free Press.

Hayward, Gerald C., and Charles S. Benson. 1993. *Vocational-Technical Education: Major Reforms and Debates, 1917–Present.* Washington: U.S. Department of Education, Office of Vocational and Adult Education.

Hoachlander, E. Gareth. 1995. "Performance Measures and Standards: Implications for Evaluating Program Improvements." In *Education Through Occupations in American High Schools: The Challenges of Implementing Curriculum Integration,* edited by W. Norton Grubb. Vol. 2. New York: Teachers College Press.

Hudson, Lisa, and David Hurst. 1999. *Students Who Prepare for College and a Vocation.* NCES Issue Brief, No. 1999-072. Washington, D.C.: National Center for Education Statistics (August).

Hughes, Katherine L., Thomas R. Bailey, and Melinda J. Mechur. 2001. *School-to-Work: Making a Difference in Education*. New York: Columbia University, Teachers College, Institute on Education and the Economy.

Levesque, Karen, Doug Lauen, Peter Teitelbaum, Martha Alt, Sally Librera, and Dawn Nelson. 2000. *Vocational Education in the United States: Toward the Year 2000*. Washington, D.C.: National Center for Education Statistics.

Levesque, Karen, Mark Premo, Robert Vergun, David Emanuel, Steven Klein, Robin Henke, Susan Kagehiro, and James Houser. 1995. *Vocational Education in the United States: The Early 1990s*. Washington: U.S. Department of Education.

Milne, Ann M., ed. 1998. *Educational Reform and Vocational Education*. Washington: U.S. Department of Education, National Assessment of Vocational Education.

National Longitudinal Survey of Youth. 1997. [Data file.] Washington: Bureau of Labor Statistics, U.S. Department of Labor.

National Research Council. 1999. *Securing America's Industrial Strength*. Washington, D.C.: National Research Council, Board on Science, Technology, and Economic Policy.

Oakes, Jeanie. 1994. "More Than Misapplied Technology: A Normative and Political Response to Hallinan on Tracking." *Sociology of Education* 67(2): 84–89.

Oakes, Jeanie, Adam Gamoran, and Reba N. Page. 1992. "Curriculum Differentiation: Opportunities, Outcomes, and Meanings." In *Handbook of Research on Curriculum*, edited by Philip W. Jackson. New York: Macmillan.

Oakes, Jeanie, Molly Selvin, Lynn Karoly, and Gretchen Guiton. 1992. *Educational Matchmaking: Academic and Vocational Tracking in Comprehensive High Schools*. Berkeley, Calif.: National Center for Research in Vocational Education.

Parnell, Dale. 1985. *The Neglected Majority*. Washington, D.C.: Community College Press.

Peng, Samuel S., DeeAnn Wright, and Susan T. Hill. 1995. *Understanding Racial-Ethnic Differences in Secondary School Science and Mathematics Achievement*. Washington, D.C.: National Center for Education Statistics.

Plank, Stephen. 2001. *Career and Technical Education in the Balance: An Analysis of High School Persistence, Academic Achievement, and Postsecondary Destinations*. St. Paul, Minn.: National Research Center for Career and Technical Education.

Plank, Stephen, Stefanie DeLuca, and Angela Estacion. 2005. *Dropping Out of High School and the Place of Career and Technical Education: A Survival Analysis of Surviving High School*. St. Paul, Minn.: National Research Center for Career and Technical Education.

Roey, Stephen, Nancy Caldwell, Keith Rust, Eyal Blumstein, Tom Krenzke, Stan Legum, Judy Kuhn, Mark Waksberg, and Jacqueline Haynes. 2001. *The 1998 High School Transcript Study Tabulations: Comparative Data on Credits Earned and Demographics for 1998, 1994, 1990, 1987, and 1982 High School Graduates*. Washington, D.C.: National Center for Education Statistics.

Roscigno, Vincent J., and James W. Ainsworth-Darnell. 1999. "Race, Cultural Capital, and Educational Resources: Persistent Inequalities and Achievement Returns." *Sociology of Education* 72(3): 158–78.

Rosenbaum, James E. 2002. *Beyond Empty Promises: Policies to Improve Transitions into College and Jobs*. Washington: U.S. Department of Education, Office of Vocational and Adult Education. Available at: http://www.ed.gov/about/offices/list/ovae/pi/hs/rosenbaum.doc (accessed on January 24, 2003).

School-to-Work Opportunities Act of 1994. 1994. Public Law 103-239. U.S. Code 20(1994).

Silverberg, Marsha, Elizabeth Warner, Michael Fong, and David Goodwin. 2004. *National Assessment of Vocational Education: Final Report to Congress*. Washington: U.S. Department of Education.

Stone, James R., III, and Oscar A. Aliaga. 2003. *Career and Technical Education, Career Pathways, and Work-Based Learning: Changes in Participation 1997–1999*. St. Paul, Minn.: National Research Center for Career and Technical Education.

Stone, James R., III, Brenda J. Kowske, and Corinne Alfeld. 2004. "Career and Technical Education in the Late 1990s: A Descriptive Study." *Journal of Vocational Education Research* 29(3): 195–223.

Stull, Judith C. 2002. *The Determinants of Achievement: Minority Students Compared to Nonminority Students*. Mid-Atlantic Regional Educational Laboratory Publication Series. Philadelphia: Temple University, Center for Research in Human Development and Education, Mid-Atlantic Regional Educational Laboratory.

Tuma, John. 1996. *Trends in Participation in Secondary Vocational Education: 1982–1992*. 96-004. Washington, D.C.: National Center for Education Statistics.

U.S. Department of Labor, Bureau of Labor Statistics. 2002. *National Longitudinal Survey of Youth 1997*. http://www.bls.gov/nls/y97summary.htm.

Wonacott, Michael E. 2002. *The Impact of Work-Based Learning on Students*. ERIC (Education Resources Information Center) Digest, no. 242. Available at: http://www.calpro-online.org/eric/docgen.asp?tbl=digests&ID=127 (accessed July 18, 2006).

— Chapter 4 —

Do School-to-Work Programs Help the "Forgotten Half"?

David Neumark and Donna Rothstein

T HE 1994 FEDERAL School-to-Work Opportunities Act (STWOA) provided around $1.5 billion to support increased career-preparation activities in the country's public schools.[1] The STWOA was spurred by a concern that youth labor markets in the United States entailed unnecessary periods of joblessness, excessive job instability, and employment in dead-end jobs (U.S. General Accounting Office 1990). The act aimed to help young people develop the skills needed in the workforce and make better connections to careers through school-to-career transition systems, which fostered partnerships among schools, employers, and others (U.S. Congress, Office of Technology Assessment 1995).

The "findings" on which the STWOA was based referred specifically to the problems that disadvantaged and minority youths face in making the school-to-work transition.[2] Furthermore, school-to-work practitioners commonly argue that school-to-work programs, policies, and institutions are particularly helpful for less-advantaged youths, or the broader group of those who in the absence of any intervention are unlikely to go on to college—often termed the "forgotten half."[3] The main goal of this paper is to use the 1997 National Longitudinal Survey of Youth (NLSY97) to examine evidence on the effectiveness of school-to-work efforts for the forgotten half—namely, those less likely, ex ante, to attend college. It is important to emphasize that the school-to-work programs covered in the NLSY97 reflect many of the types of programs that the STWOA encouraged, but that the NLSY97 was not designed specifically to evaluate the STWOA. Thus, while there is overlap in programs, there are surely cases of schools that were engaged in related school-to-work efforts prior to the STWOA, as well as schools that did not receive STWOA funds yet ran related school-to-work programs during the period in which the STWOA was in effect.[4] Thus, we are evaluating the effects of a variety of school-to-work programs, not the STWOA itself.

The actual language of the STWOA discussed three approaches to school-to-work (hereafter, STW): work-based learning, school-based learning focusing on careers, and connecting activities between the two types of learning.[5] The specific STW programs covered in the NLSY97 include job shadowing; mentoring (matching students to an individual in an occupation); cooperative education (combining academic and vocational studies);[6] work in a school-sponsored enterprise;[7] Tech Prep (a planned program of study with a defined career focus); and internships or apprenticeships.[8] Among those programs that can be interpreted as work-based learning are job shadowing, cooperative education, work in a school-based enterprise,[9] and internships and apprenticeships. Mentoring ideally is also work-based, but may not necessarily involve work. Job shadowing and mentoring are most likely considerably less intensive than these other programs (Neumark and Joyce 2001). Tech Prep is probably best classified as school-based learning, since it is a curricular arrangement rather than a program based in the workplace.[10]

Our analysis proceeds in two straightforward steps. First, to operationalize the "forgotten half" we estimate a reduced form model for attending college. We do this without incorporating information on STW participation, to establish the ex ante probabilities of college attendance. We use the estimates of this model to distinguish between those in the top half and those in the bottom half of the distribution of the predicted probability of college attendance, and interpret the latter as the "forgotten half." We then estimate regression models for the effects of participation in various STW programs on a number of postsecondary-education- and employment-related outcomes, allowing for separate effects of STW program participation for those in the top and bottom half of the predicted probability of college attendance—in other words, we estimate separate effects for the forgotten half. These estimates are then used to test which types of STW programs boost postsecondary outcomes, and which do this particularly for the forgotten half.

The NLSY97 provides researchers with the best opportunity available to date to study the impact of STW, as it covers participation in many types of STW programs and, with the data now available, begins to capture postsecondary educational and labor-market outcomes. Still, the goal of STW, "better career decision making" among young men and women completing their education and entering the labor market, is multidimensional, and its fulfillment can only be assessed using long-term observations on career trajectories. Although we cannot yet use the NLSY97 data to observe long-term career trajectories, we can use them to study the early impact of STW programs on the beginnings of the postsecondary STW transitions to employment or to higher education. We believe that this more limited perspective is still of interest to researchers and policymakers weighing the potential benefits of STW programs. After all, core concerns of STW are moving people into higher-paying jobs, encouraging skill formation among new labor-market entrants, and increasing enrollment or employment in the immediate post–high school period.

The results we obtain from the analysis provide some evidence of differences in the effects of the types of STW programs covered in the NLSY97. Specifically, the evidence suggests that for men in the forgotten half, mentoring and co-op programs increase postsecondary education, and co-op, school enterprise, and internship-apprenticeship programs boost employment and decrease idleness after leaving high school. For women in the forgotten half, there is less evidence that STW programs are particularly effective in increasing schooling, although internship and apprenticeship programs do lead to positive earnings effects concentrated among these women.

ENDOGENOUS SELECTION AND RELATIONSHIP TO PREVIOUS RESEARCH

A major challenge in studying the effects of STW programs is the traditional concern with inferring causal effects of program participation. The potential for bias from endogenous selection is clear.

For example, program participants may be those who as high school students already have the strongest career orientation, and therefore are more likely to work after participating in the program irrespective of program effects. Until recently, however, little of the existing literature has done much to control adequately for preprogram differences between participants and nonparticipants. The National Center for Research in Vocational Education (NCRVE) provided a thorough compendium of earlier research on STW programs (Stern et al. 1995). As argued elsewhere, that research provides little if any persuasive evidence of positive impacts of these programs on adult labor-market outcomes (Neumark and Rothstein 2006), often even failing to construct reasonable comparison groups, let alone to consider the problem of selection into the program on the basis of unobserved characteristics that might also be correlated with outcomes. The conclusion that existing work on STW has tended to shy away from trying to draw causal inferences is also reflected in a recent survey of published academic research on STW across the United States (Hughes, Hamilton, and Ivry 2001).

Of course, in many respects experimental evidence based on random assignment to STW programs is ideal. To the best of our knowledge, the only such study is the recent (and ongoing) evaluation of career academies by the Manpower Demonstration Research Corporation (Kemple 2001, 2004; Kemple and Snipes 2000).[11] The strength of this study is that participants were chosen randomly from applicants to the career academies in the study, and participants and nonparticipants were followed. This study has found some evidence of positive effects of participation in an STW program on employment and earnings up to four years after graduation from high school (the study extends no longer so far), although only for men, and has found some hint of possible reductions in going on to postsecondary education among those who participated in academies. This type of research is clearly valuable, although by its nature it is often restricted to studying only a single type of STW program. Moreover, such experiments are expensive and extremely difficult to implement, and when they depart from their "ideal" setting are prone to problems identified in the literature on the evaluation of other types of social programs (see, for example, Heckman, Hohmann, and Smith 2000). For both of these reasons, and because of some of the advantages afforded by secondary longitudinal data, including large and representative samples, we suspect that examination of the effects of STW programs based on longitudinal data sets such as the NLSY97 will continue to play an important role in our assessing the effectiveness of STW programs, and that ultimately the two types of evidence will be complementary.

In this chapter we study the impact of STW programs using the NLSY97, a large-scale longitudinal data set with information on participation in a variety of STW programs. With data now extending through the fifth round of interviews, the NLSY97 provides a view of individuals up to three or four years after leaving high school (or possibly more if they dropped out). In addition, the rich data available in the NLSY97 offer a number of possible approaches to controlling for endogenous selection and hence uncovering the causal impact of STW programs. In addition to simply including very rich sets of control variables including intelligence test scores, information on parents' education and socioeconomic circumstances, and school behaviors, the data set includes questions on subjective probabilities about work and schooling outcomes measured prior to STW participation, as well as repeated observations on individuals in the same school.

In an earlier paper (Neumark and Rothstein 2006), we used these data in a number of ways to address the issue of biases from endogenous selection into program participation. The overall conclusion was that in these data there is little evidence of endogenous selection into STW programs in a manner that biases the estimates of program effects. Estimates of the impact of the various STW programs are quite robust to incorporation of information on prior expectations, or school fixed effects, which provide approaches to controlling for potentially different sources of endogenous selection. Given these earlier results, in this paper we forgo all of these types of analyses and focus instead on standard cross-sectional regression estimates—albeit using the very detailed information in the NLSY97 that may, more than anything else, provide sufficient controls for the characteristics on which students are selected into STW programs.[12] Readers interested in learning more about the alternative approaches to causal inferences using the NLSY97 and the details regarding the results are referred to our earlier paper.

To summarize the overall results from the earlier research briefly, we found that certain types of programs did have positive effects on either postsecondary education or employment. Specifically, the evidence indicated that school enterprises boost post–high school education and Tech Prep may reduce it, and that cooperative education and internships and apprenticeships boost post–high school employment.[13] The magnitudes implied by the estimates were reasonable yet also sizable, suggesting that participation in these programs boosts the probabilities of enrollment or employment by about 0.05 to 0.1, relative to base probabilities of about 0.5 for college attendance and 0.6 for employment. The STW-induced increases in enrollment and employment largely come about without offsetting decreases in the other activity, suggesting that there is a net increase in skill formation from participation in STW programs that boost enrollment or employment.[14]

Our previous paper focused not only on alternative approaches to inferring causal effects of STW programs but also on the question of whether STW programs had differential effects according to race, ethnicity, or other characteristics related to socioeconomic status. For the most part, STW did not appear to be particularly beneficial for disadvantaged students. Instead, the evidence suggested beneficial effects for all groups, although the programs that deliver the benefits vary. One finding that perhaps does stand out, though, is that internship and apprenticeship programs may be particularly advantageous for the less advantaged, as these programs boost college enrollment among those with the lowest test scores and boost employment among blacks and those with less-educated mothers and in nontraditional living arrangements. These findings suggest that further efforts should attempt to establish which populations of students gain more from different types of STW programs. This is the theme we take up here, with an explicit focus on a more specific hypothesis regarding heterogeneity in the effects of STW programs that has been articulated in policy discussions about STW. Understanding the heterogeneity in the effects of STW programs is also of interest in light of the findings reported in the previous chapters about the potential need for expanded school-to-work efforts for minorities and immigrants and the higher participation rates of minorities in STW as well as in career and technical education.

DATA

In the NLSY97, individuals were surveyed about "programs schools offer to help students prepare for the world of work" (the six types of programs are listed in the introduction to this chapter). A more detailed discussion of the STW questions in the NLSY97 is provided in Mary Joyce and David Neumark (2001).

The analysis is based on data from the first five rounds of the NLSY97. When the first round was administered, in 1997, respondents were aged twelve to seventeen.[15] In round 1, the STW questions covered the types of programs in which individuals participated (at all and most recently), whereas in subsequent rounds the questions shifted to participation in the past year. The questions were asked of all ninth- to twelfth-graders in round 1. In rounds 2 to 5 the questions were asked of any respondents enrolled in school (including college), although we focus on participation while in high school by only using STW information for years in which respondents were enrolled in high school.[16] With the second round, in 1998, we begin to observe some respondents who have left high school, but we get many more such observations with the third through fifth rounds, and therefore we focus on postsecondary educational and employment outcomes measured as of the third, fourth, or fifth round.[17]

Table 4.1 gives some idea of the breakdown of the sample. Of the total 8,984 original respondents to the NLSY97, 8,609 were interviewed in 1999, 2000, or 2001 (rounds 3 to 5).[18] Of these, attention is restricted to those aged eighteen or older, which eliminates about 1,800 observations, and to those respondents with at least one post–high school observation in 1999, 2000, or 2001, yielding 5,966 observations. We restrict the sample in this way to isolate those individuals for whom information on at least the initial years of their employment or higher education after leaving high school is available. In future research we will study the longer-term career trajectories of STW participants and nonparticipants.

In addition to meeting these criteria, information on STW participation is also required. In order to get an accurate reading on STW participation during high school and to be able to measure some behaviors as of a well-defined date prior to the STW participation we study, we focus mainly on the STW information provided in the surveys after the first round (in 1997), which cover participation in the

TABLE 4.1   **Sample Construction and Analysis Samples**

Sample Inclusion Criteria	Number of Observations
(1)	(2)
Post–high school cross-sectional analysis	
Total sample in 1997	8,984
Interviewed in 1999, 2000, or 2001	8,609
Age greater than or equal to 18 at 1999, 2000, or 2001 interview	6,837
Not enrolled in high school by 1999, 2000, or 2001 interview	5,966
Answered STW questions covering high school after round 1	4,989
Complete data on baseline controls	4,810
Exclude private or vocational school students	4,292[a]
Post–high school longitudinal analysis	
Followed for at least one year from September after leaving high school	2,855[a]

Source: Authors' calculations from NLSY97.
Notes: For the post–high school enrollment or employment analysis, we use the 1999, 2000, or 2001 interview as the "post–high school interview," choosing the earliest one at which the respondent is aged eighteen or older and no longer enrolled in high school. More restrictive sample inclusion criteria are imposed in each successive row. Baseline controls include race or ethnicity, education, and family structure (whether respondent lives with one, two, or no biological parents, and which ones, and household size). When other control variables are introduced in the regression models, dummy variables indicating missing data are included. For the post–high school longitudinal analysis, we use the latest data possible, beginning with the September after respondents leave high school.
[a]For the analysis of different dependent variables the sample size is sometimes smaller because of missing data.

past year.[19] Requiring STW information after round 1 drops sample observations for those who did not answer the STW part of the survey after this round, either because they had not spent time in high school in 1997 or a subsequent year, or in subsequent years they were not enrolled as of the interview date and hence were not asked the STW questions.[20] Coupled with some final sample restrictions on availability of the other data used in the study, this takes us down to 4,810 observations. For our baseline analysis sample, we also exclude private schools, which are not the focus of STW policy, and vocational schools, which in a sense offer nothing but STW. This leaves us with 4,292 observations.

Finally, some of the analyses are based on the respondent's activities as of the first post–high school interview and others are based on longitudinal information beginning after high school, from continuous record files included in the NLSY97. We require that respondents have information available for at least one year following the September after which they left high school, and we use as much data as possible. The minimum requirement leaves us with a smaller sample of 2,855 for these analyses.

EMPIRICAL APPROACH

The basic approach with which we begin, and on which we build, is to estimate, at the individual level, the relationship between various work-related or education-related measures in the post–high school period and participation in STW.[21] STW participation is categorized in terms of participation in the six specific types of programs discussed earlier. Generically, let Y_i be the work- or education-related measure for individual i, let STW_i be a vector of dummy variables for whether the individual reports participating in each STW program, and let X_i be a vector of controls. We estimate models of the form:[22]

$$(1) \qquad Y_i = \alpha + STW_i\beta + X_i\gamma + \epsilon_i.$$

The parameters of interest are β. Consistent estimation of β requires that ϵ_i be uncorrelated with the controls in X_i as well as with STW_i. As noted earlier, Neumark and Rothstein (2006) fully explore potential biases in the NLSY97 from endogenous selection into STW program participation that could generate a correlation between ϵ_i and the independent variables. That study finds little if any evidence of such biases from using school-fixed effects or including controls for expectations prior to STW participation. Because either of these approaches limits the data set (for example, the expectations variables were asked only of a subsample), in this paper we rely instead on the full sample.

A good part of the reason for these earlier findings may be that the NLSY97 offers a rich and detailed set of control variables for characteristics of both individual respondents and their families. In addition to fairly typical demographic controls (sex, race, ethnicity, and age), the data set includes three additional sets of control variables that we view as potentially important. These include data on living arrangements and the respondent's family (including urban residence, whether one lives with both biological parents, only the biological mother or father, a biological parent and a step parent, or in some other arrangement, as well as information on household size, household income,[23] and the biological mother's schooling); Armed Services Vocational Aptitude Battery (ASVAB) scores; and self-reported measures of school behavior (whether the respondent was threatened or had gotten into a physical fight at school, and whether the respondent had been late with no excuse two or more times, or absent two or more weeks, all measured in 1997). This rich array of variables seems likely to capture many sources of variation in underlying propensities for post–high school enrollment or employment, including the quality and quantity of human capital investments in children, resources available in the household, educational norms in the family, labor-market networks, the individual respondent's academic ability, and the extent to which the respondent is learning traits such as punctuality and reliability that are valued by employers.

Given the earlier evidence that including a detailed set of control variables appears to be sufficient, and given that the question we ask in this chapter demands more of the data by testing for heterogeneity in the effects of STW programs, we do not revisit the alternative approaches to testing for biases from endogenous selection but simply work with the fullest set of control variables available for the full sample. These are listed explicitly in tables 4.2 and 4.3. Moreover, even these control variables tend to be largely uncorrelated with STW program participation. This evidence is reported in these tables, in the form of linear probability estimates for participation in each of the six types of STW programs, estimated separately by sex.

The tables present, in the first row, the proportions of students participating in each type of program covered in the individual survey, and in the remaining rows the linear probability estimates for participation in each type of program.[24] The results indicate that very few variables are significantly related to STW participation, aside from what might be considered a smattering of estimated coefficients the statistical significance of which could just reflect randomness.[25] The finding that very few variables predict STW participation reinforces the conclusion that problems from endogenous selection into STW participation may be minimal.[26]

Our particular interest in this paper, however, is in the effects of STW programs on the forgotten half and how these effects contrast with those for the rest of the population. We first estimate a linear probability model for whether the respondent attended college (two- or four-year) at any time after leaving high school (including currently), insofar as we can observe this in our data. This model includes the same set of control variables used in the preceding table and in the models for estimating the effects of STW program participation that follow. We then use this model to rank the predicted probability of college attendance and distinguish between those in the bottom and top halves of the distribution of predicted probabilities. We use sample weights in computing the median of this distribution, so that our approach identifies those whose predicted probabilities of college attendance are in the bottom half of the population distribution, not the sample distribution. In doing this, we do not include STW participation in the college-attendance model. This better aligns our approach with what might be viewed as a policy intervention of identifying those who, ex ante, have lower probabilities of college attendance, and then asking what the benefits of STW would likely be for a subpopulation chosen this way—in particular, those in the bottom half of the ex ante distribution. A more complete model of college attendance might include STW participation, but that is a different exercise from identifying which individuals are more or less likely to attend college absent STW programs.

From the estimates of the model of college attendance, we construct an indicator for those in the bottom half of the distribution of predicted probabilities, denoted FH_i (for "forgotten half"). We then estimate models of the form:

$$(2) \qquad Y_i = \alpha + STW_i\beta + STW_i \cdot FH_i\beta' + X_i\gamma + \delta FH_i + \epsilon_i.$$

Using estimates of models of this form, we can address a couple of different questions. First, whereas estimates of β in equation 2 capture the effects for those in the upper half of the distribution of the predicted probability of college attendance, the estimates of β' capture the differences between the effects of STW programs for the forgotten half and the rest of the sample, so the statistical significance of these estimates provides a test for differences in the effects.

TABLE 4.2 Linear Probability Estimates of Individual Characteristics Associated with STW Participation, Females

	Job Shadowing	Mentoring	Co-op	School Enterprise	Tech Prep	Internship or Apprenticeship
	(1)	(2)	(3)	(4)	(5)	(6)
Means	.208	.101	.150	.084	.105	.105
Regression estimates						
Demographic						
Black	-.008	.017	.024	.019	.075***	-.005
Hispanic	-.036	.014	.005	-.020	.023	.016
Age	-.002	-.000	.004	-.019**	-.009	.011
Living arrangement; family						
Urban	.027	.006	.027	.021	-.021	.007
Biological parent and stepparent	-.009	-.019	-.023	.035*	.004	.005
Biological mother only	-.047*	-.016	.005	.006	-.020	-.020
Biological father only	-.042	-.025	.029	-.031	.045	-.037
Other arrangement	-.017	.023	.002	-.017	-.013	.016
Household size	-.002	-.010***	-.004	-.007	-.009**	-.010**
Log household income	.003	.001	.001	.000	-.006	.001
Biological mother's schooling	.001	.003	.001	-.001	.001	.004

Math and verbal percentile composite score × 10^{-2}	−.085**	−.009	−.089***	.024	−.060**	−.006
School behaviors						
Threatened at school	.022	.018	.056**	.006	.014	−.008
Got into physical fight at school	−.046	−.059***	−.020	−.014	−.012	.006
Late with no excuse more than two times	−.013	−.009	−.021	.030*	−.002	.015
Absent more than two weeks	−.049*	−.011	−.032	−.029	.026	−.038*

Source: Authors' calculations.

Notes: Linear probability estimates are reported. There are 2,172 observations.
***, **, and * indicate that the estimated coefficients are significantly different from zero at the 1, 5, or 10-percent level, respectively. Dummy variables are included for missing data on some individual variables. STW participation is measured on the basis of responses from the 1998 interview and later regarding school-to-work participation while in high school. All other variables are defined as of the first round (1997), with the exception of age, which is measured (in months) at the 1999, 2000, or 2001 interview, whichever is defined as the "post–high school interview" (see notes to table 4.1). The math and verbal percentile composite score is similar to the Department of Defense's Armed Forces Qualification Test (AFQT) measure, and is based on four tests from the CAT-ASVAB. These tests were internally normed by NLSY97 survey personnel, and were used to create the aptitude score used here. Standard errors are robust to heteroscedasticity, and were adjusted to account for the clustering of observations within schools, allowing for nonindependence within schools and heteroscedasticity across schools.

TABLE 4.3 Linear Probability Estimates of Individual Characteristics Associated with STW Participation, Males

	Job Shadowing	Mentoring	Co-op	School Enterprise	Tech Prep	Internship or Apprenticeship
	(1)	(2)	(3)	(4)	(5)	(6)
Means	.189	.085	.150	.070	.137	.096
Regression estimates						
Demographic						
Black	-.017	.057***	.017	.046***	.030	.019
Hispanic	-.018	.055***	-.016	.009	.001	.020
Age	-.003	.003	.039***	.009	.019	-.004
Living arrangement; family						
Urban	-.069**	.002	.011	-.018	-.025	.011
Biological parent and stepparent	-.015	-.011	-.010	-.007	.001	-.007
Biological mother only	-.033	-.059***	-.006	-.010	-.012	.007
Biological father only	-.052	-.042	-.014	-.010	-.009	-.045
Other arrangement	-.015	.023	-.003	-.016	-.034	.009
Household size	-.007	-.006	.004	-.005	.002	-.006
Log household income	-.000	-.005	-.004	.003**	-.002	-.002
Biological mother's schooling	.003	.004	-.001	.002	-.004	-.004*
Math and verbal percentile composite score × 10^{-2}	-.131***	-.007	.003	.037	-.017	-.032
School behaviors						
Threatened at school	.002	.016	-.005	.006	.023	.023
Got into physical fight at school	.027	.020	.028	.043**	-.019	.004
Late with no excuse more than two times	.014	-.022	-.005	-.001	-.009	-.008
Absent more than two weeks	-.053*	-.040**	-.055**	-.029	-.013	-.034

Source: Authors' calculations from NLSY97.
Note: See notes to table 4.2. There are 2,120 observations.

Second, the estimates of $(\beta + \beta')$ capture the overall effects of STW programs for those in the forgotten half, and the significance of these summed coefficient estimates indicates whether there are effects for this subpopulation. The tables that follow report results regarding both types of estimates, and then present a summary of the effects of STW programs overall, the effects for the forgotten half, and the ways the effects differ for the forgotten half.

RESULTS

We first present estimates of STW effects assuming they are the same for everyone, and then report estimates allowing different effects for the "forgotten half."

Homogeneous Effects of STW Participation

We begin by briefly discussing estimates of equation 1, which excludes the direct indicator for being in the forgotten half and its interactions with STW participation. These estimates expand upon many of the findings reported in Neumark and Rothstein (2006) in two ways. First, we use an additional round of NLSY97 data, and hence have more, and later, observations. Second, we expand the set of outcomes considered. Previously, we restricted attention to transitions to higher education or employment, studying only the impact of STW programs on whether respondents were employed or had enrolled in higher education as of the first post–high school interview. Here, we also study whether the respondent attended a two-year or four-year college; was currently enrolled in either type of college; had participated in a training program; and was currently idle (neither working nor currently enrolled). More significant, we use the additional data afforded by round 5 of the NLSY97 to construct longitudinal measures of time spent in different activities, and to measure early labor-market outcomes. Specifically, we study the proportion of weeks since leaving high school spent in college, working, or idle, and average hours worked over all weeks.[27] In addition, we study earnings and wages, as well as whether the person is working full-time at the most recent job in which the respondent is observed. We study all of these outcomes in the subsequent analysis of differences in STW outcomes for the forgotten half, as well. Finally, in contrast to our previous paper, here the results are all reported disaggregated by sex.

The results are reported in tables 4.4, 4.5, and 4.6. Table 4.4 reports the results for the various outcomes defined as of the first post–high school interview, which gives us a sense of the postsecondary transitions associated with STW programs (the sole focus of our earlier work). The control variables included are the same as those in table 4.2. The first four columns in table 4.4 are for alternative measures of postsecondary education.

For females (top panel) we find that job shadowing has a significant positive effect on current enrollment and on attending a two-year college, but not on the other two measures of education. Mentoring, on the other hand, has significant positive effects on all of the education measures, with the exception of attendance at two-year colleges. In contrast, co-op education programs appear to reduce attendance at four-year colleges but to boost attendance at two-year colleges. Tech Prep appears to reduce postsecondary education (at least at four-year colleges). Finally, internship and apprenticeship programs appear to boost the likelihood of any college attendance as well as four-year college attendance. Thus, with the exception of Tech Prep, many of the STW programs appear to increase postsecondary education for women, although the effects differ across programs—in particular, with respect to two-year versus four-year college attendance. The effects are often sizable, in the range of 0.05 to 0.07 (in absolute value) relative to mean attendance or enrollment rates on the order of 0.2 to 0.5.

The results in columns 5 to 7 capture current work, training, and idleness. Here there are no significant effects for women, with a few exceptions.[28] Most significant, perhaps, is that Tech Prep—which was associated with less postsecondary schooling—has a positive effect on the likelihood of a woman student's participating in a training program, suggesting that Tech Prep leads to some substitution among opportunities for further learning.

The bottom panel reports results for males. There are quite a few similarities with the results for females. There is some evidence that for men, job shadowing, mentoring, and school enterprise programs increase postsecondary education but Tech Prep reduces it. The magnitudes are in the same range as for women.[29] For men, no effects of internship and apprenticeship programs on schooling are apparent and school enterprise programs have rather strong positive effects (in contrast to no evidence of positive effects for women).[30] There are also some sharper differences regarding the effects of STW programs on work, training, and idleness, as reported in columns 5 to 7. First, as for women, Tech Prep increases the likelihood of participating in a training program. However, for men, in contrast to women, some STW programs appear to boost employment and correspondingly to decrease idleness. This is the case for co-op programs (which also increase training participation) and for internship and apprenticeship programs. The estimated employment effects are about 0.09, relative to an employment rate of 0.61. The corresponding negative effects on idleness are of similar magnitude but represent larger percentage declines, of about 33 percent.

Table 4.5 reports results for the longitudinal measures of the percentage of weeks in school, working, or idle, as well as average hours. The education results for women do not parallel very closely the enrollment results from table 4.4, with no evidence of effects of any programs on the proportion of weeks spent in school. Similarly, in this table there is stronger evidence that STW programs boost employment for women, with job shadowing and co-op programs boosting weeks of work, and co-op programs also boosting average hours.

For men as well, the schooling evidence does not line up very well with table 4.4; a positive effect on schooling is apparent only for job-shadowing programs. In contrast, co-op, school enterprise, and internship and apprenticeship programs all have significant positive effects on weeks worked, and co-op programs, Tech Prep, and internship and apprenticeship programs appear to boost average hours. School enterprise and internships and apprenticeships also reduced weeks of idleness. Thus, the longitudinal measures, which seem that they should be more informative because they are not based on a single snapshot, tend to weaken the evidence of STW effects on schooling, but to reinforce and perhaps strengthen the evidence of positive employment effects.[31]

For the employment-related outcomes, the estimated effects of STW participation are somewhat more moderate than those in table 4.4, but are still sizable. For example, for both men and women, participation in co-op programs boosts the share of weeks worked by

TABLE 4.4 Post–High School Analysis of Effects of STW Participation on Cross-Sectional Measures Of Schooling, Employment, and Training

	Any College	Currently Enrolled	Attended Four-Year College	Attended Two-Year College	Currently Working	Participated in Training Program	Neither Working nor Enrolled Currently
	(1)	(2)	(3)	(4)	(5)	(6)	(7)
Females							
Means	.540	.481	.343	.197	.609	.083	.200
Regression estimates							
Job shadowing	.017	.049*	-.024	.041*	.026	-.014	-.036*
	(.026)	(.026)	(.025)	(.023)	(.028)	(.016)	(.021)
Mentoring	.067**	.074**	.105***	-.039	-.017	-.013	-.024
	(.034)	(.034)	(.033)	(.028)	(.036)	(.020)	(.028)
Co-op	-.014	-.044	-.079***	.065**	.033	.008	.039
	(.027)	(.027)	(.026)	(.027)	(.031)	(.019)	(.026)
School enterprise	.044	.045	.039	.005	.009	.017	-.036
	(.034)	(.035)	(.033)	(.032)	(.040)	(.023)	(.028)
Tech Prep	-.062*	-.043	-.064**	.003	-.024	.040*	.026
	(.033)	(.033)	(.028)	(.032)	(.034)	(.024)	(.028)
Internship or apprenticeship	.080***	.025	.053*	.026	-.015	-.014	.003
	(.031)	(.033)	(.029)	(.029)	(.036)	(.019)	(.028)
N	2,172	2,172	2,172	2,172	2,172	2,134	2,172

Males

	.414	.371	.260	.153	.622	.114	.222
Means							
Regression estimates							
Job shadowing	.047*	.041	.034	.013	.003	.007	-.012
	(.026)	(.026)	(.023)	(.022)	(.026)	(.020)	(.022)
Mentoring	.060*	.029	.072**	-.012	-.045	-.001	-.013
	(.036)	(.036)	(.033)	(.030)	(.039)	(.027)	(.032)
Co-op	.010	.018	-.029	.039	.089***	.046**	-.062***
	(.030)	(.030)	(.024)	(.025)	(.029)	(.023)	(.024)
School enterprise	.104***	.069*	.027	.078**	.047	-.037	-.028
	(.036)	(.037)	(.034)	(.035)	(.041)	(.025)	(.031)
Tech Prep	-.067**	-.046	-.050**	-.017	.055*	.042*	.001
	(.030)	(.029)	(.025)	(.026)	(.030)	(.025)	(.026)
Internship or apprenticeship	.023	.026	-.011	.034	.085**	.034	-.086***
	(.035)	(.035)	(.028)	(.029)	(.035)	(.029)	(.026)
N	2,120	2,120	2,120	2,120	2,120	2,080	2,120

Source: Authors' calculations from NLSY97.

Notes: All of the specifications include the demographic, living arrangement or family, math and verbal percentile composite score, and school behavior variables (see tables 4.2 and 4.3). Estimates are from linear probability models. The training programs include formal programs at schools or other centers, apprenticeships, formal company training programs, and government training programs. Standard errors of regression estimates are reported in parentheses. The standard errors allow for general heteroscedasticity, and were adjusted to account for the clustering of observations within schools, allowing for nonindependence within schools.

TABLE 4.5 Post–High School Analysis of Effects of STW Participation on Longitudinal Work and Schooling Measures

	Proportion of Weeks in School	Proportion of Weeks Working	Average Hours Worked Over All Weeks	Proportion of Weeks Idle
	(1)	(2)	(3)	(4)
Females				
Means	.545	.653	20.21	.156
Regression estimates				
Job shadowing	−.005	.037*	.91	−.030*
	(.028)	(.022)	(1.00)	(.016)
Mentoring	.035	−.030	−1.16	−.000
	(.037)	(.030)	(1.31)	(.021)
Co-op	−.034	.045*	2.54**	−.020
	(.028)	(.025)	(1.10)	(.016)
School enterprise	.053	−.016	−1.07	−.012
	(.037)	(.032)	(1.20)	(.022)
Tech Prep	−.006	−.017	.32	.015
	(.034)	(.026)	(1.24)	(.020)
Internship or apprenticeship	.038	.013	.68	−.006
	(.031)	(.027)	(1.19)	(.019)
N	1,470	1,470	1,420	1,470

Males

	.441	.677	23.75	.154
Means				
Regression estimates				
Job shadowing	.065**	.022	-.32	-.020
	(.028)	(.024)	(1.13)	(.018)
Mentoring	.024	-.028	.41	.019
	(.045)	(.033)	(1.69)	(.027)
Co-op	-.014	.053**	3.03**	-.026
	(.036)	(.025)	(1.32)	(.019)
School enterprise	.037	.066*	1.63	-.039*
	(.046)	(.034)	(1.67)	(.023)
Tech Prep	.012	.042	3.09**	-.030
	(.036)	(.027)	(1.41)	(.020)
Internship or	.008	.079***	2.48*	-.043*
apprenticeship	(.039)	(.030)	(1.47)	(.023)
N	1,336	1,337	1,235	1,336

Source: Authors' calculations from NLSY97.

Notes: See notes to table 4.4. All estimates are from linear regressions. The variables are based on the period beginning with the first September since leaving high school; the specifications include a control for the total number of weeks from that time until the interview.

about five percentage points, an increase of a bit less than 10 percent. And the negative effect on weeks idle of internship and apprenticeship programs for males is still over 25 percent.

Table 4.6 presents measures related to the quality of employment on the most recent job (for those observed employed), including earnings and wages and full-time status. The results for wages and log earnings are reported both without and with conditioning on schooling, experience, and full-time status, with the idea being that the unconditional estimates capture the full effects of STW programs including those acting through schooling, experience, and so forth. For women (top panel), the co-op programs that were associated with increased work appear to boost hourly earnings as well, as do the internship and apprenticeship programs that increase schooling. In contrast, mentoring programs, which increase education for women based on the estimates in table 4.4, if anything, reduce earnings and full-time status, although it is conceivable that this is partly attributable to combining work with schooling, given the young ages of respondents.

For men, only the effects of co-op programs appear to carry over to the job, and even then not always; co-op programs increase some measures of work, training, and hours (tables 4.4 and 4.5) and earnings (unconditional) and full-time status (table 4.6). These results must be interpreted cautiously, however, as they pertain to jobs held early in the life cycle and may be contaminated by such factors as ongoing schooling and lower current wages associated with greater opportunities for human-capital investment.

STW Effects for the Forgotten Half

Having examined the evidence on the overall effects of STW programs, we now turn to the core of our new analysis, examining how effects differ for the "forgotten half," those who are less likely, ex ante, to attend college. Table 4.7 presents the results from the first step in this analysis, estimates of models for the likelihood of college attendance (excluding information on STW participation). These estimates are used to compute the probability of college attendance for each respondent in the sample.

These estimates do not contain any surprises. Blacks are more likely to attend college than non-black, non-Hispanics, which is not true in the raw means but is not an uncommon result conditional on socioeconomic status, test scores, and so forth (for example, Cameron and Heckman 2001). Respondents living with their biological mother only and, more generally, living in an arrangement other than with two biological parents are considerably less likely to attend college, which may partly reflect socioeconomic status. For both males and females, household size is negatively associated with college attendance, and respondents with more-educated mothers are more likely to attend college. Test scores are strongly positively associated with college attendance. Finally, troublesome school behaviors including both violence and absences are generally associated with a lower likelihood of college attendance. In general, these models predict college attendance correctly (based on the predicted probability being above or below the median) in a high fraction of cases, between 70 and 73 percent.

The next three tables report models for the same outcomes covered in tables 4.4 to 4.6, but now expanded to include the indicator for whether the predicted probability of college attendance—based on the estimates in table 4.7—was below the median, and its interaction with the dummy variables for participation in each type of STW program (equation 2).[32] Table 4.8 covers the education- and work-related outcomes as of the first post–high school interview; table 4.9 covers the longitudinal measures of schooling, work, idleness, and hours; and table 4.10 covers wages, earnings, and full-time status on the most recent job. In each of these tables, the main effects of STW programs (β) measure the effects for those in the top half of the distribution of predicted probabilities, while the interactive coefficients (β') measure the difference in the effects for the bottom half. For each STW program the sum of these—not reported in the table, but summarized later—measures the effect for those in the forgotten half. However, in the tables the statistical significance of the results for those in the forgotten half is reported in two ways. First, with asterisks we denote whether the interactive coefficients are significantly different from zero—that is, whether the effects of STW programs are different for those in the forgotten half. And second, with plus signs we denote whether the overall effects for those in the forgotten half—($\beta + \beta'$) in equation 2—are significantly different from zero.

The estimates in the top half of table 4.8, for women, indicate that the overall effects of mentoring and internship and apprenticeship

Males

	2.15	2.09	.578	2.15	2.09
Means					
Regression estimates					
Job shadow	.017	.001	-.018	.027	.008
	(.033)	(.033)	(.039)	(.032)	(.032)
Mentoring	-.021	.010	-.022	-.007	.026
	(.051)	(.052)	(.059)	(.046)	(.047)
Co-op	.063*	.026	.073*	.054	.014
	(.036)	(.036)	(.040)	(.035)	(.036)
School enterprise	-.001	.020	-.018	-.044	-.020
	(.049)	(.047)	(.062)	(.042)	(.040)
Tech Prep	-.015	.029	.061	-.027	.014
	(.036)	(.034)	(.043)	(.035)	(.032)
Internship or apprenticeship	.025	.017	.015	.004	-.005
	(.041)	(.037)	(.047)	(.041)	(.036)
N	1,073	1,160	1,219	1,056	1,142
Condition on schooling, experience and its square, and full-time	No	No	No	Yes	Yes

Source: Authors' calculations from NLSY97.

Notes: See notes to table 4.4. All estimates are from linear regressions. The definition of full-time is thirty-five or more hours per week. Earnings include tips, bonuses, and overtime. Earnings, wages, and full-time status are for the most recent job, for jobs held during or after the September after leaving high school. Only those observed in a job are included in the analysis. The specifications include a control for the total number of weeks since leaving high school.

TABLE 4.7   **Estimates of Equations for College Attendance**

	College Attendance, Females (N = 2,172)	College Attendance, Males (N = 2,120)
	(1)	(3)
Regression estimates		
Demographic		
Black	.088***	.051*
Hispanic	.024	.025
Age	.073***	.037
Living arrangement; family		
Urban	.019	.045*
Biological parent and stepparent	−.024	−.111***
Biological mother only	−.114***	−.106***
Biological father only	−.075	−.122**
Other arrangement	−.117**	−.097**
Household size	−.014**	−.015**
Log household income	.002	.009
Biological mother's schooling	.025***	.032***
Math and verbal percentile composite score × 10^{-2}	.603***	.625***
School behaviors		
Threatened at school	−.049*	−.080***
Got into physical fight at school	−.136***	−.094***
Late with no excuse more than two times	−.034	−.008
Absent more than two weeks	−.133***	−.094***
Share correctly predicted	.701	.729

Source: Authors' calculations from NLSY97.
Notes: All estimates are from linear probability models. See notes to table 4.2 for additional details. The means are weighted. The specifications include a control for the total number of weeks since leaving high school. Share correctly predicted, in last row, is based on a comparison between actual outcomes and whether predicted probability of outcome is above or below median probability (weighted). Estimates reported here are for the samples in table 4.4. Results were very similar for the samples used in tables 4.5, 4.6, 4.9, and 4.10.

programs on any college attendance persist for those in the top half of the distribution of predicted probabilities of college attendance, and appear no different for the forgotten half. However, there are some differences for the effects of internship and apprenticeship programs, which do not increase the likelihood that those in the bottom half will attend a four-year college but do increase the likelihood that

TABLE 4.8 Post-High School Analysis of Effects of STW Participation on Cross-Sectional Measures of Schooling, Employment, and Training by Position in Distribution of Predicted Probability of College Attendance

	Any College	Currently Enrolled	Attended Four-Year College	Attended Two-Year College	Currently Working	Participated in Training Program	Neither Working nor Currently Enrolled
	(1)	(2)	(3)	(4)	(5)	(6)	(7)
Females							
Job shadowing	-.011	.039	-.048	.036	.021	-.008	.004
	(.033)	(.035)	(.038)	(.033)	(.040)	(.018)	(.023)
x Lower half	.050	.015	.048	.002	.004	-.006	-.069*++
	(.050)	(.051)	(.048)	(.047)	(.054)	(.030)	(.039)
Mentoring	.102***	.118***	.154***	-.053	-.012	-.031	-.055**
	(.038)	(.045)	(.048)	(.041)	(.051)	(.024)	(.028)
x Lower half	-.063	-.080	-.093	.031	-.002	.032	.054
	(.061)	(.067)	(.065)	(.057)	(.072)	(.038)	(.055)
Co-op	-.037	-.059	-.120**	.082*	.100**	-.003	.022
	(.045)	(.046)	(.050)	(.045)	(.047)	(.026)	(.031)
x Lower half	.042	.028	.077	-.034	-.111*	.020	.030
	(.057)	(.058)	(.057)	(.055)	(.059)	(.036)	(.046)
School enterprise	.027	.038	.054	-.027	-.067	.056	.005
	(.048)	(.051)	(.054)	(.042)	(.060)	(.035)	(.033)
x Lower half	.027	.009	-.027	.054	.142*	-.074	-.071
	(.072)	(.072)	(.067)	(.061)	(.079)	(.046)	(.056)

(continued)

TABLE 4.8 Continued

	Any College	Currently Enrolled	Attended Four-Year College	Attended Two-Year College	Currently Working	Participated in Training Program	Neither Working nor Currently Enrolled
	(1)	(2)	(3)	(4)	(5)	(6)	(7)
Tech Prep	-.034	-.014	-.104*	.070	.014	.045	-.020
	(.049)	(.053)	(.055)	(.048)	(.053)	(.036)	(.032)
x Lower half	-.041+	-.044	.065	-.106*	-.052	-.012	.068
	(.064)	(.066)	(.060)	(.055)	(.073)	(.046)	(.053)
Internship or apprenticeship	.068*	-.012	.113**	-.045	-.038	.017	.034
	(.038)	(.046)	(.045)	(.036)	(.051)	(.026)	(.032)
x Lower half	.016+	.070	-.125**	.141**,++	.044	-.062+	-.054
	(.063)	(.067)	(.058)	(.059)	(.071)	(.038)	(.055)
Males							
Job shadowing	.063	.049	.052	.012	.054	.001	-.039
	(.044)	(.043)	(.046)	(.035)	(.044)	(.031)	(.026)
x Lower half	-.026	-.011	-.029	.003	-.085	.010	.045
	(.052)	(.052)	(.052)	(.044)	(.059)	(.041)	(.042)
Mentoring	.022	-.004	.064	-.041	-.044	.012	-.040
	(.054)	(.056)	(.054)	(.044)	(.058)	(.040)	(.034)
x Lower half	.063+	.056+	.011++	.051	-.008	-.022	.051
	(.073)	(.075)	(.066)	(.062)	(.079)	(.054)	(.059)

114

Co-op	-.087*	-.104**	-.099**	.012	.102**	.086**	.005
	(.047)	(.048)	(.045)	(.037)	(.045)	(.035)	(.031)
x Lower half	.171***,++	.215***,+++	.128**	.043+	-.025++	-.070	-.118***,++
	(.059)	(.061)	(.052)	(.049)	(.058)	(.046)	(.046)
School enterprise	.143***	.124**	.056	.087*	.067	-.068**	-.042
	(.055)	(.060)	(.060)	(.053)	(.061)	(.031)	(.040)
x Lower half	-.072	-.104	-.052	-.020	-.044	.057	.027
	(.075)	(.078)	(.068)	(.072)	(.082)	(.049)	(.062)
Tech Prep	-.129**	-.096*	-.127***	-.002	.129***	.064	.015
	(.051)	(.051)	(.048)	(.045)	(.047)	(.040)	(.039)
x Lower half	.105	.086	.132**	-.028	-.127**	-.037	-.022
	(.065)	(.062)	(.055)	(.053)	(.061)	(.051)	(.053)
Internship or apprenticeship	-.007	.038	.055	-.061	.017	.028	-.075***
	(.056)	(.056)	(.054)	(.041)	(.055)	(.040)	(.028)
x Lower half	.042	-.029	-.119**,++	.161***,++	.123*,+++	.012	-.017++
	(.071)	(.068)	(.061)	(.060)	(.074)	(.054)	(.049)

Source: Authors' calculations from NLSY97.
Notes: See notes to tables 4.4 and 4.7. In constructing the lower half of the distribution of predicted probabilities of college attendance, the weighted median of the predicted probability of college attendance based on the model in table 4.7 is used.
***, **, * Indicate that the estimated coefficients are significantly different from zero at the 1, 5, or 10-percent level, respectively.
+++, ++, + Indicate, for the interactions with the lower half, that the overall effects for the lower half (the sums of the main and interactive effects) are significantly different from zero at the 1, 5, or 10-percent level, respectively.

TABLE 4.9 Post–High School Analysis of Effects of STW Participation on Longitudinal Work and Schooling Measures by Position in Distribution of Predicted Probability of College Attendance

	Proportion of Weeks In School	Proportion of Weeks Working	Average Hours Worked Over All Weeks	Proportion of Weeks Idle
	(1)	(2)	(3)	(4)
Females				
Job shadowing	-.022	.045	.59	-.019
	(.038)	(.032)	(1.30)	(.013)
x Lower half	.032	-.016	.51	-.019
	(.052)	(.046)	(1.96)	(.030)
Mentoring	.052	-.012	-.77	-.012
	(.049)	(.045)	(1.73)	(.020)
x Lower half	-.038	-.027	-.45	.018
	(.068)	(.060)	(2.37)	(.040)
Co-op	-.104**	.056	2.19	.008
	(.047)	(.040)	(1.63)	(.021)
x Lower half	.114*	-.021	.51+	-.043
	(.064)	(.050)	(2.13)	(.032)
School enterprise	.074	-.058	-2.73*	-.011
	(.053)	(.045)	(1.41)	(.021)
x Lower half	-.033	.067	2.62	-.000
	(.073)	(.062)	(2.20)	(.041)
Tech Prep	-.065	.030	2.25	.017
	(.052)	(.045)	(1.85)	(.029)
x Lower half	.087	-.071	-3.00	-.002
	(.069)	(.058)	(2.23)	(.041)
Internship or apprenticeship	.039	-.013	.24	.015
	(.041)	(.041)	(1.79)	(.023)

x Lower half	−.010	.049	.70	−.036
	(.063)	(.055)	(2.39)	(.038)
Males				
Job shadowing	.031	.042	1.61	.006
	(.045)	(.039)	(1.71)	(.023)
x Lower half	.058++	−.035	−3.36	−.045
	(.057)	(.049)	(2.20)	(.034)
Mentoring	.034	.002	.22	−.016
	(.060)	(.047)	(2.19)	(.028)
x Lower half	−.036	−.047	.67	.063
	(.080)	(.067)	(3.36)	(.051)
Co-op	−.040	.065	4.73**	−.012
	(.054)	(.043)	(1.96)	(.024)
x Lower half	.044	−.029	−2.94	−.015
	(.068)	(.052)	(2.54)	(.036)
School enterprise	.029	.041	.15	.002
	(.069)	(.051)	(2.25)	(.033)
x Lower half	.035	.035+	2.20	−.077*,++
	(.099)	(.069)	(3.31)	(.045)
Tech Prep	−.087	.083**	5.43**	.001
	(.063)	(.042)	(2.48)	(.025)
x Lower half	.162**,+	−.068	−4.01	−.051+
	(.076)	(.052)	(2.87)	(.037)
Internship or apprenticeship	−.009	.075*	4.01*	−.031
	(.060)	(.045)	(2.11)	(.029)
x Lower half	.031	.007++	−2.52	−.023+
	(.073)	(.059)	(2.81)	(.042)

Source: Authors' calculations from NLSY97.
Note: See notes to tables 4.4, 4.5, 4.7, and 4.8.

TABLE 4.10 Post–High School Analysis of Effects of STW Participation on Earnings, Wages, and Full-Time Status of Most Recent Job, by Position in Distribution of Predicted Probability of College Attendance

	Log Hourly Earnings	Log Hourly Wage	Full-Time	Log Hourly Earnings	Log Hourly Wage
	(1)	(2)	(3)	(4)	(5)
Females					
Job shadowing	.071*	.058	−.022	.064	.056
	(.043)	(.045)	(.051)	(.043)	(.044)
x Lower half	−.042	−.037	.093	−.055	−.048
	(.056)	(.061)	(.069)	(.055)	(.059)
Mentoring	−.138***	−.085*	−.084	−.120***	−.070
	(.046)	(.051)	(.066)	(.045)	(.052)
x Lower half	.124*	.111	−.005	.121*	.103
	(.066)	(.072)	(.091)	(.066)	(.074)
Co-op	.053	.029	−.008	.034	.021
	(.046)	(.051)	(.059)	(.045)	(.051)
x Lower half	−.012	−.031	.050	.011	−.026
	(.056)	(.064)	(.077)	(.056)	(.065)
School enterprise	−.022	.041	.006	.004	.060
	(.065)	(.063)	(.078)	(.065)	(.065)
x Lower half	.051	−.039	.069	.016	−.077
	(.084)	(.082)	(.105)	(.082)	(.084)
Tech Prep	.043	.044	.142*	.011	.014
	(.052)	(.068)	(.083)	(.049)	(.063)
x Lower half	−.050	−.057	−.163	−.015	−.006
	(.067)	(.076)	(.100)	(.065)	(.073)
Internship or apprenticeship	.063	.073	−.017	.072	.084
	(.058)	(.057)	(.059)	(.057)	(.056)

x Lower half	.064+++ (.073)	.026++ (.074)	.009 (.085)	.036++ (.072)	.029++ (.073)

Males

Job shadowing	-.035 (.051)	-.045 (.056)	.034 (.064)	-.035 (.050)	-.045 (.052)
x Lower half	.099 (.065)	.079 (.067)	-.085 (.085)	.113*+ (.065)	.091 (.064)
Mentoring	-.049 (.084)	.038 (.089)	-.056 (.080)	-.014 (.069)	.069 (.076)
x Lower half	.068 (.100)	-.042 (.101)	.069 (.106)	.025 (.090)	-.076 (.094)
Co-op	.085 (.061)	.031 (.063)	.109 (.068)	.059 (.058)	.007 (.061)
x Lower half	-.039 (.076)	-.009 (.077)	-.071 (.084)	-.011 (.074)	.012 (.076)
School enterprise	.036 (.089)	.116 (.086)	-.121 (.088)	-.035 (.067)	.057 (.069)
x Lower half	-.067 (.104)	-.167* (.099)	.174 (.114)	-.018 (.085)	-.131 (.083)
Tech Prep	-.045 (.066)	.006 (.067)	.072 (.076)	-.045 (.060)	.001 (.061)
x Lower half	.053 (.075)	.042 (.075)	-.026 (.092)	.039 (.071)	.032 (.071)
Internship or apprenticeship	.025 (.080)	-.049 (.072)	.036 (.071)	-.008 (.076)	-.085 (.067)
x Lower half	-.003 (.095)	.112 (.086)	-.026 (.094)	.016 (.089)	.133* (.080)
Conditional or schooling, experience and its square, and full-time	No	No	No	Yes	Yes

Source: Authors' calculations from NLSY97.
Note: See notes to tables 4.4, 4.6, 4.7, and 4.8.

they will attend a two-year college. The effects of co-op programs on education are similar for both parts of the distribution. In contrast, the adverse effects of Tech Prep on attending any college are present only for those in the forgotten half, although this is not the case for the other college attendance measures.[33] In the four outcomes covered in columns 1 to 4, there are only a few cases where plus signs indicate statistically significant effects for the forgotten half—namely, for the negative effect of Tech Prep on college attendance, and the positive effect of internship-apprenticeship programs on any college attendance and especially on attending a two-year college.

As in table 4.4, for women there is not much evidence of effects of STW on current work, training, and idleness. There is evidence of a positive effect of co-op programs on current employment only for those more likely to attend college. On the other hand, there is evidence that job shadowing reduces idleness only for those in the lower half of the distribution of the predicted probability of college attendance.

For men, there is stronger evidence of different effects of STW programs for the forgotten half. The first four columns indicate that mentoring, co-op, and internship and apprenticeship STW programs boost postsecondary education only for the forgotten half, whereas school enterprise programs tend to have effects that are stronger for those more likely to go to college. In the last three columns, there is evidence that co-op programs increase employment overall and for the forgotten half, but co-op programs decrease idleness only for the forgotten half. The effects of internship and apprenticeship programs in increasing employment and reducing idleness are quite strong, with the employment effect present only for those less likely to attend college.

The evidence on the longitudinal measures of schooling, work, hours, and idleness is reported in table 4.9. For women, the evidence of beneficial effects for the forgotten half (or the rest of the sample) appears quite weak, as there is only one case of a significant beneficial effect for the forgotten half—for the effect of co-op programs on hours—and the effect is small. For men, though, paralleling the previous table, there is stronger evidence. In particular, we now find that school enterprise programs increase weeks worked and reduce weeks idle only for the forgotten half, whereas internship and apprenticeship programs boost the proportion of weeks worked for both parts of the sample but reduce weeks idle only for the forgotten half.

Table 4.10 shows effects on wages, earnings, and full-time status. For women, the one set of results that stands out is that internship and apprenticeship programs boost wages and earnings (unconditional and conditional) for those in the forgotten half only. For men, paralleling the simpler analysis in table 4.6, there is little evidence of effects of STW programs on these outcomes; an exception is the effect of job shadowing on hourly earnings for the forgotten half (column 4).

Summary of the Findings

The three preceding tables present a large number of estimates, and it is difficult to get a sense of their overall message by perusing the tables. Therefore, in table 4.11 we offer a summary of the results from tables 4.8 to 4.10. In columns 1 and 3 we summarize the results for the forgotten half, and in columns 2 and 4 we summarize the results for those in the top half of the distribution of the predicted probability of college attendance. We list all effects that are significantly different from zero for each half of the distribution of predicted probabilities of college attendance. Plus signs indicate a positive effect and minus signs a negative effect. These signs appear three times, two times, or one time, depending on whether the result is significant at the 1, 5, or 10-percent level. We also distinguish two important cases for the estimates for the forgotten half. First, if the evidence points to effects that are significant only for the forgotten half, the result is reported in boldface. Second, for the subset of these cases where the estimate for the forgotten half was significantly different from that for the rest of the sample—that is, where we reject equality for the two halves of the sample—the entry is underlined as well. Both of these types of results are of interest: the first indicates that for the forgotten half only, the effects are significant or of a particular sign; the second indicates the stronger result, that the effects are significantly stronger for the forgotten half. Finally, we have shaded results for either half that are most likely viewed as beneficial: increasing schooling, work, skills (training), or earnings. This shading helps highlight where estimates of beneficial effects, and not just statistically significant effects, are more prevalent.

TABLE 4.11 Summary of Differences in Effects of STW Participation

	Schooling-Related, Forgotten Half (1)	Schooling-Related, Top Half (2)	Work-Related, Forgotten Half (3)	Work-Related, Top Half (4)
Females				
Job shadowing			Idle: – –	**Earnings, unconditional: +** Idle: – – Earnings, unconditional: – – Wage, unconditional: – Earnings, conditional: – – Currently working: +
Mentoring		Any college: +++ Currently enrolled: +++ Attended four-year college: +++		
Co-op		Attended four-year college: – – Attended two-year college: + Weeks in school: – –	Hours: +	
School enterprise				
Tech Prep		Attended four-year college: – Any college: + Attended four-year college: ++		Hours: – Full-time: +
Internship or apprenticeship	**Any college: –** Any college: + **Attended two-year college: ++**		**Training: –** **Earnings, unconditional +++** **Wage, unconditional ++** **Earnings, conditional ++** **Wage, conditional ++**	

122

Males

Program	Schooling	Schooling	Earnings, conditional: +	Work and training
Job shadowing	Weeks in school: ++			
Mentoring	Any college: + Currently enrolled: + Attended four-year college: ++			
Co-op	Any college: ++ Currently enrolled: +++ Attended two-year college: +	Any college: – Currently enrolled: – – Attended four-year college: – –	Currently working: ++ Idle: – –	Currently working: ++ Training: ++ Hours: ++
School enterprise		Any college: ++ Currently enrolled: ++ Attended two-year college: +	Weeks working: + Weeks idle: – –	Training: – –
Tech Prep	Weeks in school: +	Any college: – – Currently enrolled: – Attended four-year college: – – –	Weeks idle: –	Currently working: +++ Weeks working: ++ Hours: ++ Idle: – – – Weeks working: + Hours: +
Internship or apprenticeship	Attended four-year college: – – Attended two-year college: ++		Currently working: +++ Idle: – – Weeks working: ++ Weeks idle: –	

Source: Authors' calculations from NLSY97.

Notes: Results are from tables 4.8–4.10. Only statistically significant results are shown. The sign is as indicated, appearing three, two, or one times to indicate that the estimate for the indicated group is significantly different from zero at the 1, 5, or 10-percent level, respectively. In columns 1 and 3, entries appearing in bold are statistically significant at the 10-percent level (or significant with the opposite sign). Those underlined as well are significantly different from zero and significantly different from the effects for those in the rest of the distribution, at the 10-percent level or better. In all cases, effects that increase schooling, work, skills, or earnings are highlighted by shading, to emphasize estimated effects of STW that are presumably beneficial.

Looking first at the results for females, for the schooling-related outcomes the impression given by table 4.11 is that STW programs are generally less effective for those in the forgotten half. There are considerably more significant beneficial effects for those in the top half, with generally positive effects for mentoring and internship-apprenticeship programs. And the negative effects of Tech Prep on postsecondary education appear for both halves of the distribution. The findings are different for the work-related outcomes, the most striking contrast being that internship and apprenticeship programs boost wages and earnings for the forgotten half—and only for the forgotten half.

For men, the situation is somewhat reversed, although overall there is more evidence of beneficial effects of STW programs on those in the forgotten half. For the schooling-related outcomes, there are roughly equal numbers of significant effects in the two halves of the distribution of predicted probabilities of college attendance. But note that for those in the forgotten half these effects are almost always positive (with the exception of internship and apprenticeship programs, which reduce attendance at four-year colleges but boost it at two-year colleges). In contrast, for those in the top half, many more of the estimated effects on postsecondary schooling are negative (and hence unshaded). For the work-related outcomes there is particularly strong evidence that internship and apprenticeship programs boost employment and decrease idleness among men in the forgotten half, with similar results for co-op and school enterprise programs (although co-op programs and Tech Prep also boost employment for those in the top half). At the same time, there are also numerous cases of evidence of beneficial effects of STW participation, in particular Tech Prep, among men in the top half.

Overall, then, this summary points to some evidence that STW programs are advantageous for men in the forgotten half with respect to both schooling and work-related outcomes, but for women only with respect to work-related outcomes. Moreover, for the work-related outcomes for women and the schooling-related outcomes for men there is some evidence that STW programs are particularly advantageous for those in the forgotten half. Among the strongest evidence for men in the forgotten half is that mentoring and co-op programs increase postsecondary education, and that co-op, school enterprise, and internship and apprenticeship programs boost employment and decrease idleness. Among the strongest evidence for women in the forgotten half is that internship and apprenticeship programs increase earnings.

CONCLUSIONS

In this chapter we explore whether school-to-work (STW) programs are particularly beneficial for those who would be less likely to go to college in the absence of STW programs. This group is often termed the "forgotten half" in the STW literature. The empirical analysis is based on the NLSY97, which provides the best data available to date on participation in a wide array of STW programs. The NLSY97 data allow us to study six types of STW programs, including job shadowing, mentoring, co-op, school enterprises, Tech Prep, and internships and apprenticeships.

The data provide some evidence that STW program participation is particularly advantageous for men in the forgotten half with respect to both schooling and work-related outcomes. Among these men, mentoring and co-op programs increase postsecondary education, and co-op, school enterprise, and internship and apprenticeship programs boost students' employment and decrease their idleness after they leave high school;[34] there is less evidence of such beneficial effects for other men, especially with respect to schooling. The evidence that STW programs are particularly beneficial for women in the forgotten half is more limited to work-related outcomes, especially the finding that internship and apprenticeship programs lead to positive earnings effects concentrated among these women, measured early in the life cycle.

Overall, then, especially for men there is rather compelling evidence that participation in some STW programs increases education and employment and decreases idleness among the forgotten half. Returning to the policy issue that helped frame this chapter, these findings suggest that there may be substantial benefits to STW efforts targeting male high school students whose characteristics and backgrounds make them less likely to attend college, and there may also be labor-market benefits for women in this group.

Of course, some qualifications to these conclusions or further clarifications are necessary. First, the empirical analysis in this chapter only weighs some of the benefits of a set of programs. It does not consider the costs of these programs, nor does it compare the benefits with the potential benefits of other programs. For example, it is important to ask whether national policy changes downgrading STW efforts and emphasizing testing serve the forgotten half. But we have not presented evidence that test-based reforms are not particularly helpful to those in the forgotten half.[35]

Second, as noted in the text, we have not revisited all of the issues of endogenous selection that we studied earlier (Neumark and Rothstein 2006) to analyze the effects of STW programs on a more limited set of outcomes. In that study we found that biases from endogenous selection into STW programs were minimal, and we strongly believe that these results would carry over to the more detailed analyses that we conduct here. However, the more demanding nature of the specifications estimated in this study makes it difficult to address both selectivity issues and heterogeneous effects of STW programs simultaneously, in part because addressing selection issues eliminates many observations that we can otherwise use.

And finally, while the NLSY97 provides, in our view, the best available data for studying the effects of a wide array of STW programs, the data set has two limitations. First, of necessity in a large-scale data set, there is much unmeasured variation in the nature and intensity of the STW programs in which individuals participate. It seems likely that we might obtain sharper evidence of effects of STW programs—or at least of some types of programs—if we had richer data.[36] Second, the data set does not yet follow respondents very far into their careers or even all the way through their postsecondary education, but at best into their early twenties. Therefore, firmer conclusions clearly await analysis five or more years down the road, when the NLSY97 data will permit a more detailed characterization of the developing careers of sample members.

We are grateful to Chris Jepsen and Heather Rose for helpful comments. The views expressed are those of the authors and do not reflect the views or policies of the Public Policy Institute of California or the Bureau of Labor Statistics.

NOTES

1. The STWOA focused on high school students. The roughly $300 million annual spending is a trivial share of total federal high school spending. But it is larger relative to what might be considered related spending, such as $900 million annual federal spending on career and technical education, mainly through the Perkins Act (see National Association of State Boards of Education, n.d.).

2. Specifically, the act notes that a "substantial number of youths in the United States, especially disadvantaged students, students of diverse racial, ethnic, and cultural backgrounds, and students with disabilities, do not complete high school," and "Federal resources currently fund a series of categorical, work-related education and training programs, many of which serve disadvantaged youths, that are not administered as a coherent whole" (*School-to-Work Opportunities Act* 1994).

3. See, for example, Debra Donahoe and Marta Tienda (1999) and the references therein and William T. Grant Foundation (1988).

4. Stephen F. Hamilton and Mary A. Hamilton (1999) note that the schools and states that appeared to make the most progress toward creating STW systems were those that began building them prior to the STWOA and drew on more resources than those made available by the STWOA. However, Neumark (2006) documents the substantial overlap in one state (California) between programs supported by the STWOA and those covered in the NLSY97.

5. See, for example, http://www.fessler.com/SBE/act.htm (accessed June 26, 2005).

6. See David Stern et al. (1997) for a description.

7. See Stern et al. (1994).

8. The NLSY97 does not explicitly ask about participation in career academies, although it seems likely that students in career academies would have responded affirmatively to some of the other types of activities included in the STW questionnaire items.

9. These are student-run businesses based in schools. Examples include banks, auto repair, and "spirit shops" selling school sweatshirts, etc.

10. Career academies have a large school-based learning component, but typically also some work-based experiences such as internships.

11. The study covers nine schools across the country, all located in or near urban areas.

12. In addition to focusing on the forgotten half, here we study a considerably broader set of outcomes than in Neumark and Rothstein (2006).

13. There is also some evidence that job shadowing boosts college enrollment, but this finding is not as robust across the alternative statistical analyses.

14. David Neumark and Mary Joyce (2001) attempted to evaluate the effects of STW using only the first round of the NLSY97, but given the newness of the data set they were restricted to estimating effects on work- and education-related expectations of high-school students.

15. Respondents were aged twelve to sixteen as of December 31, 1996.

16. The manner in which the STW data are collected raises two issues. First, because some (and most likely the larger share of) STW participation occurs in the later high school years, we cannot use the NLSY97 to study the effects of STW on high school completion. Because high school dropouts would by construction report less STW participation, there would be a spurious negative correlation between STW participation and dropping out of high school. Second, a moderate share of individuals report some college enrollment in the last year in which they are enrolled in high school, so in principle these individuals could be reporting STW during their short initial spell of college. In past work, we have examined the sensitivity of the results to excluding the STW information for that interview year when calculating our STW measures, and found that our qualitative conclusions were unaffected.

17. Postsecondary enrollment is based on the NLSY97's definition of "regular schooling." This refers to enrollment in a college, graduate school, law school, or nursing program leading to an RN degree, but not training in technical institutes, programs for trade licenses, and so forth, unless the credits can be transferred to a regular school and would count toward a diploma or degree.

18. Like any longitudinal study, the NLSY97 suffers from some attrition, as indicated by the dropoff in number of interviews. In general, though, the National Longitudinal Surveys have been very successful at following cohort members over time. It is quite plausible that attriters differ from non-attriters with respect to their STW transitions—for example, those who become idle after leaving high school may be more like to attrit. However, only if attriters differ from non-attriters with respect to the effects of STW will the parameter estimates of interest be biased. This question can be explored using methods paralleling those in Evangelos M. Falaris and H. Elizabeth Peters (1998), who test for attrition bias by comparing estimates of behavioral equations of "eventual" attriters and non-attriters in the period prior to attrition of the former. However, such an analysis will not be useful for the NLSY97 until quite a few more rounds of data are available.

19. The school behaviors are measured as of round 1. This approach also helps avoid the problem of early STW participation affecting the

test scores that we use as controls. The ASVAB was administered in 1997 or 1998, so at worst this leaves open the possibility of some overlap between the period to which round 2 STW questions refer and time prior to the administration of the ASVAB.

20.   The implication of using the data on STW participation in this way is that we ignore variation in participation reported in round 1. If past participation has an effect and is associated with future participation, then this introduces a source of correlation between the STW participation that we measure and the error term. However, we are not too concerned about the potential bias that this creates, since it is generated from a correlation of the treatment variable with past STW participation, rather than with something that might spuriously generate an effect (or lack thereof) of STW. In addition, in our past work we have verified the robustness of the results to using information on any STW in which the respondent had ever participated.

21.   When we define employment, those who report their employer as the military are coded as employed.

22.   When the dependent variable is dichotomous, in the models for the effects of STW participation we report linear probability estimates. We verified that results were very similar using logit or probit models (as well as a probit model for the college attendance equation for identifying the "forgotten half," described later). Using the linear probability model simplifies the presentation and avoids distributional assumptions that underlie the logit or probit model. Throughout the empirical analysis, reported standard errors are robust to heteroscedasticity. Also, because there are often multiple observations on students within the same school, the reported standard errors allow for heteroscedasticity of the error term across schools and nonindependence of an arbitrary nature within schools, which typically results in somewhat larger standard errors.

23.   Household income is from round 1, and is from the parent questionnaire except in the rare event that the youth is defined as independent in 1997.

24.   Note that these participation rates are broadly consistent with estimates of individual participation rates in STW from other data sources (Brown 2000; Hershey et al. 1999; WestEd and MPR Associates, Inc. 2002).

25.   The one exception, perhaps, is the differences between blacks and whites. Neumark and Rothstein (2006) also found some evidence of higher STW participation for blacks. The evidence suggested that this is a within-school phenomenon, as there was no significant evidence that schools with more black students were more likely to offer STW.

At the same time, evidence in that paper did not point to particularly stronger benefits of STW program participation for blacks, with the exception of internship and apprenticeship programs.

26. Colinearity among the other variables in the models in tables 4.2 and 4.3 could obscure significant coefficients. But the R-squares are also extraordinarily low, ranging from 0.010 to 0.022. These may be low in part because of the dichotomous nature of the dependent variable. But in our earlier paper we found much higher R-squares for regressions for school-level offerings of STW programs as functions of school characteristics.

27. This is computed on a weekly basis, with zeros for weeks with no work; the average overall weeks is then computed. When we estimate equation 1 for these longitudinal measures, we include a control for the total number of weeks from the first September after leaving school until the interview.

28. Note that a program that affects schooling (such as mentoring) need not have offsetting effects on work, because individuals can engage in both work and schooling.

29. One striking finding for both men and women is that the effects of job shadowing and mentoring appear relatively large, despite these programs being considerably less intense in terms of hours devoted to them than, for example, co-op or internship and apprenticeship programs. That could indicate that there are problems with the data or that the effectiveness of different programs is not that closely related to their intensity.

30. Research by Stern (1984) and Stern et al. (1994) reports that enterprise-based jobs are more closely related to students' education than are out-of-school jobs, and that enterprise-based jobs provide more opportunity to apply what students are learning in school. Thus, school enterprises may be a particular type of STW program that enhances the educational experience and therefore encourages higher education.

31. One possible explanation for this is that the continuous history files capture schooling experiences with more error, although it is not obvious why this would be the case, and we leave it to future work to explore this possibility more fully. Another possibility is that estimates are biased because of the incidence of zeros for the dependent variables. We reestimated the models in table 4.5 (and table 4.9, which studies the same dependent variables distinguishing effects for those in the forgotten half) using Tobits. In most cases the results were very similar. Finally, we considered the possibility that the results in table 4.5 are weaker because of

the smaller samples. Reestimating the models in table 4.4 for the table 4.5 sample did in fact point to weaker effects of STW participation than indicated in table 4.4 (and similarly for the models with the forgotten-half interactions that come later). Our best estimates come from using the largest sample possible. What this indicates, then, is that we may need more rounds of the NLSY97 to better pin down the effects of STW on the longer-term measures of postsecondary outcomes, something we will pursue in future research.

32. We also estimated augmented models in which we included interactions between the forgotten-half indicator and all of the other control variables, to be sure we were not picking up omitted interactions in the forgotten-half–STW interactions. The results were very robust to the inclusion of these interactions.

33. The adverse effects of Tech Prep on college attendance are also found in other research using these data, although with refinements. Neumark and Rothstein (2006) also report negative effects of Tech Prep on college enrollment, in analyses of the NLSY97 data that take careful account of selection into Tech Prep participation.

   Stephanie Riegg Cellini (2006), using within-family differences to net out some unobservables, finds that Tech Prep may increase overall educational attainment by encouraging high school completion but may divert students from four-year to two-year colleges. Results for men, reported in the bottom panel of table 4.8, echo these results in part, finding evidence of negative effects of Tech Prep on four-year but not on two-year college attendance. Debra D. Bragg et al. (2002) report results from a study of eight Tech Prep consortia, in each of which Tech Prep participants were compared to samples of similar nonparticipants. In seven of the eight consortia, participants were more likely to attend two-year colleges and less likely to attend four-year colleges, paralleling the results reported previously (see their tables K1 to K8).

34. Because these results for the effects of STW on idleness appear mainly for men, we doubt that they reflect substitution between work and parenting.

35. Heather Rose (2006) presents some evidence that, for men, test-score gains achieved during high school have a positive impact on post–high school earnings for those whose eighth-grade test scores were in the bottom quartile.

36. But in a setting with dummy variables, multiple measures, and interactions, standard results for classical measurement error need not apply.

REFERENCES

Bragg, Debra D., Jane W. Loeb, Yuqin Gong, Chi-Ping Deng, Jung-sup Yoo, and Jerry L. Hill. 2002. *Transition from High School to College and Work for Tech Prep Participants in Eight Selected Consortia.* St. Paul, Minn.: National Research Center for Career and Technical Education.

Brown, Carrie H. 2000. "A Comparison of Selected Outcomes of Secondary Tech Prep Participants and Non-Participants in Texas." *Journal of Vocational Education Research* 25(3). Available at http://scholar.lib.vt.edu/ejournals/JVER/v25n3/brown.html (accessed August 7, 2006).

Cameron, Stephen V., and James J. Heckman. 2001. "The Dynamics of Educational Attainment for Blacks, Hispanics, and Whites." *Journal of Political Economy* 109(31):455–99.

Cellini, Stephanie Riegg. 2006. "Smoothing the Transition to College? The Effect of Tech-Prep Programs on Educational Attainment." *Economics of Education Review* 25(4): 394–411.

Donahoe, Debra, and Marta Tienda. 1999. "Human Asset Development and the Transition from School to Work: Policy Lessons for the 21st Century." Unpublished paper. Princeton University, Office of Population Research.

Falaris, Evangelos M., and H. Elizabeth Peters. 1998. "Survey Attrition and Schooling Choices." *Journal of Human Resources* 33(2): 531–54.

Hamilton, Stephen F., and Mary A. Hamilton. 1999. *Building Strong School to Work Systems: Illustrations of Key Components.* Washington, D.C.: National School-to-Work Office.

Heckman, James, Neil Hohmann, and Jeffrey A. Smith. 2000. "Substitution and Dropout Bias in Social Experiments: A Study of an Influential Social Experiment." *Quarterly Journal of Economics* 115(2): 651–94.

Hershey, Alan M., Marsha K. Silverberg, and Joshua Haimson. 1999. *Expanding Options for Students: Report to Congress on the National Evaluation of School-to-Work Implementation.* Princeton, N.J.: Mathematica Policy Research, Inc.

Hughes, Katherine L., Stephen F. Hamilton, and Robert J. Ivry. 2001. *School-to-Work: Making a Difference in Education.* New York: Columbia University, Teachers College, Institute on Education and the Economy.

Joyce, Mary, and David Neumark. 2001. "School-to-Work Programs: Information from Two Surveys." *Monthly Labor Review* 124(8): 38–50.

Kemple, James J. 2001. *Career Academies: Impacts on Students' Initial Transitions to Post-Secondary Education and Employment.* New York: Manpower Demonstration Research Corporation.

———. 2004. "Having an Impact on the Transition from School to Work: Evidence from Career Academies." Unpublished manuscript, Manpower Demonstration Research Corporation.

Kemple, James J., and Jason C. Snipes. 2000. *Career Academies: Impacts on Students' Engagement and Performance in High School.* New York: Manpower Demonstration Research Corporation.

National Association of State Boards of Education. n.d. "Vocational Education." *Policy Update* 10(8). Available at http://www.nasbe.org/Educational_issues/New_Information/Policy_Updates/10_08.html (accessed May 17, 2006).

Neumark, David. 2006. "Evaluating Program Effectiveness: A Case Study of the School-to-Work Opportunities Act in California." *Economics of Education Review* 25(3): 315–26.

Neumark, David, and Mary Joyce. 2001. "Evaluating School-to-Work Programs Using the New NLSY." *Journal of Human Resources* 36(4): 666–702.

Neumark, David, and Donna Rothstein. 2006. "School-to-Career Programs and Transitions to Employment and Higher Education." *Economics of Education Review* 25(4): 374–93.

Rose, Heather. 2006. "Do Gains in Test Scores Explain Labor Market Outcomes?" *Economics of Education Review* 25(4): 430–46.

School-to-Work Opportunities Act of 1994. 1994. Public Law 103-239, *U.S. Statutes at Large* 108 Stat 568.

Stern, David. 1984. "School-Based Enterprise and the Quality of Work Experience." *Youth & Society* 15(4): 401–27.

Stern, David, Neal Finkelstein, James R. Stone, John Latting, and Carolyn Dornsife. 1995. *School to Work: Research on Programs in the United States.* London and Washington, D.C.: Falmer Press.

Stern, David, Neal Finkelstein, Miguel Urquiola, and Helen Cagampang. 1997. "What Difference Does It Make If School and Work Are Connected? Evidence on Co-operative Education in the United States." *Economics of Education Review* 16(3): 213–29.

Stern, David, James Stone III, Charles Hopkins, Martin McMillion, and Robert Crain. 1994. *School-Based Enterprise: Productive Learning in American High Schools.* San Francisco: Jossey-Bass.

U.S. Congress, Office of Technology Assessment. 1995. *Learning to Work: Making the Transition from School to Work.* OTA-HER 637. Washington: U.S. Government Printing Office.

U.S. General Accounting Office. 1990. *Training Strategies: Preparing Noncollege Youth for Employment in the U.S. and Foreign Countries.* Washington: U.S. Government Printing Office.

WestEd and MPR Associates, Inc. 2002. *California School-to-Career: Helping Students Make Better Choices for Their Future.* San Francisco and Berkeley: WestEd and MPR Associates, Inc.

William T. Grant Foundation. 1988. *The Forgotten Half: Pathways to Success for America's Youth and Young Families.* Washington: U.S. Government Printing Office.

— Chapter 5 —

Learning by Doing
Career Academies

David Stern, Christopher Wu,
Charles Dayton, and Andrew Maul

F OR A NUMBER of years, we have been helping high schools and districts that are attempting to create or improve career academies—hence our title: "Learning by Doing Career Academies."[4] Our assistance includes developing the schools' capacity to keep track of results for students by relying mainly on information that is ordinarily available from student transcripts. We believe it is essential for schools themselves to continuously gauge results of career academies and other educational programs, because even if such programs have been found to be effective somewhere, they are unlikely to be effective everywhere. Therefore, one of our aims here is to describe how schools can self-monitor, and what they can learn in the process of operating career academies. Second, we wish to add to general knowledge about career academies by testing some ideas about why they may be more effective in some locations and situations than in others. Specifically, we conduct a cross-site analysis to explore whether sites that implement certain features of the academy model to a greater degree also obtain bigger gains in performance of academy students. Both parts of the analysis in this chapter focus on student performance during high school, not post–high school outcomes such as employment or college attendance.

Longevity and solid evidence of effectiveness distinguish career academies from other programs, practices, and policies that were bundled under the "school-to-work" or "school-to-career" rubric in the United States during the 1990s. The first known career academies were started in 1969, well in advance of more recent initiatives such as Tech Prep or job shadowing, though much later than co-op or vocational education (Stern et al. 1995). Relatively persuasive evidence of career academies' effectiveness comes from several quasi-experimental studies, and especially from a random-assignment evaluation conducted by MDRC (Manpower Demonstration Research Corporation). The second part of this paper spells out what we mean by a career academy, and summarizes career academies' history and existing research. (Chapter 6 in this volume, by Margaret Terry Orr and her colleagues, provides additional information about the purposes and pedagogical practices of career academies, especially those associated with the National Academy Foundation.)

Despite evidence that career academies can produce positive results for students, success is never automatic. Local circumstances may enhance or undermine the effectiveness of a particular career academy, within a particular school at a particular time. The career-academy model has several elements, all of which require planning and effort to put in place and keep in place. In 1997 we established the Career Academy Support Network (CASN) to help high schools and districts that want to develop and improve career academies. CASN provides professional development, on-site coaching, and other kinds of implementation assistance.

As part of its service, CASN uses available data from student transcripts to monitor implementation and to determine whether academy students are improving more or less rapidly than nonacademy students in the same high schools. Nonrandom selection of students into academies and nonrandom attrition make it impossible for this analysis to determine whether academy participation causes greater improvement in students' performance.[2] But the available data can nevertheless inform academy stakeholders about the kinds of students who are participating and how their performance is changing over time. The third and fourth sections of the chapter illustrate this kind of analysis.

The second question we seek to answer in this paper is whether academy students' growth, relative to nonacademy students in the same school, is associated with implementation of certain key features of the model. We focus on measures having to do with scheduling and course taking because these are considered fundamental to the academy design and they can be computed from student transcripts. This analysis, using a hierarchical model, is reported in the fourth and fifth sections of the chapter. Although the differences between academy and nonacademy students may be attributable in part to nonrandom selection or attrition, this exercise demonstrates a new procedure for estimating how much implementation matters.

CAREER ACADEMIES: DEFINITION, HISTORY, AND RESEARCH RESULTS

Teachers and community groups in Philadelphia first put the essential elements of contemporary career academies into practice in 1969.[3] For a decade or more this structure and related practices were known as the Philadelphia academy model. Before elaborating on the definition and history, we note that teachers had an indispensable role in creating the first such ventures. The subsequent spread and development of this approach also have depended on teachers' initiatives. But teachers have seldom been involved in analyzing data on academies, and part of CASN's purpose is to equip the teachers who are responsible for academies to participate in monitoring outcomes for students.

History of the Career Academy

The term "career academy" was coined by David Stern, Marilyn Raby, and Charles Dayton (1992) to describe the kind of high school configuration that originated in Philadelphia, then spread to California, New York City, and eventually nationwide. In 1981 the academy idea was exported from Philadelphia to California, starting with two academies near Silicon Valley. A series of evaluations, ending with that by Dorothy J. Reller (1987), found improved student performance, and spurred California to pass legislation in 1984 supporting ten replications of the model. The number of state-supported academies eventually grew to about three hundred in 2004. Also in the 1980s, New York City created the first Academies of Finance, sponsored by the American Express Company, which subsequently joined with many other companies to create the National Academy

Foundation (NAF). The foundation added academies for training in the travel and tourism field in 1987, public service in 1990, and information technology in 1999. As of 2004, NAF supported about four hundred academies in about thirty states (see also chapter 6, this volume).

In addition to the Philadelphia, California, and NAF academies, many other academies have sprung up independently, and new organizations have sprung up to support them (for example, the National Career Academy Coalition). Common themes for career academies are health, business and finance, arts and communications, computers, engineering, law, and government.

There is no authoritative uniform definition of the career academy, and as the term has become popular the variation among programs that call themselves career academies has increased.[4] In 1993 MDRC began the first random-assignment evaluation of career academies (Kemple and Rock 1996). MDRC identified three main features of the career academy:

- School-within-a-school organization in which at each grade level a group of students takes a set of classes together and stays with the same small group of teachers for at least two years.
- Curriculum that combines academic courses that meet college entrance requirements with technical classes, all related to the academy theme.
- Employer partnerships to provide internships and other experiences outside the classroom, related to the academy theme.

The Philadelphia academies began with a focus on dropout prevention and vocational preparation, but they soon evolved to include preparation for enrollment in four-year colleges and universities. The NAF academies have been college oriented since their inception. Our impression from the field is that most career-academy teachers explicitly aim to prepare students for both college and careers.

Until the 1990s, career academies existed only as small separate units within larger high schools. For example, a typical career academy might serve two hundred students in a school containing two thousand. Since the mid-1990s, however, some schools have converted themselves entirely into groups of career academies or of various small learning communities (SLCs), some of which are career academies. Valerie E. Lee, Douglas D. Ready, and David J. Johnson (2001) conducted an informal national canvass to identify high schools where all students and teachers belonged to small learning environments. They identified fifty-five such schools, of which 80 percent were using career academies as their model. In the Talent Development High School model developed by the Center for Research on the Education of Students Placed at Risk (CRESPAR), for example, every student in grades ten to twelve belongs to a career academy. Chicago now uses the term "career academies" for entire high schools that have, or did have, a vocational focus, but these do not seem to fit the definition we are using.

Research Evidence on Career Academies

Six different researchers or research teams, using longitudinal data from different sets of academies between 1985 and 2000, compared performance of academy and nonacademy students from the same high schools. These studies are described and summarized by Stern (2003). None of these studies randomly assigned students to the academy or nonacademy groups. Most researchers used regression techniques to control for some observed differences between academy and nonacademy students. In some studies the researchers and teachers chose each comparison student individually to match one of the academy students.

All of these studies reported academy students performing significantly better while in high school. Salient findings are as follows:

- Reller (1984, 1985) studied the first two career academies in California. Academy students earned significantly more course credits than a matched comparison group from the same high schools. One-year attrition rates ranged from 2 to 6 percent in academies, and from 10 to 21 percent in the comparison group.
- Stern and colleagues (1988, 1989) studied ten state-funded academies in California. Academy students tended to perform significantly better than matched comparison groups from the same high schools in attendance, credits earned, average grades, and likelihood of staying in school. The three-year attrition rate for the cohort entering in 1985 was 7.3 percent from academies, and 14.6 percent from the comparison group.

- Becky Hayward and G. Talmadge (1995) evaluated ten different programs that used some form of vocational education to
  promote success in high school. The two sites that were career
  academies showed generally better results than other programs
  in terms of students' improved attendance, credits, grades, and
  likelihood of completing high school.
- James M. McPartland and colleagues (1996, 1998) reported on
  the reorganization of Patterson High School in Baltimore in
  1995, which included the creation of career academies for all
  students in grades ten through twelve. Attendance in the first
  implementation year rose from 71 to 77 percent, contrasting
  with a districtwide decline from 73 to 70 percent in grades nine
  through twelve. A survey of teachers found great improvement
  in the reported school climate.
- Nan L. Maxwell and Victor Rubin (1997, 2000) analyzed 1991-to-
  1995 school records for three cohorts of students in grades ten to
  twelve in an urban district, including nine career academies.
  Controlling for other characteristics of students, academy students
  received significantly better grades than nonacademy students, in
  both academy and nonacademy classes. Ninety-two percent of
  the academy students graduated from high school within the
  study period, compared to 82 percent of nonacademy students.
- Marc. N. Elliott, Lawrence. M. Hanser, and Curtis. L. Gilroy (2000)
  compared 1994-to-1996 data from three Junior Reserve Officers
  Training Corps (JROTC) career academies in large cities with
  student data from other career academies or magnet schools in
  the same or similar schools, and data on JROTC students not in
  academies and on students not in any academy or magnet program. Propensity-weighted regression was used in an attempt
  to offset possible selection bias. Students in JROTC career academies and in other career academies or magnets generally
  received higher grades, had better attendance, completed more
  credits, and were less likely to drop out than statistically similar
  students not in academies.

Three of these studies also gathered data on post–high school
outcomes, resulting in the following salient findings:

- Reller (1987) surveyed students fifteen months after graduation.
  She found that 62 percent of academy graduates were enrolled

in postsecondary education, compared with 47 percent of the comparison group. Fifty-five percent of academy graduates expected to complete a bachelor's degree, versus 22 percent of the comparison group. Another survey, undertaken twenty-seven months after graduation, found no significant differences between academy and comparison students in employment status, wages, or hours worked.

- Stern, Raby, and Dayton (1992) conducted follow-up surveys ten and twenty-two months after graduation. They found no consistent differences between academy and comparison graduates in postsecondary attendance or degree aspirations. Academy graduates on average were working three more hours per week, but there was no consistent difference in hourly earnings.

- Maxwell and Rubin (1997, 2000) found no significant differences in wages or hours worked between former academy and non-academy students. Former academy students more often said that their high school program had prepared them well for further education and work; moreover, participation in postsecondary education was higher among former academy students: 52 percent were attending four-year colleges, compared to 36 percent of the nonacademy students. In a subsequent study of students at a public university campus, Maxwell (2001) found that academy graduates were less likely to need remedial course work, and were more likely to complete bachelor's degrees than statistically similar nonacademy graduates from the same district.

In sum, different researchers studying different sets of career academies have consistently found that academy students are outperforming their nonacademy schoolmates on various measures of academic success while in high school. Post–high school differences in further education and employment have been less consistent, but where significant differences have been found they have favored the academy students.

Although these studies statistically controlled for measured differences between academy and nonacademy students, the possibility remains that unobserved differences account for the results. For example, the academy students may have been more motivated or better organized to begin with, and that may explain why they did better. Indeed, there might be a systematic tendency for more motivated or better-organized students to join career academies.

The classic method for eliminating bias due to selection or self-selection is for researchers to use a random procedure to assign some subjects to the "treatment group" and the others to the control group. This procedure ensures that the average difference between the two groups will be negligible, given a large enough sample. Despite this great advantage, there are well-known drawbacks and limitations to using random assignment in educational field studies. Denying a beneficial treatment to a control group may raise ethical questions. Some important educational variables—for example, completing high school—cannot be experimentally manipulated. Even when random assignment is feasible and ethical, absence of a placebo means that Hawthorne effects and other biases may influence the result. Nevertheless, a well-designed random-assignment study can eliminate the problem of selection bias that plagues much educational research. (For a fuller discussion, see Stern and Wing 2004.)

In 1993, MDRC began its random-assignment evaluation of career academies, initially with ten sites, but one academy ceased operating. All nine remaining academies are in high schools with large proportions of low-income and minority students. Each was the only career academy in its high school.

At the start of the MDRC evaluation, the academies recruited more applicants than they could accommodate. Applicants knew they might not be admitted. MDRC randomly assigned about two-thirds of the applicants to the academy; the others became the control group. For more than ten years since the evaluation began, MDRC has collected student records, surveyed students during each of their high school years, and conducted follow-up surveys one year and four years after high school.

During the high school years, the career academies studied by MDRC produced several positive impacts on students' experience and achievement. Compared to the control group, academy students reported receiving more support from teachers and from other students (Kemple 1997). They were more likely to combine academic and technical courses, engage in career development activities, and work in jobs connected to school (Kemple, Poglinco, and Snipes 1999). As of spring of senior year, academies retained a larger fraction of the students whose initial characteristics made them more likely to drop out. And among students at less risk of dropping out, academies increased participation in technical courses and career development activities without reducing academic course credits (Kemple and Snipes 2000).

The first follow-up survey, one year after scheduled graduation, found no significant impacts on students' high school completion, GED acquisition, or participation in postsecondary schooling. It also showed no significant impact on employment or earnings, though students who had been assigned to career academies were working and earning somewhat more than the control group (Kemple 2001).

However, MDRC's most recent follow-up, about four years after scheduled graduation from high school, found large and significant impacts on employment and earnings, and no difference in educational attainment (Kemple and Scott-Clayton 2004). In the full sample, students assigned to career academies earned higher hourly wages, worked more hours per week, had more months of employment, and earned about 10 percent more per month than the control group. Similar differences were estimated for both males and females, but they were not statistically significant for females. Impacts on high school completion or postsecondary education were not significantly positive or negative for the sample as a whole or for any subgroup, but James J. Kemple and Judith Scott-Clayton (2004) note that both the academy and control groups had high rates of high school completion and postsecondary enrollment compared to national (NELS) data on urban high school students.

DESCRIBING STUDENT COMPOSITION AND PERFORMANCE IN A SINGLE ACADEMY

Evaluations of career academies have found that they can produce positive impacts on students, but it does not follow that every academy does produce such impacts. The career-academy model is not a surefire recipe for success. Much may depend on the particular people involved, local circumstances, and the degree of implementation. Consequently, to know whether a career academy is yielding the desired results it is necessary to keep collecting the data. In this section and the next we illustrate the kinds of information that can be obtained from student records.

Student transcript data have the great virtue of being readily available in all schools, but they also have serious limitations as a data source. Generally they are messy and full of anomalies. For example, it is common to find students on the rolls despite having zero attendance for the year. We eliminated such students from our analysis. We kept students who had fifty or more days of attendance, even though some of these are only marginally involved in the school. Since state funding is determined by attendance counts, attendance may be one of the more accurately recorded variables. Credits earned, grades, suspensions, and demographic data may be subject to even greater inaccuracies. We weeded out anomalies we could find, but we had to take most of the data at face value. Despite these problems, we think it is worth trying to find out what schools might be able to learn from the data in their own files.

Are Academy Students Representative?

One of the first questions raised by academy teachers and their nonacademy colleagues is whether students in the academy are representative of the student body in their schools, or different from the rest of the school. This is a contentious issue. Nonacademy teachers would resent an academy that recruited only the school's "best and brightest" students. Furthermore, many large high schools are now grouping students and teachers into smaller learning communities (SLCs), and an inequitable distribution of students among these smaller units can be a cause of divisiveness that undermines the strategy (Muncey and McQuillan 1996). In order to know whether students are being assigned to academies or SLCs in some unfair way, schools are beginning to develop routines that enable them to monitor the data.

For example, consider a simple analysis of ethnic and gender data from a biotechnology academy and its home high school, which we call Wyles High School (all school names are fictitious). Grade ten is the first year of the three-year biotech academy sequence. In 2002, Hispanic students were overrepresented and Asian students were underrepresented in this academy when compared to nonacademy tenth-graders in the academy. But this imbalance disappeared a year later, in grade eleven. At the same time, the academy enrolled a disproportionately large number of females in both years. The gender imbalance may or may not be considered problematic, but the data at least call attention to the fact. Similar analysis can be done on other student characteristics that are usually recorded in district records, including proficiency in English, eligibility for subsidized lunch, and participation in special education.

Student Mobility

An important fact of life in schools is that students come and go. Keeping track of mobile students is difficult, but it may be a crucial part of the story. For instance, an academy or SLC that pushes out low-performing students would not be considered as effective as one that retains those students and improves their performance. As high schools face growing pressure to raise test scores, and as more high schools divide students and teachers into smaller groupings, the temptation to deselect low-performing students may increase.

Table 5.1 illustrates how we can account for student mobility semester by semester. We are especially concerned about students reported as leaving the school district for unknown reasons. Many of these may have dropped out of school entirely, although others may have transferred to schools outside the district without informing anyone in the district where they went. The number leaving the district for unknown reasons therefore can be considered an upper bound on the number of dropouts.[5] Dividing that number by the number of students who ever enrolled gives an upper bound for the dropout rate. The number ever enrolled includes students who were there at the beginning of the period plus those who transferred in. During the two years covered in table 5.1, no biotech academy students left the district for unknown reasons, but a total of 198 (107 + 91) nonacademy students did. These 198 are 32 percent of the nonacademy students ever enrolled in this cohort.

Table 5.2 summarizes results of similar computations for several other academies (school names are fictitious). In most of those cohort comparisons, academies had lower proportions of students leaving the district for unknown reasons compared to nonacademy students at the same schools and grade levels. In many cases the differences are quite large. Academies, like other SLCs, are intended to encourage stronger ties among students, and between students

TABLE 5.1   **Accounting for Student Mobility at Wyles High School, Grades 10 and 11, 2001 to 2003**

	Biotech Academy	Non-academy	School Total
Number of students at beginning of grade 10, 2001	40	476	516
Transfers in from outside school	1	65	
Left district for unknown reasons		(107)	
Number of students at end of first semester, grade 10	41	434	475
Transfers in from outside school		13	
Transfers from nonacademy to academy			
Transfers from academy to nonacademy			
Left district for unknown reasons			
Number of students at end of second semester, grade 10	41	447	488
Transfers in from outside school	1	52	53
Transfers from nonacademy to academy	10	(10)	
Transfers from academy to nonacademy	(2)	2	
Left district for unknown reasons		(91)	
Number of students at end of first semester, grade 11	50	400	450
Transfers in from outside school		7	
Transfers from nonacademy to academy			
Transfers from academy to nonacademy			
Left district for unknown reasons			
Number of students at end of second semester, grade 11, 2003	50	407	457

Source: Authors' analysis of data from the school.

and teachers, in part on the basis of their shared interest in the academy theme. The results in tables 5.1 and 5.2 may reflect the holding power of those stronger relationships and shared interests. But it is also possible that the academies initially selected students who were already more likely to stay in school.[6]

Year-to-Year Changes in Attendance, Credits, and Grades

Students staying in school is an important outcome in its own right. In addition, differences in the rate of attrition between academy and

TABLE 5.2   **Students Leaving the District for Unknown Reasons, as a Percentage of Students Ever in the Academy or Nonacademy Group, for Various Schools and Cohorts**

School and Cohort	Academy	Nonacademy
Bantam High School, 9, 1999–2000, to 11, 2001–2002	Biotech 4.0%	18.7%
Bantam High School, 9, 2000–2001, to 10, 2001–2002	Biotech 4.4	2.1
Bantam High School, 9, 2001–2002 to 10, 2002–2003	Biotech 0.0	12.6
	Maritime 15.4	
Bantam High School, 11, 2001–2002 to 12, 2002–2003	Biotech 3.5	8.0
Bantam High School, 10, 2001–2002 to 11, 2002–2003	Biotech 10.9	16.1
Blizzard High School, 11, 2001–2002 to 12, 2002–2003	Media 10.0	41.0
Ohio High School, 9, 2000–2001, to 10, 2001–2002	Information technology 0.0	29.3
Ohio High School, 10, 2001–2002, to 11, 2002–2003	Information technology 9.1	34.3
Pierce High School, 9, 1999–2000, to 11, 2001–2002	Public service 8.5	21.5
Pierce High School, 9, 2000–2001 to 10, 2001–2002	Public service 0.0	9.2
	Construction 4.2	
Rollo High School, 10, 2001–2002, to 11, 2002–2003	Teaching and learning 17.7	26.5
Rollo High School, 11, 2001–2002, to 12, 2002–2003	Futures 15.0	13.5

Source: Authors' analysis of data from the schools.

TABLE 5.3   **Attendance and Credits Earned by Wyles High School Academy and Nonacademy Students in Grade 10, Compared to Previous Year**

	Grade 9, 2000–2001	Grade 10, 2001–2002
Average percentage attendance, biotech academy	96.9	96.1
Average percentage attendance, nonacademy	96.4	96.0
Average credits earned, biotech academy	4.93	4.83
Average credits earned, nonacademy	4.68	4.33

Source: Authors' analysis of data from the schools.

nonacademy students also affect the interpretation of other results. On average, students who leave the district for unknown reasons are probably not doing as well in high school as students who stay, so comparisons of performance trends between academy and nonacademy students are probably biased against the academy. In other words, performance trends for the academy would look better if more low-performing students left the academy. As we compare trends over time in various student outcomes, it is important to keep this possible attrition bias in mind.

Comparing both academy and nonacademy students' performance at the same grade levels with their own previous performance is a simple but instructive procedure schools can use to gauge an academy's results over time. Attendance, credits earned, and grades are three outcomes that schools measure periodically and record in students' transcripts. For example, table 5.3 shows average attendance and credits earned during tenth grade by the cohort of academy and nonacademy students. Table 5.3 also shows attendance and credits earned by those same students during ninth grade, before the biotech academy students had entered that program. Both attendance and number of credits declined during tenth grade for both academy and nonacademy students. The biggest drop was in credits earned by the nonacademy group. Academy students declined slightly more than nonacademy students in attendance but slightly less in credits earned. Again, if attrition among academy students had been the same as among nonacademy students, these average performance measures for academy students at the end of grade ten would probably have been higher. In other words, it is likely that holding on to more students lowered the academy's averages.

ACADEMY STUDENTS' PERFORMANCE

Do academy students perform better, when prior performance and other factors are controlled for? It is apparent from table 5.3 that students who entered the biotech academy in grade ten had in grade nine already compiled better records of attendance and credits earned than nonacademy students in grade nine at the school. It is necessary to include students' prior performance in the analysis in order to gauge whether academy students are doing better than expected compared to nonacademy students. The analysis also can control for other student characteristics.

Table 5.4 shows results from a series of regressions predicting cumulative GPA at the end of grade ten for these same cohorts of academy and nonacademy students at Wyles High School. In model 1, the only performance predictor is GPA at the end of grade nine. As expected, the coefficient on grade nine GPA is positive and highly significant, and this remains true in subsequent models. Model 2 adds demographic characteristics to the list of predictors: gender, age, and race (African American, Asian, or Hispanic—whites are the comparison group). Only the coefficient on gender is significant, and it indicates that males receive lower grades, controlling for the other predictors in the model. The coefficients on demographic characteristics also do not change much in subsequent models. Model 3 adds a variable indicating whether a student was in the academy or not. A positive coefficient would mean that academy students on average are receiving better grades than nonacademy students, holding constant the other predictors. In this case the academy coefficient is positive, but barely so, and it is far from significant statistically. Finally, model 4 adds a multiplicative interaction between the academy variable and grade nine GPA. A positive coefficient here would mean students with high GPA at the end of grade nine are receiving higher grades in grade ten if they are in the academy. In Table 5.4 this coefficient turns out to be negative, but not statistically significant.

TABLE 5.4 Regressions Predicting Cumulative GPA at End of Grade 10, Wyles High School, 2001–2002

Variables	Model 1		Model 2		Model 3		Model 4	
	Coefficient	Standard Error	Coefficient	Standard Error	Coefficient	Standard Error	Coefficient	Standard Error
Constant	.450**	.099	.814	1.288	.795	1.291	.793	1.293
GPA, grade 9	.755**	.036	.672**	.042	.670**	.042	.670**	.044
Male			-.161*	.076	-.159*	.077	-.159*	.077
Age			-.0082	.081	-.0071	.081	-.007	.081
African American			-.211	.251	-.214	.252	-.214	.252
Asian			.235	.160	.239	.160	.238	.160
Hispanic			-.070	.151	-.071	.151	-.071	.152
Academy					.047	.127	.060	.398
Academy × GPA, grade 9							-.005	.136

Source: Authors' analysis of data from the school.
**p < .01, *p < .05

We conclude from table 5.4 that students in their first year of the biotech academy in the 2001–2002 school year did not show significant improvement in grades relative to nonacademy students, on average. And this is true whether GPA in the prior year was high or low.

We have estimated the models in table 5.4 with data from various schools and districts. Tables 5.5 and 5.6 show coefficients on the academy variable from regressions on several cohorts in this and other academies, using model 3 from table 5.4 to predict each year's GPA, attendance, credits earned, and suspensions. For predicting GPA, the academy coefficient is significant in five out of the twenty-six cases and negative in four of those five. In the other twenty-one cases, compared to nonacademy students in the same schools and grade levels, academy students on average are not getting higher or lower GPAs than would be predicted from their prior GPAs and demographic characteristics. In three out of twenty-two regressions predicting attendance, the coefficient on academy participation is significant and positive. Of the twenty-one regressions for credits earned during the year, the coefficient on academy participation was significant and positive in one case and significant and negative in three. Finally, none of the twenty-one regressions run for suspensions revealed a significant coefficient on the academy variable.

Our intent in this and the preceding sections has been to illustrate how teachers, administrators, and community partners can "learn by doing" career academies. Transcript data reveal whether academy students represent a cross-section of the school in terms of gender, race, ethnicity, or other characteristics. The same data also can be used to calculate attrition rates and to monitor the performance of academy students over time as compared to nonacademy students in the same school. We have seen that the academies analyzed here have relatively few students leaving the district for unknown reasons. If students who leave the district for unknown reasons tend to be worse performers, then holding on to more of these students may reduce the apparent effectiveness of academies on other measures. In spite of that, several of the academies analyzed here do show some relative gains in student attendance, which can be seen as another indicator of academies' holding power.

Students' gains in attendance, credits earned, GPA, or (reducing) disciplinary suspensions generally do not differ significantly

TABLE 5.5 **Coefficients on Academy Variable from Regressions Predicting GPA and Attendance, for Various Academies and Cohorts**

Academy, Cohort, and Year	GPA		Attendance	
	Coefficient	Standard Error	Coefficient	Standard Error
Ohio, info tech, 10, 2001–2002	.033	.056	3.505*	1.499
Ohio, info Tech, 10, 2002–2003	.054	.056	.276	1.731
Bantam, biotech, 10, 2002–2003	−.008	.035	.890	.682
Bantam, biotech, 11, 2002–2003	.028	.046	.516	.890
Bantam, biotech, 12, 2002–2003	−.036	.028	.140	1.339
Bantam, public service, 10, 2001–2002	.107*	.043	2.012*	1.005
Bantam, public service, 11, 2001–2002	−.090**	.000	−.535	.810
Bantam, public service, 10, 2002–2003	−.002	.038	.674	.860
Bantam, public service, 11, 2002–2003	−.067**	.034	−.478	1.021
Bantam, public service, 12, 2002–2003	−.010	.023	1.621	1.343
Bantam, construction, 10, 2001–2002	−.011	.058	−1.151	1.279
Bantam, construction, 10, 2002–2003	−.114*	.050	−1.290	1.172
Bantam, construction, 11, 2002–2003	−.064*	.031	−.134	1.298
Wyles, biotech, 10, 2001–2002	.047	.127	−.122	.787
Wyles, biotech, 12, 2001–2002	.006	.119	1.533	1.027
Wyles, biotech, 10, 2002–2003	.103	.119	−1.049	.613
Wyles, biotech, 11, 2002–2003	.056	.111	.136	.631
Wyles, biotech, 12, 2002–2003	.066	.120	.943	.704
Rollo, teaching and learning, 10, 2001–2002	−.033	.046		
Rollo, teaching and learning, 11, 2001–2002	−.018	.026		
Rollo, teaching and learning, 11, 2002–2003	−.035	.045		
Rollo, teaching and learning, 12, 2002–2003	−.018	.026		
Blizzard, media, 10, 2001–2002	.034	.067	3.212	1.687
Blizzard, media, 11, 2001–2002	.016	.032	1.977	1.161
Blizzard, media, 11, 2002–2003	.023	.062	3.801*	1.859
Blizzard, media, 12, 2002–2003	.005	.030	1.350	.807

Source: Authors' analysis of data from the schools.
**$p < .01$, *$p < .05$

TABLE 5.6 Coefficients on Academy Variable from Regressions Predicting Credits Earned and Suspensions, Various Academies and Cohorts

Academy, Cohort, and Year	Credits Earned		Suspensions	
	Coefficient	Standard Error	Coefficient	Standard Error
Ohio, info tech, 10, 2001–2002	.140	.202	.021	.062
Ohio, info tech, 10, 2002–2003	−.564*	.222	−.031	.073
Bantam, biotech, 10, 2002–2003	−.106	.125	−.062	.038
Bantam, biotech, 11, 2002–2003	.100	.216	.000	.043
Bantam, biotech, 12, 2002–2003	.336	.352	−.029	.050
Bantam, public service, 10, 2001–2002	.204	.174	.026	.030
Bantam, public service, 11, 2001–2002	.271	.176	−.004	.028
Bantam, public service, 10, 2002–2003	.143	.131	−.005	.050
Bantam, public service, 11, 2002–2003	.261	.200	−.064	.041
Bantam, public service, 12, 2002–2003	−.036	.239	−.066	.047
Bantam, construction, 10, 2001–2002	−.500*	.227	.017	.038
Bantam, construction, 10, 2002–2003	−.093	.171	−.032	.069
Bantam, construction, 11, 2002–2003	.241	.260	.015	.057
Wyles, biotech, 10, 2001–2002	−.001	.147		
Wyles, biotech, 12, 2001–2002	−.039	.130		
Wyles, biotech, 10, 2002–2003	.460**	.144		
Wyles, biotech, 11, 2002–2003	.015	.149		
Wyles, biotech, 12, 2002–2003	.180	.132		
Rollo, teaching and learning, 10, 2001–2002	−.351	1.086	−.092	.066
Rollo, teaching and learning, 11, 2001–2002	−2.823**	.873	.036	.064
Rollo, teaching and learning, 11, 2002–2003	−.347	1.063	−.094	.059
Rollo, teaching and learning, 12, 2002–2003			.006	.054
Blizzard, media, 10, 2001–2002			−.073	.055
Blizzard, media, 11, 2001–2002			−.061	.048
Blizzard, media, 11, 2002–2003			−.064	.055
Blizzard, media, 12, 2002–2003			−.069	.048

Source: Authors' analysis of data from the schools.
**p < .01, *p < .05

between these academies and the rest of their host high schools. In a few academies, the "value added" in terms of GPA or credits earned appeared to be significantly negative. Teachers in these situations would want to probe for explanations and, if the data are accurate, determine what corrective action to take.

RELATIONSHIP OF RESULTS TO DEGREE OF IMPLEMENTATION

In addition to providing information to teachers and other stakeholders in individual academies, we are also interested in making comparisons across sites. In particular, we would like to know whether outcomes for academy students are related to how thoroughly the academy model is implemented. To explore that question, we have devised several new measures of implementation, which this section explains. In the following section, we present results from a hierarchical model that tests whether those implementation measures are associated with student outcomes.

One of the key features of career academies, like some other SLCs, is that academy students at a given grade level are scheduled to take a set of classes together. Typically, academy sections of English, social studies, science, and a technical or lab class related to the academy theme are scheduled so that academy students can take them together. This allows teachers to design lessons, projects, and assignments that connect some of the different subjects the students are taking. In contrast to the usual high school schedule, the intent is to create more intellectual coherence among the various concepts and bodies of knowledge students are learning. Having a group of students take a set of classes together also adds to social cohesion among students, and with the teachers who share responsibility for this group.

This kind of cohort scheduling is a major departure from standard practice in American high schools.[7] Scheduling academy students into academy classes therefore requires persistent effort by the academy teachers and school administration, especially given the varying scheduling systems and constraints in school districts. As a result, the actual implementation of this scheduling design is seldom perfect.

We have developed three "course metrics" to indicate how closely students' actual course taking comes to the academy model. We usually compute these measures for one year at a time, but they could also be calculated by semester or for more than one year.

- *Course taking:* The average percentage of the academy courses in which academy students actually enrolled. For example, suppose the intended academy course sequence includes four classes during sophomore year, but because of scheduling conflicts the average academy student ended up enrolling in only three of these classes. Our course-taking measure would then be three-fourths, or 75 percent. A low number here means academy students have actually experienced a low portion of the intended academy curriculum.
- *Course purity:* The percentage of students enrolled in the average academy class who are actually academy students. For example, if academy classes on average have thirty students and twenty-four of these are academy students, course purity would be four-fifths (24/30), or 80 percent. A low number on this index means it is more difficult for teachers to connect lessons or assignments from different classes, because the different classes do not contain the same set of students.
- *Course coverage:* Credits earned in academy courses as a percentage of all credits earned by academy students, on average. For example, suppose that the academy schedule called for academy students to take four classes during tenth grade, and that this actually happened. If the total course load all students took was six classes, then course coverage would be two-thirds (4/6), or 67 percent. This measure was first used by B. J. McMullan, C. L. Sipe, and W. C. Wolf (1994) to indicate how big a part the academy or SLC curriculum represents in the total course load.

These three measures are independent in the sense that knowing two of them does not allow you to compute the third. Conceptually, low course coverage together with high course taking would indicate that the academy is designed to offer only a relatively small number of classes, but the average academy student is successfully scheduled to enroll in a high percentage of those classes.

To take another scenario, low course taking and high purity would mean that the average academy student misses out on a substantial part of the intended academy curriculum, but few nonacademy students are enrolled in the academy classes.

Although individual students have some degree of choice about which courses they take, we view these course metrics primarily as resulting from administrative structures and processes within the school rather than from individual student choices. The third metric, course coverage, is limited by how many courses are included in the academy sequence; this is a school decision, not a student decision. The second metric, purity, is determined by how well organized the school's scheduling process is—in some schools it can be chaotic!—and by the priority given to academy membership when the school's master schedule is constructed. Similarly, the first measure, academy-course taking, depends on the degree to which schedulers try, and are able, to avoid forcing academy students to choose between taking an academy core course and some other required course.

In our sample, all but one of the twenty-two academy cohorts have values within the range of 0.67 to 1.0 for course taking, 0.55 to 1.0 for purity, and 0.22 to 0.57 for coverage. The standard deviations among all twenty-two cohorts are 0.14, 0.19, and 0.12, respectively. These measures do indeed vary, but does this variation matter?

RESULTS OF HIERARCHICAL
MODELING ACROSS SITES

To test whether our measures of academy implementation are associated with improvement in academy student performance, we shifted to a hierarchical modeling framework (Bryk and Raudenbush 1992). At level 1, individual students are the units of observation. The level 1 predictors are the prior-year outcome for that student, along with gender, age, and race or ethnicity. At level 2 the unit of observation is a cohort of students who belonged to a particular academy or a cohort that belonged to the nonacademy part of the high school, at a particular grade level in a particular year. The analysis reported here involves twenty-two academy groups and twenty-two nonacademy groups for the same grade level, calendar year, and high school, for which we have the necessary data (from seven academies).[8]

Tables 5.7 to 5.10 show results from estimating a sequence of five models for each outcome. The level 1 regressions, not shown here, are the same as model 2 in table 5.4.[9] In each of the level 2 models reported in tables 5.7 to 5.10, the level 1 intercept is treated as a random coefficient that varies among the forty-four level 2 cohorts. The first level 2 model uses only one predictor, a variable indicating whether the student belonged to an academy or not.

More explicitly, the level 1 regression can be written as $y_{ijt} = b_{0j} + b_1 y_{ij,t-1} + x'_{ij} b_x$, where y_{ijt} is the predicted value of an outcome (for example, attendance) for the ith student in the jth cohort during year t; b_{0j} is the intercept for cohort j; b_1 is the coefficient on last year's outcome for that student, $y_{ij,t-1}$; and b_x is a set of coefficients on a student's demographic characteristics x_{ij}.

Coefficients b_1 and b_x do not vary across cohorts, but b_{0j} does. The level 2 model in which the academy variable is the only predictor would be written as $b_{0j} = g_0 + g_1 A_j$, where $A_j = 1$ if cohort j is in an academy, 0 otherwise; and g_1 is the coefficient reported for model 1 in tables 5.7 to 5.10.

The next three models add the course metrics one at a time. The last model uses all three course metrics in addition to the academy variable itself. The course metrics are defined only for academies and are given a value of 0 for nonacademy students. The level 2 coefficients on the course metrics therefore tell us whether and to what extent student outcomes are better in academies that have higher scores on the course metrics.

Tables 5.7 to 5.10 show the estimated coefficients and robust standard errors, corrected for clustering of students within the twenty-two groups. In table 5.7, the academy coefficient by itself is a significantly positive predictor of attendance. But when course metrics are added, neither the academy coefficient nor the course metrics appear significant. In table 5.8, no variable is significant in predicting credits earned. In predicting GPA, table 5.9 shows a negative coefficient on the course-coverage metric, meaning that students tend to receive lower grades in academies where the academy curriculum represents a larger proportion of the total course work. But when this is the only course metric in the model, this negative association is partly offset by a positive coefficient on the academy variable itself. We do not have an explanation for this finding, other than randomness in the data. Finally, table 5.10 suggests that being

TABLE 5.7 Level 2 Coefficients on Academy Variable and Course Metrics, Predicting Level 1 Intercept in Model for Attendance

Model	Academy		Course Taking		Purity		Coverage	
	Coefficient	Standard Error	Coefficient	Standard Error	Coefficient	Standard Error	Coefficient	Standard Error
1	0.713*	0.301						
2	−1.493	1.360	2.554	1.532				
3	0.371	0.947			0.394	1.049		
4	0.888	0.759					−0.398	1.585
5	−1.211	1.565	2.693	1.504	0.080	1.204	−1.069	1.807

Source: Authors' analysis of data from the schools.
*p < .05; N = 6,017

TABLE 5.8   Level 2 Coefficients on Academy Variable and Course Metrics, Predicting Level 1 Intercept in Model for Credits Earned

Model	Academy		Course Taking		Purity		Coverage	
	Coefficient	Standard Error	Coefficient	Standard Error	Coefficient	Standard Error	Coefficient	Standard Error
1	0.085	0.104						
2	0.546	0.367	−0.541	0.449				
3	0.162	0.263			−0.091	0.291		
4	0.388	0.392					−0.732	0.909
5	0.679	0.438	−0.597	0.548	0.415	0.422	−1.054	1.046

Source: Authors' analysis of data from the schools.
*p < .05; N = 5,477

TABLE 5.9   Level 2 Coefficients on Academy Variable and Course Metrics, Predicting Level 1 Intercept in Model for GPA

Model	Academy		Course Taking		Purity		Coverage	
	Coefficient	Standard Error	Coefficient	Standard Error	Coefficient	Standard Error	Coefficient	Standard Error
1	0.002	0.041						
2	−0.103	0.089	0.123	0.103				
3	0.064	0.076			−0.072	0.083		
4	0.194*	0.072					−0.440*	0.178
5	0.006	0.110	0.178	0.100	0.116	0.121	−0.590*	0.224

Source: Authors' analysis of data from the schools.

*p < .05; N = 6,017

TABLE 5.10 **Level 2 Coefficients on Academy Variable and Course Metrics, Predicting Level 1 Intercept in Model for Suspensions**

	Academy		Course Taking		Purity		Coverage	
Model	Coefficient	Standard Error	Coefficient	Standard Error	Coefficient	Standard Error	Coefficient	Standard Error
1	−0.005	0.019						
2	0.0276	0.083	−0.038	0.087				
3	−0.081*	0.039			0.087	0.059		
4	−0.023	0.038					0.043	0.080
5	−0.028	0.061	−0.077	0.101	0.139	0.120	−0.075	0.153

Source: Authors' analysis of data from the schools.
*p < .05; N = 4,119.

160

in an academy may be associated with fewer suspensions—a positive result—but none of the course metrics is significant.

On the whole, tables 5.7 to 5.10 do not reveal any consistent association between our measures of academy implementation and outcomes for students. However, it would be premature to conclude from these results that implementation makes no difference. We have measured only a few implementation variables that we could calculate from student transcript data, and these may not be the most important. In 2004 several organizations that provide technical assistance to academies published a set of standards containing ten key elements, each with three to five separate components, amounting to thirty-eight distinct practices in all.[10] Some of these other practices, or interactions among them, may be more important than the three indicators we were able to calculate.

Furthermore, even the three implementation variables we did measure might have more explanatory power if we had data on a larger number of academies. More observations would give us more precise estimates, as would including academies with a wider range of values on our course metrics. Differences in the range we observed may not matter, but bigger differences might.

Finally, the effectiveness of a given career academy may depend less on the absolute degree of implementation than on the contrast between the academy and the rest of the school (see Kemple and Snipes 2000). A perfectly implemented career academy may not help students much if the rest of the high school also offers similar benefits as the academy, but an imperfectly implemented academy may help students a lot if the quality of the surrounding high school is poor. Unfortunately, we did not have the data necessary to compare students' experiences in the academy with those in the rest of the high school.

CONCLUSIONS AND CAUTIONS

In this chapter we analyzed data collected as part of an ongoing project to develop and improve career academies in various high schools and districts. We presented two kinds of analysis, single-site and cross-site. The purpose of the single-site analysis was to inform the efforts of individual career academies. The cross-site analysis explored whether better-implemented academies showed bigger changes in the performance of academy students relative to their nonacademy counterparts.

We placed this analysis in the context of earlier studies, which have found fairly consistent and persuasive evidence of positive effects for career-academy students at different times and places. However, the fact that academies have produced positive results in some places does not imply that such results are inevitable or automatic. Implementing the career-academy model is not easy. That is why several organizations and projects, including CASN, offer help to schools that request it (see note 10). As part of CASN's service, we collect student transcript data and report findings back to the teachers, administrators, and others involved. We presented examples of the kind of analysis we give back to schools to inform the self-guidance of individual academies. For instance, comparing the gender and racial-ethnic composition of academy students with that of nonacademy students in the same school tells the stakeholders whether academy students represent a reasonable cross-section of the school.

The most substantive finding from the analysis of individual academies is that most academies have fewer students who leave the district for unknown reasons than the nonacademy parts of their high schools. This suggests that academies tend to have stronger holding power, a finding that is consistent with previous research. However, unlike previous studies, our data on twenty-six different academy cohorts do not show that academy students generally receive higher grades than their nonacademy peers, when we control for prior grades and demographic variables. Nor do we find relative improvement among academy students in terms of credits earned or disciplinary suspensions during the year. This failure to find positive effects may be attributable to the stronger holding power of academies exerting a downward influence on measures of academy students' relative gains. In spite of that, we do find some evidence that academy students' attendance improves relative to nonacademy students. This seems consistent with the idea that academies have stronger holding power than the rest of the school: academy students are less likely to leave for unknown reasons, and they show bigger year-to-year gains in the number of days they actually come to school.

In addition to reporting results that may be used to inform individual academies, we also did a cross-site analysis to explore whether academies that are better implemented tend to show bigger gains (or changes generally) in student performance. For that analysis we had to construct measures of implementation. The most innovative piece of this chapter is the development of three implementation measures indicating (1) what percentage of the designated academy courses the average academy student actually takes; (2) what percentage of students in the average academy class are actually academy students; and (3) what percentage of the average academy student's total course credits are earned in academy classes. We refer to these metrics as "course taking," "purity," and "coverage." Results from a hierarchical model did not find significant associations between these measures and student performance. However, we do not view this result as conclusive, because we measured only a few aspects of implementation, had data for only a small sample of academies, observed a fairly narrow range of variation in our implementation measures, and could not assess the quality of academy students' experience relative to the rest of the school, which may be more important than the absolute degree of implementation.

We end with two cautionary observations. First, the information in school files is not always accurate. It is not collected for research purposes, and may not be checked or audited for accuracy. For instance, we had to exclude from the analysis some students who appeared in the data files despite having zero attendance for the year.

A particularly vexing problem is how to know exactly which students are in an academy during any given term. Accurately identifying academy and nonacademy students in the database is essential for comparing their performance, but schools and districts do not have routine procedures to flag academy students in their databases. As foundations and federal and state authorities induce more high schools to regroup students and teachers into academies or other SLCs, accountability pressures will require schools and districts to institute such procedures for identifying students by academy or SLC—at the beginning and end of each term the academy or SLC leader must give the district a list of students. Further, to construct the kind of course metrics developed here, it will also be necessary to flag every course or every section of a course that is designated for students from a particular academy or SLC.

Our second caution has to do with implementation standards. Many school-reform organizations, funders, government agencies, and researchers publish advice about how to improve student performance. Unfortunately, too little of that advice is based on firm evidence. Our analysis illustrated one way to test whether particular aspects of implementation are associated with results for students. This kind of analysis is only a beginning. In the particular case of career academies, most previous evaluations have treated an academy as a "black box" and have offered little or no data on the mechanisms or processes through which academies may affect student performance or on the influence of the social, historical, cultural, or institutional context. The MDRC evaluation is an exception (see, for example, Kemple and Snipes 2000; see also chapter 6, this volume, which measures a range of outcomes related to different features of the academy). More studies of this kind would be highly desirable.

Obtaining desired results from career academies, other kinds of SLCs, or generally any kind of reform requires a better understanding of how and under what conditions a given strategy or approach actually works. Until much more such analysis has been done, researchers and policymakers should be humble about telling schools how to improve.

We are grateful for suggestions from James Kemple, David Neumark, Terry Orr, James Rosenbaum, other conference participants, and anonymous reviewers. We also want to express our continuing admiration for the teachers, administrators, community partners, and students who seek, and sometimes find, ways to make high school more worthwhile. We hope our work will support theirs. As always, as authors we retain responsibility for any shortcomings in this paper.

NOTES

1. Readers who are unfamiliar with career academies should not construe the title to imply that career academies themselves are designed to sub-

stitute "doing" for "learning." To the contrary, as the text describes, most course work in career academies is in academic subjects, and the intent is to prepare students for college.

2. This chapter also does not attempt to test whether CASN's efforts are producing positive results.

3. Some text in this section is from Stern (2003) and Stern and J. Y. Wing (2004).

4. The state of California provides grants to school districts for "partnership academies," which are defined by statute, but this definition does not apply to the hundreds of academies in California that do not receive state funding. A few other states also have funded such academies. The federal School-to-Work Opportunities Act of 1994 included career academies on a list of seven "promising practices," but did not define them. Building on the MDRC definition, the Career Academy Support Network (http://casn.berkeley.edu) helped negotiate a common definition among several networks currently promoting career academies.

5. Students who did transfer to other schools are also at greater risk of not completing high school. See R. W. Rumberger and K. A. Larson (1998).

6. The possibility that academies select students with lower propensities to move is also consistent with the finding in table 5.1 that the academy accepts few transfers from outside the school. On the other hand, the academy did take a substantial number of transfers from the rest of the school.

7. Cohort scheduling for secondary school students is common practice in other countries. The individualistic, shopping mall approach to scheduling seems to prevail only in the United States.

8. The four missing cohorts are the 2001-to-2002 grades ten and eleven from Rollo and Blizzard. They were excluded from tables 5.7 to 5.10 because course metrics were not available for these cohorts.

9. Results in tables 5.7 to 5.10 are not exactly comparable to those shown in tables 5.5 and 5.6 because the samples are somewhat different as a result of missing data; and coefficients on student characteristics were free to vary across academies in the equations for which academy coefficients are reported in tables 5.5 and 5.6, but not in tables 5.7 to 5.10.

10. The organizations involved were the National Career Academy Coalition, National Academy Foundation, National Center for Education and the Economy, Southern Regional Education Board, Center for Research on the Education of Students Placed at Risk, and CASN. The standards are available at each organization's web site, for example, http://casn.berkeley.edu/resources/national_standards.html.

REFERENCES

Bryk, Anthony S., and Stephen W. Raudenbush. 1992. *Hierarchical Linear Models: Applications and Data Analysis Methods.* Newbury Park, Calif.: Sage Publications.

Elliott, Marc N., Lawrence M. Hanser, and Curtis L. Gilroy. 2000. *Evidence of Positive Student Outcomes in JROTC Career Academies.* Santa Monica, Calif.: RAND Corporation.

Hayward, Becky, and G. Talmadge. 1995. *Strategies for Keeping Kids in School.* Washington: U.S. Department of Education.

Kemple, James J. 1997. *Career Academies: Communities of Support for Students and Teachers. Emerging Findings from a 10-Site Evaluation.* New York: Manpower Demonstration Research Corporation.

———. 2001. *Career Academies: Impacts on Students' Initial Transitions to Post-Secondary Education and Employment.* New York: Manpower Demonstration Research Corporation.

Kemple, James J., Susan M. Poglinco, and Jason C. Snipes. 1999. *Career Academies: Building Career Awareness and Work-Based Learning Activities Through Employer Partnerships.* New York: Manpower Demonstration Research Corporation.

Kemple, James J., and JoAnn L. Rock. 1996. *Career Academies: Early Implementation Lessons from a 10-Site Evaluation.* New York: Manpower Demonstration Research Corporation.

Kemple, J. J., and Judith Scott-Clayton. 2004. *Career Academies: Impacts on Labor Market Outcomes and Educational Attainment.* New York: Manpower Demonstration Research Corporation.

Kemple, J. J., and J. C. Snipes. 2000. *Career Academies: Impacts on Students' Engagement and Performance in High School.* New York: Manpower Demonstration Research Corporation.

Lee, Valerie E., Douglas D. Ready, and David J. Johnson. 2001. "The Difficulty of Identifying Rare Samples to Study: The Case of High Schools Divided into Schools-Within-Schools." *Educational Evaluation and Policy Analysis* 23(4): 365–79.

Maxwell, Nan L. 2001. "Step to College: Moving from the High School Career Academy Through the Four-Year University." *Evaluation Review* 25(6): 619–54.

Maxwell, Nan L., and Victor Rubin. 1997. *The Relative Impact of a Career Academy on Post-Secondary Work and Education Skills in Urban, Public High Schools.* Hayward, Calif.: California State University, Hayward, School of Business and Economics, Human Investment Research and Education Center.

————. 2000. *High School Career Academies: A Pathway to Educational Reform in Urban Schools?* Kalamazoo, Mich.: W. E. Upjohn Institute for Employment Research.

McMullan, B. J., C. L. Sipe, and W. C. Wolf. 1994. *Charters and Student Achievement: Early Evidence from School Restructuring in Philadelphia.* Philadelphia: Center for Assessment and Policy Development.

McPartland, James M., Robert Balfanz, Will Jordan, and Nettie Legters. 1998. "Improving Climate and Achievement in a Troubled Urban High School Through the Talent Development Model." *Journal of Education for Students Placed at Risk* 3: 337–61.

McPartland, James M., Nettie Legters, W. Jordan, and Edward L. McDill. 1996. *The Talent Development High School: Early Evidence of Impact on School Climate, Attendance, and Student Promotion.* Baltimore: Johns Hopkins University and Howard University, Center for Research on the Education of Students Placed at Risk.

Muncey, Donna E., and Patrick J. McQuillan. 1996. *Reform and Resistance in Schools and Classrooms: An Ethnographic View of the Coalition of Essential Schools.* New Haven: Yale University Press.

Raudenbush, Stephen W., and Anthony S. Bryk. 2001. *HLM5: Hierarchical Linear and Nonlinear Modeling.* Lincolnwood, Ill.: Scientific Software International.

Reller, Dorothy. 1984. *The Peninsula Academies: Final Technical Evaluation Report.* Palo Alto, Calif.: American Institutes for Research.

————. 1985. *The Peninsula Academies, Interim Evaluation Report, 1984–85 School Year.* Palo Alto, Calif.: American Institutes for Research in the Behavioral Sciences.

————. 1987. *A Longitudinal Study of the Graduates of the Peninsula Academies, Final Report.* Palo Alto, Calif.: American Institutes for Research in the Behavioral Sciences.

Rumberger, Russell W., and Katherine A. Larson. 1998. "Student Mobility and the Increased Risk of High School Dropout." *American Journal of Education* 107(1): 1–35.

Stern, David. 2003. "Career Academies and High School Reform Before, During, and After the School-to-Work Movement." In *The School-to-Work Movement, Origins and Destinations,* edited by William J. Stull and Nicholas M. Sanders. Westport, Conn.: Praeger.

Stern, David, Charles Dayton, Il Woo Paik, and Alan Weisberg. 1989. "Benefits and Costs of Dropout Prevention in a High School Program Combining Academic and Vocational Education: Third-Year Results from Replications of the California Partnership Academies." *Educational Evaluation and Policy Analysis* 11(00): 405–16.

Stern, David, Charles Dayton, Il Woo Paik, Alan Weisberg, and John Evans. 1988. "Combining Academic and Vocational Courses in an Integrated Program to Reduce High School Dropout Rates: Second-Year Results from Replications of the California Peninsula Academies." *Educational Evaluation and Policy Analysis* 10(00): 161–70.

Stern, David, Neal Finkelstein, James R. Stone III, John Latting, J., and Carolyn Dornsife. 1995. *School to Work: Research on Programs in the United States*. London and Washington, D.C.: Taylor & Francis/Falmer Press.

Stern, David, Marilyn Raby, and Charles Dayton. 1992. *Career Academies: Partnerships for Reconstructing American High Schools*. San Francisco: Jossey-Bass.

Stern, David, and Jean Y. Wing. 2004. "Is There Solid Evidence of Positive Effects for High School Students?" Prepared for the conference "High School Reform: Using Evidence to Improve Policy and Practice," organized by Manpower Demonstration Research Corporation, New Orleans (January 22–23). Paper available on-line at http://www.mdrc.org/publications/391/conf_report.pdf.

—— Chapter 6 ——

The National Academy Foundation's Career Academies: Shaping Postsecondary Transitions

Margaret Terry Orr, Thomas Bailey,
Katherine L. Hughes,
Gregory S. Kienzl,
and Melinda Mechur Karp

T HE CAREER-ACADEMY model—a school-within-a-school, career-focused high school program of study often with related work experience—has spread rapidly throughout the United States since the mid-eighties, in large part because educators and policymakers believe it to be a promising approach for encouraging better academic achievement and facilitating students' transition to college and careers. Learning to what extent well-designed career academies deliver on this promise is the focus of this chapter.

As defined in chapter 5 of this volume and other sources, career academies generally include school-based and work-based components, make use of an industry-themed, contextualized curriculum, have a paid summer internship, and offer supplemental career readiness and exploration activities (Kemple and Rock 1996; Stern, Dayton, and Raby 2000; Stern, Raby, and Dayton 1992). In this chapter we look further at the learning theories and instructional strategies of career academies. Academies integrate strategies for student career and college preparation, including organizing learning around a thematic, career-focused curriculum; extending learning experiences outside of the classroom to the workplace; and preparing all students for college, regardless of their college-going intentions (Cannon and Reed 1999; Maxwell and Rubin 2000; Stern, Dayton, and Raby 2000; Stern, Raby, and Dayton 1992). Unlike conventional vocational education, career academies expose students to a whole industry rather than merely to a job, including the industry's academic foundations and its range and distribution of career opportunities, particularly as related to different levels of postsecondary education attainment. Career academies commonly emphasize innovative instructional strategies that develop high-performance workplace skills—project-based and cooperative learning, in particular—and stress critical thinking and problem solving. These structural and pedagogical characteristics all reflect the current consensus on secondary-educational reform strategies for improving the engagement and learning of students (Balfanz, Jordan, and McPartland 2002; Castellano, Stringfield, and Stone 2003; Kaufman, Bradby, and Teitelbaum 2000; Useem, Neild, and Morrison 2001).

With the expansion of career academies has come considerable variation in implementation. The National Academy Foundation (NAF), which sponsors hundreds of academies nationwide, endeavors to limit variation and sustain quality. Career academies in the NAF network are to implement all recommended elements of the NAF career-academy model to engage students academically, help them prepare for their postsecondary career and college transition, and support them personally while they are in school. For NAF career-academy students, the primary program experiences are four or more core academy courses that are career-contextualized, project-based, and offer student-centered instructional practices during the junior and senior years (although some programs begin earlier); a computer or technology course; a paid six-week summer internship with a private company; a college-level course taken while in high school; and exposure to a variety of activities for college and career planning and preparation.

The first NAF academy was founded in 1982, and NAF as a central organization was established in 1989. One of the largest career academy networks in the country and the only one that is national in scope, NAF currently sustains a national network of 619 career academies focusing on finance, travel and tourism, and information technology. It also provides curricular support, professional development, and technical assistance.[1] NAF's emphasis is on the inclusion of all core career academy components and the provision of quality contextualized curriculum to its network members; teacher professional development through NAF conferences, materials, and local activities; and business involvement through high-profile national-level firms as well as local advisory boards who provide paid student internships.

Career-academy teachers receive NAF curriculum and related materials that are frequently updated and adapted for their local industry context, and they can attend an annual professional development conference. They typically have designated classroom spaces, an area of the school for the academy program, and some autonomy in program management and delivery. In an analysis of the impact on teachers of the academy experience, Margaret Terry Orr (2005) found that the career-academy approach encourages teachers to focus more collectively on preparing students through their curriculum, instructional practices, and working relationships. Academy teachers were more likely than nonacademy teachers to have a strong commitment to the academy-program focus and to the use of organizational supports (such as common teacher meeting time), and to work collaboratively with other teachers, all of which were positively related to their perceived effectiveness with students.

Local business participation in career academies varies widely and can include advisory board membership; providing paid summer internships to students; assisting with work-readiness activities for students, such as mock job interviews; offering work experiences or other professional development to teachers; and making in-kind contributions of business-related materials for instruction. Generally, businesses do not directly fund the program. Our analysis of employer participation in the NAF academies found that, judging by the depth and breadth of employers' participation, NAF has been particularly effective in recruiting and retaining quality support from them. As in other research on employer participation, the NAF employers cited philanthropic, public relations, and employee-recruitment as reasons for their involvement (Hughes, Karp, and Orr 2002).

NAF acts as an intermediary between schools and businesses, and supports the implementation of all the components noted earlier in its programs. As a result of their membership in a national network and their agreement to adhere to common program characteristics, NAF-affiliated academies are likely to offer a more homogeneous and comprehensive experience than are nonaffiliated, stand-alone academies.

Other studies have examined academies in general, as reviewed in chapter 5 of this volume, but this study was the first to look specifically at NAF academies. The multipart study examined the practices of teachers in the program, employer participation, and the views and experiences of alumni and high school seniors in the program. Using data from student transcripts and surveys as well as qualitative evidence from site visits, this chapter summarizes findings regarding graduating seniors' college and career planning and preparation from a study of nine long-standing NAF academies.[2]

NAF funded the Institute on Education and the Economy (IEE) to undertake the study and NAF officials served as advisers and encouraged local site cooperation. Although the research was funded by NAF, we took considerable measures to ensure the validity and independence of the results.[3] The conclusions reflect the authors' views and not necessarily those of NAF.

THE RATIONALE FOR CAREER ACADEMIES

Current national concerns about high school curriculum and structure make close examination of the academy model critical. Perhaps the most prominent concern is related to curriculum content. Building on the call for higher standards in the early 1980s (National Commission on Excellence in Education 1983), the current trend has been to promote rigorous academics for all students (Bottoms n.d.; Education Trust 2001). Although this emphasis might seem to preclude career-oriented and technical courses, research has shown that high-quality courses of the latter type—offering challenge, academic skill development, and complex assignments—can increase student motivation and achievement (Bottoms n.d.).

A related concern of high school teachers is engagement: how to keep students motivated and interested in doing well in school. Prior research has shown that student engagement, as measured by identification with and participation in school, is predictive of student retention (Finn 1989). Educators have been exploring ways to create more options for high school students, in the hopes of increasing their engagement in school and thereby increasing their academic achievement, particularly during the senior year (National Commission on the High School Senior Year 2001a, 2001b). Curricular and organizational options such as magnet programs, academic houses, and career academies are promising reform approaches to adding variety and challenge to the secondary curriculum (see American Youth Policy Forum 2000; Cannon and Reed 1999; Castellano, Stringfield, and Stone 2003; Legters, Balfanz, and McPartland 2002; McPartland et al. 1998; Useem, Neild, and Morrison 2001).

Researchers have looked at how the organization and structure of high schools interacts with student learning. Much research has already demonstrated the benefits of smaller high schools for student engagement and retention (Natriello, McDill, and Pallas 1990; Oxley 1997; Wehlage et al. 1989) and academic achievement (see Lee and Smith 1995). There is a growing movement to replicate these benefits by implementing small learning communities (SLCs) within high schools.

Facilitating young people's transition from secondary to post-secondary education is also assuming greater importance.[4] Although the college-going rate has increased, the college completion rate has not (Jennings and Rentner 1998; U.S. Department of Education 1998; Wirt et al. 2004). Getting into and through college successfully is dependent in part on the quality of preparation while in high school. First, the intensity and quality of high school course taking strongly predicts degree attainment. Specifically, Clifford Adelman (1999), in analyzing a longitudinal study of youth ("High School and Beyond"), found that a composite measure of academic resources (curriculum intensity and quality,[5] test scores, and class rank or GPA) strongly predicted college entry and bachelor's degree attainment by age thirty, with curriculum being the primary component. Yet, as Adelman reported, a large percentage of students in academic and college-preparatory programs do not take advanced course work. In addition, having access to information about college is instrumental to college going, but the sources available vary by students' family income: low-income students have the least access and hence depend almost exclusively on their high school counselors for this information (Carbrera and La Nasa 2000).

Career academies, by design, address these concerns. NAF in particular has expended significant resources developing its curricula, which include college-level course work. The integration of industry- and work-related content with academics aims to make the latter more relevant and meaningful. Educators hope the program's design strengthens student engagement and facilitates transition into college and careers, enabling them to focus their plans and consider the academy-affiliated industries as career choices without limiting students' career aspirations to these industries. This early insight into promising career opportunities exposes students to a range of jobs, and could both shape students' college and employment pursuits and motivate them to complete their college degree in order to pursue gainful employment.

As noted in chapter 5 of this volume, there is a small body of research on the career academy model's benefits to students, particularly beyond high school graduation. There is evidence that career academies promote a close and personal academic experience for students and teachers (Kemple 1997), provide quality academic experiences (Kemple 1997; Orr and Fanscali 1995; Orr et al. 1987), and can help improve student achievement (Elliott, Hanser, and Gilroy 2000; Foothill Associates 1997) and post–high school success (Maxwell 2001; Orr 1990; Orr and Fanscali 1995; Reller 1987).[6] Much of this research was conducted in the early years of program implementation or on career academy programs that varied in purpose, structure, and focus.

Recent research on short-term educational outcomes has found somewhat contradictory results. Nan L. Maxwell (2001) examined the postsecondary outcomes of individuals who applied to a local noncompetitive four-year university from 1990 to 1998 for a degree program, comparing a subset of academy-program completers from one school district with a sample of nonacademy comparison students from the same district.[7] Maxwell looked backward at the effect of enrollment in a diverse set of academies on subsequent college experiences, for just those who went to the local college. She found that having been in a career academy reduced the participants' need for English remediation in college and increased their chances of graduating, as compared with nonacademy graduates then in college. In contrast, the MDRC longitudinal study (see a fuller discussion of the study's design and findings in chapter 5 of this volume, in Kemple 1997, and in Kemple and Snipes 2000), which randomly assigned applicants to be in the academy program or not (thereby creating a control group),[8] found no effect of academy participation on standardized achievement test scores or initial postsecondary outcomes. Both the academy students and those who applied to the academies but did not attend (the control group) had relatively high levels of high school graduation and college enrollment when compared to national samples of high school students.

OVERVIEW OF METHODOLOGY

To analyze the NAF career-academy program and participants' high school experiences and college and career plans, we conducted a multimethod, multisite study.[9] The study sought to answer whether the academy (1) created a distinctive experience for participating students in contrast to others; (2) was positively associated with students' engagement and achievement in high school; and (3) was positively related to students' college and career aspirations and plans.

Study Population and Sample Selection

To select individual NAF programs for study, we limited the site population to those that were most likely to have seniors who had had full program experiences and comparison seniors who had not. We selected sites with fully implemented, long-running academy programs, defined as containing the core programmatic features of the NAF model. Thus, the results do not generalize to all NAF academies or all academies. According to NAF officials, by 1999 one hundred fifty NAF-affiliated career academies had been in operation a minimum of five years and approximately fifty—several in a number of cities—had been in operation for ten years, when the study was initiated. With the assistance of NAF staff, we chose ten programs in nine locations (two programs were in New York City) to reflect geographic and racial and ethnic diversity, and eliminated programs that, according to NAF's review, were not sustaining good implementation or were experiencing turnover in school or program leadership. Seven were Academies of Finance (AOF) and three were Academies of Travel and Tourism (AOTT). One program did not provide comparison student information and so was dropped from the student study. The ten sites, listed by letter rather than name, are listed in table 6.1.

Our visits to the program sites revealed additional variability among the sites, in their setting and focus, which could influence students' high school experiences and their subsequent college and career planning. For example, the programs were located in high schools with student enrollments ranging from eight hundred to three thousand, which could influence the perceived level of school support and engagement generally. The programs differed somewhat in their organization, in their focus (more academic or more vocational), and in the presence or absence in the schools of other similar programs (ranging from none to several others).

The study used two samples of seniors: graduating seniors who were completing an NAF career-academy program experience and graduating seniors who were not. We used all graduating academy seniors as our program participant sample, which was the number of transcripts school staff provided for all academy students (N = 305). We wanted to maximize "treatment" differences between the two groups and not have treatment-like experiences vary widely within the treatment and comparison groups. Working with school staff, we selected a comparable number of classes of nonacademy seniors at each site that were demographically and academically similar to the academy seniors. All classes were in academic fields (English or social studies) that were not part of a career-focused program.

Sampling comparison students by courses enabled us to select students who were not part of other uniquely focused programs and who were not academically advanced or deficient compared to the academy class. For example, at the school in which the academy is considered an honors program, the comparison was a class of students enrolled in a nonacademy honors course. More important, by drawing our comparison group from among seniors, we excluded the least academically able nonacademy students (who would not have reached senior status in credit accumulation). We assumed that since both groups had reached senior-year status by means of credit accumulation, the groups' members had similar high school completion motivation and did not include poorly per-

TABLE 6.1 Characteristics of Sampled Sites

Sites	Type of Academy	First Year of NAF Operation	State	Predominant Racial or Ethnic Group Served
A	Academy of Finance	1988	Washington	White
B	Academy of Finance	1988	California	Asian and Pacific Islander
C	Academy of Finance	1989	Florida	White
D[a]	Academy of Finance	1982	New York	Multi-ethnic
E	Academy of Finance	1988	Utah	White
F	Academy of Finance	1986	New York	African American
G[b]	Academy of Finance	1987	Maryland	African American
H	Academy of Travel and Tourism	1991	Florida	Hispanic
I	Academy of Travel and Tourism	1991	California	Hispanic and White
J[a]	Academy of Travel and Tourism	1987	New York	Multi-ethnic

Source: Authors' compilations from the National Academy Foundation Evaluation Study, conducted by the Institute on Education and the Economy.
[a]Not included in analyses with GPA or attendance data, because transcripts were not provided, or were incomplete or unusable.
[b]Did not provide a comparison sample.

177

forming students. Notwithstanding the chance that unaccounted-for characteristics may exist and may skew results, this method served to maximize the difference between the two samples' program experiences while minimizing other differences, such as in academic strength, between the two samples. Sampling comparison groups by class rather than individually probably reduced the likelihood of refusal and increased cooperation, since students completed the surveys during class time rather than personal time.

Procedures and Respondents

Our primary methods of data collection were site visits during the spring and fall of 2000 to the sample academies, including interviews with teachers, administrators, and employers; written surveys of academy and nonacademy seniors administered in school by program staff in late spring 2000; and the collection of student transcripts compiled by program staff in spring and summer 2000. To ensure that we were accurately measuring program characteristics, IEE and NAF staff collaborated in designing the survey questions to identify the core program components and intended program outcomes.

Program staff members administered surveys to students in academy classes and were encouraged to administer the survey later to students who had been absent. A total of 233 usable surveys were returned from respondents (see table 6.2). We received completed surveys from 215 nonacademy comparison seniors from the nine sites.

We collected student attendance and transcript information for the academy and nonacademy students for the year prior to the first academy year and throughout the academy years, which provided us with pre- and postprogram data on school-related outcomes. We received 305 academy student transcripts from ten schools and 183 nonacademy student transcripts from seven schools, as shown in table 6.2.

We used the transcript information and returned surveys to calculate the survey response rates. Since the survey was voluntary and we assume that 100 percent of the sample was contacted, we have concluded that any difference between the numbers of transcripts and surveys is due to refusal to participate and errors in

TABLE 6.2 Number of Student Transcripts Obtained, by School and Academy Status

School	Transcripts Received		Surveys Received		Usable Surveys		Usable Surveys Included in All Analyses	
	Non-academy	Academy	Non-academy	Academy	Non-academy	Academy	Non-academy	Academy
A	17	24	11	23	11	23	11	23
B	32	16	24	12	21	9	21	9
C	42	39	40	43	38	42	38	42
D	[a]	61[a]	31	26	30	23	[c]	23
E	26	13	11	11	10	10	10	10
F	37	37	19	27	17	25	17	25
G	[b]	20	[b]	11	Omitted from Study			
H	13	28	22	25	14	22	14	22
I	16	42	41	37	39	33	39	33
J	[a]	25[a]	16	18	10	12	[c]	[c]
Total	183	305	215	233	190	199	150	164

Source: Authors' compilations from the National Academy Foundation Evaluation Study, conducted by the Institute on Education and the Economy.
[a] Did not provide usable student transcripts.
[b] Did not provide a comparison sample.
[c] Not included in transcript analyses.

TABLE 6.3   **Number of Completed Surveys and Surveys with Available Transcripts by Program**

Program	Completed Surveys		Completed Surveys and Transcripts	
	Academy	Comparison	Academy	Comparison
Academy of Finance	132	127	109	97
Academy of Travel and Tourism	67	63	55	53
Total	199	190	164	150

Source: Authors' compilations from the National Academy Foundation Evaluation Study, conducted by the Institute on Education and the Economy.

record keeping. Using the transcript and survey response information, we concluded that we had obtained a 76 percent response rate for academy participants.[10] We received transcript information for 175 nonacademy seniors from seven schools, and 172 completed surveys from those schools (see table 6.2). From some schools we received more transcripts than surveys; from others the opposite was true.

We restricted our sample further in order to have complete measures for statistical comparisons. We dropped twenty-three academy seniors' and twenty-five regular seniors' surveys (forty-eight, or 11 percent of the original sample) because of missing demographic information that was needed for some of the analyses.[11] With these adjustments, our final sample of 389 comprised 199 academy seniors, of whom 66 percent were in high schools with Academy of Finance programs, and 190 nonacademy seniors, of whom 67 percent were in schools with an Academy of Finance program (see table 6.3).

For some of our analyses that required transcript data, we restricted our sample even further, eliminating the groups from two other sites, D and J, because their transcript data were either incomplete or not usable for our purposes.[12] For the analyses using just the seven sites our sample was 314, comprising 164 academy students and 150 comparison students (shown in table 6.3), of whom 66 and 65 percent, respectively, attended high schools with Academy of Finance programs.

We compared the two groups on selected demographic and achievement attributes. In all nine selected schools, both samples of students attended classes in the same building and had the opportunity to take several courses together throughout their high school career, use the same support services, and participate in the same extracurricular activities. Using our program site visits and student survey and interview feedback, we verified that the academy seniors had the full or almost full career academy experience available and that the nonacademy senior samples did not, and that academy and other students were not mixed in the core academy courses.

Measuring Outcomes

Although there is general agreement that career-academy programs should improve students' transitions into college and careers and may contribute to improved attendance and achievement, there is no agreement on appropriate measures of programs' success. Several have been used in other studies, and their appropriateness may differ depending on the outcomes on which programs focus. Alternatives include academic achievement, in all courses or just in academy-related courses; transition to any postsecondary education program, that is, to a program that is consistent with the academy focus, or specifically to a four-year college; and career transition to quality employment in an academy-related industry.

Given these ambiguities, and the multiple options encouraged by program officials and staff, we designed the study to examine several possible academic outcomes (the alumni survey, not reported here, explored career outcomes). First, we included an examination of the program's relationship to improvements in overall GPAs and attendance, using pre- and postprogram transcript data. Although the NAF program's purpose is not explicitly to raise GPAs and attendance, these indicators are commonly used in career-academy program evaluations, and some previous academy research has found positive effects on student attendance (Hanser and Stasz 1999; Kemple and Snipes 2000). In addition, we wanted to know whether there is any negative program effect on these academic outcomes. As a second set of outcome measures we looked at four-year and two-year college going, using the student survey data, and included separate analyses by type of career academy to underscore our expectations for differential college going. Finally, we also included college-planning and college-acceptance rates among the outcome measures because we expected the program to enable its students to be better prepared for college.

Our primary independent measure was a participant's academy status as either an academy program completer or nonacademy participant. For some analyses, academy status was further subdivided into Academy of Finance participants and Academy of Travel and Tourism participants. We used two additional sets of independent measures: For the transcript data analyses, we only had school affiliation. For the survey data analyses, we had gender, race or ethnicity, parents' education, and the GPA averages of the high schools with whom the academies were affiliated. The only preprogram data we had were transcript information on GPA and attendance, and survey data on students' recollections of their reasons for enrolling or not enrolling in the career academy.

Analyzing Program Outcomes

Our two data sets were separately analyzed for relationships between academy participation and outcomes. For confidentiality reasons, we could not collect the transcript and survey data in a manner that would permit their integration at the level of the individual student. Using the survey data collected from the academy and nonacademy seniors, we report on the differences in their high school experiences, to confirm that the former students experienced the academy model. We also report what both groups planned to do after graduation. The analysis conducted in this section is a combination of descriptive tables and regression with a parsimonious set of controls. No causal relationship should be inferred from the former, and limited causality should be gleaned from the latter.

Using the transcript data, we compared attendance and GPAs between academy and nonacademy seniors, first descriptively and then using OLS regressions in which attendance and GPA were the dependent variables. For these regressions we controlled for the type of academy (finance or travel and tourism), and for pre-academy attendance and GPAs.

Using the survey data, we conducted logistic regressions on college plans, in which the dependent variable was whether or not the student planned to attend a four-year college in the summer or fall after graduation. We used demographic data collected in the survey to control for some of the factors other than academy status that might influence college plans. These included gender, race or ethnicity, parents' education, and an aggregate school-level measure of GPA in the grade prior to academy eligibility—either ninth or tenth grade.

FINDINGS

The findings presented below are grouped as follows: selection and motivation of academy students; comparison of the experiences of academy and nonacademy students; their postsecondary educational plans and college acceptance; and the academy influence on four-year college plans.

Selection and Motivation of Academy Students

How do students become academy participants and what are initial differences between academy students and nonacademy students? Enrollment in all of the academies in the sample was voluntary; students chose to enroll. In order to be considered for admission, students submit written applications in the spring of their freshman or sophomore year (or eighth grade, for admission to a four-year program), and obtain parental permission and letters of recommendation from teachers. Program staff review the applications and select students who they think have the potential to succeed in the program.[13]

The NAF-affiliated career-academy program is designed to target students in the academic middle who may be interested in careers in finance or in travel and tourism.[14] The program is not designed exclusively for either college-bound or non-college-bound students. Students do have to be on track for graduation in terms of credits earned, since much of the academy course work uses up elective credits. The program also targets youths who, as one teacher said, need a "hook" to stay engaged in school. Thus the program is not intended for the most or least academically able students, but instead seeks students who could benefit from a career-focused program of study that is believed to be motivating and enriching.

Interviews with academy staff revealed that teachers play an important role in encouraging students to apply, often recruiting prospective students from their courses. Some teachers deliberately recruited students who they believed would benefit from the program (such as the "reluctant learners" described by one principal), while others focused on students who would "gel" with the program staff and fit the program's goals. Thus, program enrollment requires active selection by both students and teachers, and teachers' encouragement may contribute as much to the likelihood of enrollment as students' own initial motivation. We also asked the academy students their main reason for applying to the program, and nonacademy students for the main reason they did not apply. No single reason for applying stood out—academy students cited interest in subject matter, their friends applying, and the challenge of the program, among other reasons. Twelve percent said they could not give a particular reason. For the nonacademy students, 41 percent said they were not interested in the topic area and 34 percent said they did not know that applying was an option. Thus, neither participation nor nonparticipation in the program was associated with strong career-related motivations.

What relationship exists between the mutual selection process and the demographic and academic characteristics of the academy and nonacademy students? There is no statistically significant difference between the two groups with respect to age, gender, race, and measures of family stability such as whether the student had moved or changed schools. The comparison group did have more students who had at least one parent whose education had not gone beyond high school, yet the academy seniors were more likely to be unsure of their parents' educational backgrounds (table 6.4).[15]

We also measured the most commonly identified personal and family risk factors (Natriello, McDill, and Pallas 1990), and found that career-academy seniors were as likely as nonacademy seniors to have had any of nine family or personal changes or issues over the previous two years (shown in table 6.4). In addition, the two groups varied unsystematically in their differences on these items. Finally, in the seven schools with transcript information, academy seniors had slightly higher pre-academy GPAs than the comparison seniors (2.97 versus 2.52, which is between a B and C+), but the difference is not significant. Taken together, it appears that the two

senior samples were similar on most critical personal and academic attributes.

Comparison of the Experiences of
Academy and Nonacademy Students

Most career-academy students had all the primary career-academy
program experiences called for in the NAF academy model: four or
more career-focused courses, a paid private-sector summer internship, at least one college-level course, and at least one year of computer technology, along with a greater number of career-, college-
and job-related planning activities (see table 6.5). Other seniors were
statistically significantly less likely to have these, if at all, verifying
that the two groups differed on the characteristic academy features.[16]

The internship, a six-to-eight-week paid position within the
industry, which usually takes place during the summer between
the junior and senior years of high school, is a fundamental characteristic of the NAF career-academy model.[17] As shown in table 6.6,
65 percent of academy seniors had a paid summer internship, 5 percent had an unpaid summer internship, and 15 percent had a more
individualized experience tailored to students who were ineligible
for paid positions because they lacked proper documentation.
Taken together, 85 percent of the academy seniors had a school-
sponsored internship or work experience. In contrast, only 34 percent of the nonacademy seniors had a school-sponsored internship
or work experience and only 8 percent had a paid summer internship. This academy student internship participation rate is greater
than findings for career-academy students in general. In MDRC's
study of various career academies, only about 45 percent of students still enrolled in an academy at the end of the twelfth grade
had had a work-based learning experience, and about one-quarter
of all the students had had a job with high work-based learning
content (Kemple, Poglinco, and Snipes 1999).

Table 6.6 shows that the NAF-affiliated internships differ qual-
itatively from what seem to be more typical school-based work
experiences as reported by the comparison seniors. Most NAF
career-academy students had someone from their school visit their
work sites and rotated across several jobs for broader career exposure. Most academy students found their internship to be mean-

TABLE 6.4 Personal and Academic Characteristics of Academy and Nonacademy Seniors

Characteristic	Academy Seniors	Nonacademy Seniors
Demographic characteristics		
Academy of Finance student	66%	—
Female	71	65%
Asian American or Pacific Islander	21	28
Black or Hispanic	35	32
White, non-Hispanic	44	40
Do not know parents' educational attainment	22	14*
High school completion only for one or both parents	25	35*
Some college education, but not completion, for one or both parents	12	14
College completion for one parent	26	20
College completion for both parents	15	16
Moved one or more times in the last six years	22	26
Changed schools two or more times in six years	9	13
N	199	190
Personal risk characteristics that occurred within the last two years		
One parent lost a job	15%	20%
A family member was disabled or ill	22	17
One parent got married or remarried	7	11

Family member was a victim of a crime	14	17
Family received welfare	9	6*
Parents divorced or separated	11	9
A sibling dropped out of school	3	5
A parent who died	4	5
Became seriously ill or disabled personally	6	7
N[a]	180	189
Academic characteristics		
Pre-academy GPA	2.97	2.52
N[b]	196	180
Pre-academy attendance	170.3	167.1
N[b]	170	153

Source: Authors' compilations from the National Academy Foundation Evaluation Study, conducted by the Institute on Education and the Economy.
Note: Totals may not add up to 100 percent because of rounding.
[a]Only eight schools are included in this analysis; due to concerns over confidentiality and privacy, one site, school E, refused to allow us to ask these questions of either the academy or the comparison group.
[b]Only six schools had attendance data for analysis purposes. One additional school had GPA data for analysis purposes.
*Statistically significant p < .10, chi-squared test.

TABLE 6.5   **Core Academy Program or Equivalent Experiences, and Other Academic High School Experiences of Students, by Academy Status (Percentage and Number)**

Academy Components	Academy Seniors	Other Seniors
Primary components		
Four or more career-academy courses	83%	—
Paid summer internship, connected to school	65	8%*
Unpaid summer internship, connected to school	5	6
Alternative work-based learning experience	15	0
One or more college-level courses	67	33*
One or more years of computer technology	96	67*
Strongly encouraged enhancements		
Number of career-related activities and classes in school	5.4	3.0**
Number of college-planning activities	5.9	5.1
Number of school-related job seeking activities	2.6	1.5
Other academic high school experiences		
Took at least one remedial course	9.6	14.2
Took at least one college or AP course	77.9	54.7
Number of algebra I or high math courses	3.2	2.8
Number of foreign language courses	2.2	2.3
N	199	190

Source: Authors' compilations from the National Academy Foundation Evaluation Study, conducted by the Institute on Education and the Economy.
*Statistically significant $p < .05$, chi-squared test.
**Statistically significant at $p < .01$, t-test of independent sample means.

ingful and important, while only half of the nonacademy seniors with an internship did.

Another core program feature is career and college preparation. The academy program encourages teachers to incorporate a wide variety of related work-based learning experiences and co-curricular activities into their courses in order to help students learn about the industry, explore careers, plan for college, and develop their social and interpersonal skills. The survey results generally confirm that academy students were more likely than nonacademy students to have had work-based learning experiences other than an internship and, to a lesser extent, to have engaged in job-seeking activities, but not necessarily more college- and job-planning activities (see table 6.7). In particular, academy seniors were much more likely than the comparison seniors to engage in community service,

TABLE 6.6   **School-Based Internship Experiences, by Academy Status (Percentages)**

Attribute	Academy Seniors	Nonacademy Seniors
Had internship or school-based work experience	85	34%**
Paid, summer	65	8**
Unpaid, summer	5	6
Other school-based work experience	15	20
Had no school-based work experience	16	65**
Quality of the internship[a]		
Sometimes or always spent at least half time in training	62	62
Rotated across several jobs	60	38**
Completed one or more projects for the business	75	57*
Received a performance evaluation	91	83
Had school-based supervision	74	27**
Learned new things	85	70*
Was meaningful and important	82	52**
N	190	199

Source: Authors' compilations from the National Academy Foundation Evaluation Study, conducted by the Institute on Education and the Economy.
Note: Percentages may not add up to 100 because of rounding.
[a]Quality ratings are based on samples of 140 academy seniors and 48 other seniors who had some type of internship or school-related work experience. The percentages reflect those who sometimes or always had these qualities in their internship.
*Statistically significant at $p < .05$, chi-square test of independence between academy and nonacademy seniors
**Statistically significant at $p < .01$, chi-square test of independence between academy and nonacademy seniors

job shadowing, and work-site visits, to participate in employer talks at school and work readiness classes, and to talk with teachers and counselors about careers. Finally, academy seniors were more likely to have used interest inventories and to have participated in practice and real job interviews as part of their school program, making it unsurprising that they were more likely to have secured a job offer by graduation.

Program Impact on Students in School and Beyond

The primary goals of the NAF career-academy model—improving students' postsecondary and employment planning, so that students have a smoother and better transition into further education and

TABLE 6.7   **Percentage of Students Participating in College- and Career-Planning Activities in High School, by Academy Status**

Activities	Participation in Activities	
	Academy Seniors	Nonacademy Seniors
College-planning activities		
Talked with a teacher about postsecondary institutions	67%	57%
Talked with a guidance counselor about postsecondary institutions	61	61
Discussed college in class	73	62
Looked at college catalogs	78	73
Visited a college campus	71	54
Took the SATs or ACTs	81	73
Had a college interview	27	18
Talked with parents about how to pay for school	75	68
Talked with a knowledgeable adult about financial aid	61	46**
Career-related work-based learning experiences		
School-based business or enterprise	59	31***
Community service	74	47***
Job shadowing	43	15***
Work-site visit	53	16***
Employer talks at school	68	38***
Work-readiness class	55	19***
Talked with teachers about careers	78	56***
Talked with counselors about careers	57	48*
Job-planning and -seeking activities		
Submitted a job application	56	58
Had a job interview	51	43
Applied for college work-study	20	17
Talked with a teacher about a career	42	28
Talked with an adviser about a career	26	29
Has been offered a job	48	39*
Currently work for or has worked for the employer respondent is planning to work for after graduation	32	31
Job-planning and -seeking activities engaged in as part of school		
Interest inventories	12	6*
Job listings	22	22

TABLE 6.7   *Continued*

	Participation in Activities	
Activities	Academy Seniors	Nonacademy Seniors
Job fairs	19	8
Career placement	10	8
Letters of recommendation from teachers	21	19
Letters of recommendation from other school staff	19	11**
Practice interviews	35	14***
School-arranged job interviews	24	6**
Career exploration	26	15
Job rotations	15	6
Job shadowing	22	9
Mentor	17	6
Career day	22	17

Source: Authors' compilations from the National Academy Foundation Evaluation Study, conducted by the Institute on Education and the Economy.
*p < .10
**p < .05
***p < .01, chi-squared test

careers—can be thought of both broadly and narrowly. Broadly, academy teachers and administrators want to help students think more consciously about their futures, to help them make more explicit educational and career plans for achieving their goals, and to help them understand the varied opportunities within an industry for their own career decision making and gain the capacity to analyze opportunities in other industries. In addition, the academy model is designed to promote college attendance.

More narrowly, academy staff and especially employer partners also encourage students to consider careers in the particular industries around which the academies are organized—finance, or travel and tourism in the academies that we studied. Such career encouragement, however, should not limit students' future career options because the program design is not intended to limit postsecondary education options and pursuits. Thus, we focus in part on student outcomes that should reflect this deeper understanding of career opportunities and their relationship to education.

School Engagement, Attendance, and Achievement

The program's thematic focus and structure as a partial school-within-a-school aims to foster a supportive learning environment for students and thus to improve their engagement with school. The NAF academy model is designed to give the students a more personal educational experience than is typical in high school. It accomplishes this by creating a cohort of students enrolling together in several commonly focused courses, and by fostering closer relationships with individual adults by having one or more teachers who teach at least two courses to each cohort. In a previous study of NAF Academy of Travel and Tourism (AOTT) seniors, students attributed their greater incentive to attend school regularly and apply themselves to academic work to the sense of community and support they received from their fellow AOTT students and their AOTT teachers (Orr and Fanscali 1995).

In the present study, academy seniors were somewhat more likely to feel motivated by and engaged in schooling than were the other seniors (see table 6.8), but these differences in motivation and engagement may have existed prior to program enrollment. What can be said of the program, however, is that academy students feel more supported by their academy peers than regular students do, suggesting that the program does create a more supportive environment, at least among the student cohorts.

Student attendance patterns also give some sense of their engagement in school. Six schools provided yearly attendance data for the academy and the comparison students. Our analyses of the transcript data (table 6.9) show that academy students had slightly higher attendance than nonacademy students in earlier high school grades before academy enrollment and smaller decreases in attendance by the senior year, but these differences are not statistically significant. Further analysis using OLS regression (not shown) shows some academy influence independent of pre-academy attendance, but the influence was also not significant.

We also investigated whether academy participation was positively related to GPA. Prior research found mixed results concerning

TABLE 6.8   **Percentage of Students Who Agree or Strongly Agree with Various School Engagement and Importance Measures, by Academy Status**

Measures	Academy Seniors	Nonacademy Seniors
Doing well in school is important	96%	96%
The things learned in school are going to be important later in life	90	85*
Does not think about dropping out	92	84
Enjoys coming to school	75	64**
Feels like they belong in this school	73	60
Students feel connected to this school	54	46
Average school engagement and importance scale score (1 to 6)	3.8	3.7***
Other students (in the academy, for academy students) encourage you to work hard and do well	58	38**
N	199	190

Source: Authors' compilations from the National Academy Foundation Evaluation Study, conducted by the Institute on Education and the Economy.
The average scale score is based on a four-point scale, with strongly agree = 4, and refers to the measures in the six lines above it.
*$p < .10$
**$p < .05$, chi-squared test
***$p < .05$, t-test of independent sample means

the effect of academy enrollment on a student's GPA. Lawrence Hanser and Cathleen Stasz (1999) found positive academic outcomes for academy students, at least in the short term, but others did not (see Bishop, Mane, and Ruiz-Quintinella 2000; Kemple and Snipes 2000). Any presumed academy effect on GPA would be indirect, working through the greater motivation or focus provided by the contextualized pedagogy and more personalized educational experience. In this study, we compared pre-academy and twelfth-grade GPAs for academy and nonacademy students, using transcripts provided by seven of the schools in our sample (see table 6.9). In both cases, the differences in GPA were not significant. We further sought to estimate whether academic participation had an effect on twelfth-grade GPA after controlling for students' pre-academy GPAs. Once again, the results showed no difference between academy and nonacademy students (results not shown).[18]

TABLE 6.9 **Pre- and Postprogram Attendance Rates and GPA, by Academy Status**

Measures	Academy Seniors	Nonacademy Seniors
Tenth-grade average daily attendance	170.4	166.9
Twelfth-grade average daily attendance	169.2	162.1
N[a]	171, 177	154, 157
Pre-academy GPA	3.0 (0.24)	2.5 (0.36)
Senior-year GPA	2.9 (0.21)	2.6 (0.29)
N[a]	196, 198	180, 183

Source: Authors' compilations from the National Academy Foundation Evaluation Study, conducted by the Institute on Education and the Economy.
[a]The two figures shown represent the number of tenth grade and twelfth grade observations.

Postsecondary Educational Plans and College Acceptance

To what extent is the career-academy experience related to post–high school college plans for graduating seniors? Academy seniors completed slightly more college-level courses than did the comparison seniors (see table 6.10), and nearly all (90 percent) believe they will complete at least a four-year college degree—slightly higher than for nonacademy seniors. These modest differences suggest that academy participation may encourage more focused college planning, but academy students may have been somewhat more college-oriented than nonacademy students when they initially enrolled.

Given the college and career orientation influences, career academies can potentially have a variety of influences on students' post–high school plans, and there are many possible postsecondary pursuits, including full- or part-time employment and full- or part-time college or other postsecondary education. Academy graduates would be expected to have more attractive employment opportunities (in the primary, rather than secondary, labor market)[19] immediately after high school than the average high school graduate, because of their academy experience and contact with employers. Such opportunities might look attractive particularly to lower-income students who would have trouble financing college. Academy graduates are also likely to be better prepared to pursue post–high school employment because of their internships, other career-related expe-

TABLE 6.10 Comparison of Career Academy and Nonacademy Seniors on Their College Preparation, and College Attendance Plans

Preparation and Long-Range Plans	Academy Seniors	Nonacademy Seniors	Finance Academy Seniors	Travel Academy Seniors
	(1)	(2)	(3)	(4)
Number of college-planning actions	5.9	5.1	6.3	5.3
Average number of AP courses already completed	0.73	0.82	0.89	0.40
Average number of college-level courses already completed	1.05	0.61#	1.14	0.87
Average number of colleges applied to	2.85	2.65	2.89	2.75
Believe they will complete a four-year college degree or more	90%	84%	91%	88%
Aspire to an advanced degree	55	46	55	57
Planning to go to college in the summer or fall and have applied already	93	89	96	84**
Accepted to and planning to go to college	77	64	88	57**
Planning to go and accepted to a four-year college	64	45	76	40**
Planning to go and accepted to a two-year college	14	19	12	16
Planning to work and not go to college	13	27	5	28***
N	199	188	126	70

Source: Authors' compilations from the National Academy Foundation Evaluation Study, conducted by the Institute on Education and the Economy. Comparisons are made between columns 1 and 2, and between columns 3 and 4.

*p < .10
**p < .05
***p < .01, chi-squared test
#Statistically significant difference p<.01, t-test for independent means

riences, and job-planning and -seeking activities. A period of full-time employment that does not preclude later college enrollment might be a good option for some graduates. Thus, working immediately after high school is not necessarily a negative outcome, and does make evaluating the quality of postsecondary outcomes difficult.

We would expect that the college orientation and preparation experiences of the academies coupled with exposure to how postsecondary education influences career opportunities would encourage academy students to pursue postsecondary education after high school graduation. Different career opportunities are available in the finance and travel and tourism industries to those who complete postsecondary education. The AOF exposes students to a wide range of skilled and semiskilled employment opportunities within quite clearly defined financial-services-industry segments, such as accounting, investment banking, and financial planning. Without a college degree, employees in this industry have limited promotion opportunities and earning potential. The AOTT, on the other hand, focuses on a very broad industry that encompasses work involved with hotels, event and meeting planning, spas and other health resorts, cruise lines, entertainment, airlines, travel planning, sports and recreation, restaurants, and tourist attractions. This industry also offers a wide range of skilled, semiskilled, and unskilled employment opportunities, many of which require only a two-year college degree or professional certification. It is also considered a common practice in this industry for companies to hire high school graduates and then pay for their college tuition, as long as the employees maintain good work and academic records.

Because attending a two-year college or going directly into employment may very well be considered appropriate outcomes for graduates of the AOTT, whereas attending a four-year college would be a preferable outcome for graduates of the AOF, there is no one single outcome measure that reflects an academy program's effectiveness. Despite these ambiguities and options, we analyzed the four-year college-going patterns of the AOF and AOTT seniors and compared the patterns for program-related differences. We narrowed our outcomes analysis to whether seniors had applied to and been accepted at four-year colleges, to learn what differences exist that could be related to career academy participation.

Table 6.10 displays information about college plans for the seniors in our samples. By May of their senior year, 93 percent of the academy seniors and 89 percent of nonacademy seniors had applied to attend some postsecondary institution in the summer or fall following graduation.[20] In addition, 77 percent of the academy seniors and 64 percent of the comparison seniors had already been accepted and planned to attend four-year, two-year, or technical postsecondary institutions. The two groups contrasted with respect to the types of colleges they expected to attend. The academy seniors were much more likely than those in the comparison group to expect to attend a four-year college, but this difference is not statistically significant. However, there are statistically significant differences between students from the two types of academies. Finance academy seniors were more likely to have applied to college and to have been accepted by and to be planning to matriculate at a four-year college. Travel academy seniors were much more likely than finance academy seniors to be planning to work after high school and not to attend college.

The Academy Influence on Four-Year College Going

These simple comparisons, and other survey findings, suggest that academy seniors had planned for and taken more specific actions than their peers to gain admission to a four-year college. Sixty-four percent of academy seniors planned to attend a four-year college after high school graduation compared with only 45 percent of nonacademy seniors. Although the difference is not statistically significant at the 5-percent level, the near 20 percent difference in the two groups' college plan rates warranted further examination. Therefore, we decided to test whether a significant relationship between academy participation and four-year college plans would emerge when controlling for a limited number of student background variables and school-level characteristics. We also considered examining the two other outcomes, planning to attend a two-year college and entering the workforce, but the relatively small sample sizes available— twenty-six and twenty-seven academy seniors, respectively, who went to a community college or work—provided unreliable estimates.

We analyzed the determinants of the probability that a student by the end of his or her senior year had been accepted at a four-year college and was planning to attend.[21] Our focus is on the influence of attending an academy and of the type of academy attended on college plans; we are in effect comparing seniors who have received the complete academy experience to seniors who have not received an academy-like high school experience, for the overall academy effect (columns 1 and 2 in table 6.11) and for travel and tourism and finance separately (columns 3 and 4 of table 6.11).

Since the dependent variable was dichotomous (a student planned either to attend or not to attend), we used logistic regression. To further isolate the specific effect of academy status, we included demographic variables such as gender, race, ethnicity, parental education (which were found to be significant in prior research; see Wirt et al. 2001), and an aggregate pre-GPA average of the schools both academy and nonacademy students attended. Coefficients are reported as marginal effects to improve interpretability. According to results displayed in column 1 of table 6.11, the school-level pre-academy GPA and the academy status are statistically significantly associated with plans to go to a four-year college. However, while the overall academy effect is significant, when it is divided by academy type, a rather substantial effect—an increase in probability of twenty-seven percentage points—emerges for students in finance academies relative to nonacademy students, whereas for travel and tourism students, there is little effect.

Hence the positive relationship between college plans and academy status is attributable to the finance academy students, not to those from the travel and tourism academies.[22] Travel and tourism academy students are no more likely than comparison students to have planned to go to a four-year college and been accepted at one, perhaps a result of industry-related career opportunities for those with less than a four-year college degree.[23]

The positive results for the finance academy seniors contrast with the findings from MDRC's random-assignment career-academies evaluation (Kemple 2001). MDRC found no statistically significant relationship between academy enrollment and college-going. Several factors might account for this difference. First, MDRC used a random-assignment strategy to eliminate systematic initial differences between the academy and control groups, whereas we relied on using measured personal and family characteristics to control for initial group differences. Nevertheless, since students in our sample must choose

TABLE 6.11   Probability of Planning to Attend a Four-Year College

	Academy b/se (1)	Academy ME/se (2)	Finance and Travel b/se (3)	Finance and Travel ME/se (4)
Academy seniors	0.768** (0.30)	0.177** (0.07)		
Finance academy students			1.153** (0.44)	0.271** (0.10)
Travel academy students			0.210 (0.26)	0.044 (0.05)
Female students	0.306 (0.22)	0.066 (0.05)	0.381 (0.22)	0.082 (0.05)
Black or Hispanic	0.148 (0.23)	0.031 (0.05)	0.227 (0.19)	0.048 (0.04)
One parent with at least some college	0.420 (0.48)	0.093 (0.10)	0.393 (0.46)	0.085 (0.10)
PREGPA[a]	1.661*** (0.45)	0.339*** (0.06)	1.538*** (0.33)	0.308*** (0.05)
Constant	−5.647*** (1.61)		−5.337*** (1.23)	
Adjusted R-squared	0.181		0.191	
N	312		312	

Source: Authors' compilations from the National Academy Foundation Evaluation Study, conducted by the Institute on Education and the Economy.
Notes: These analyses are based on the seven schools with both transcript and survey information for surveyed seniors. Columns 1 and 2 report the coefficients and marginal effects, respectively, and standard errors, with an academy indicator. Columns 3 and 4 report the coefficients and marginal effects, respectively, and standard errors, with finance and travel and tourism indicators.
[a]PREGPA is an aggregate school-level measure of GPA taken from the grade prior to academy eligibility—either ninth or tenth grade.
**p < .05
***p < .01

to join an academy, must be accepted by the staff, and must persist in the program until graduation, it is possible that unmeasured differences between the academy and comparison groups might explain the positive findings in our study.

Second, the student samples also differed in the two studies. MDRC randomly selected program and control groups from a pool of academy applicants. But of the group that entered the program through random assignment, 33 percent left the academy before the end of their senior year. Of the students in the control group, 6 percent eventually had a program experience that was similar to the career academy. The authors of the MDRC report adjusted their coefficients for attrition from the treatment group and academy enrollment for the control group, and even after this adjustment they found no measured academy effect (Kemple 2001, 18).

Finally, the MDRC study included several different types of career-academy programs in their sample, which varied dramatically in their type of affiliation with an industry, related course work, internship experiences, and professional development and technical support—variability that was not taken into account. Our study included only NAF-affiliated programs, which have a more prescribed set of program features, yet we found different effects of the finance programs as compared to the travel and tourism programs. Still, as a group, the NAF-affiliated academies may, because of their program coherence, integration, and intensity, have a stronger influence on postsecondary experiences than do the more diverse group of academies included in the MDRC study.

CONCLUSIONS

What has emerged from the various debates in recent years about high schools and their role in college preparation and workforce development are three converging objectives for transitioning adolescents: (1) to improve their academic skills and performance; (2) to increase college-going and college completion; and (3) to shorten the early floundering period between high school completion and securing quality employment. These objectives both overlap and are complementary, yet they are often addressed separately in policy, programs, and research. At the same time, many high school reform recommendations contain similar institutional transformation features such as small, more intimate learning communities; thematic, contextualized, and challenging curricula; the use of student-centered instructional practices; and engagement of learning resources from beyond the high school itself, namely, through businesses and the community at large.

Our study shows that it is possible to create an intensive and coherent academy program that embodies these objectives. In this study, all the sampled programs provided the core career-academy components for their academy seniors as stressed by the NAF model, and these were markedly distinguishable from the high school experiences of nonacademy seniors. Participating in the academy seems to improve students' high school engagement, which is consistent with the model's cohort design, school-within-a-school structure, and focus on integrated content. The career-academy experience did not have any positive or negative measured influence on student GPAs. The program had positive achievement benefits, however, because academy seniors reported completing more college-level courses while in high school, which is encouraged by the program design.

Academy seniors, especially those in finance academies, were more likely than comparison seniors to have been admitted to a four-year college and to plan to attend by the time they graduated from high school. This difference remained even after controlling for a variety of demographic and achievement-related variables, suggesting that at least participation in finance academies is positively related to post–high school four-year educational plans. Given the higher rates of two-year college attendance or work plans among travel and tourism academy students (in contrast to finance academy students), it appears that academy students are appropriately varying their postsecondary educational plans according to the requirements of the different industries and career-related opportunities.

The recent study by MDRC found no academy effect on college going; the different results presented here may be attributable to differences in the sample of academies and the intensity of the academy experience the participants had. Our study examined only NAF academies, which provide a more uniform experience, including a private-sector summer internship, whereas the MDRC study used a more heterogeneous sample of programs that were less uniform and did not always include similarly intensive internships. Although our results on post–high school plans and transitions are encouraging, the analysis is complicated by two factors: (1) ambiguity about the optimal postsecondary outcome when aggregating academy students who are focusing on different industries with differing postsecondary-education requirements; and (2) the possibility that unmeasured initial differences between the academy and nonacademy seniors may explain differences in measured outcomes.

The results presented in this chapter parallel some of the findings in chapter 5, "Learning-by-Doing Career Academies," on career academies' positive influence on student attendance but neutral influence on GPAs. These results underscore the importance of quality implementation for student postsecondary transition outcomes and the instrumental role an intermediary organization can play in setting program standards, developing and updating curriculum, and providing linkages to businesses for program support. Together, this and the previous chapter provide useful insights into the measurement of implementation and the importance of accounting for program-model fidelity when examining outcomes.

This study shows that well-implemented NAF academies are accomplishing many of the goals that they were established to achieve by engaging students in learning and helping them plan for and pursue college and careers. The findings are most readily generalizable to other well-implemented academy programs. Further research is needed to compare well-implemented and prescriptive academy models such as NAF's with other academies, but available comparative evidence suggests that simultaneous attention to program focus, curriculum content, instructional practices, and a quality internship is influential for student outcomes. As an educational strategy, the academy model is consistent with other high school–reform initiatives such as recent efforts to create smaller high schools and to link high schools more closely with community colleges and other postsecondary institutions.

The authors wish to acknowledge the directors, staff, teachers, and students of the programs studied. The authors are particularly grateful to Bonnie Silvers of the National Academy Foundation for her insights. Paula Ko served as a statistical consultant on the project. James Kemple, Nan Maxwell, David Stern, David Neumark, Hilary Steedman, Francisco Rivera-Batiz, Dale

Whittington, and several anonymous reviewers all provided comments on earlier drafts. The authors also thank Lauren Koch for editorial assistance.

NOTES

1. For further information, see http://www.naf-education.org.
2. The original sample included ten sites, but we were not able to secure all of the requested data from each site. Therefore, some of the analyses use different numbers of sites, depending on the availability of the relevant data. For more information on the sites, see table 6.2.
3. The research, analysis, and reporting were carried out by IEE staff independently, according to appropriate professional standards and without censorship. To further ensure objectivity, the study results were subjected to three rounds of professional review from unaffiliated content and methodological experts. With NAF's permission, the data can be made available to other researchers.
4. Exemplified by the interinstitutional consortium Pathways to College; see http://www.pathwaystocollege.net for further information.
5. Academic intensity, a scaled variable created by Adelman (1999, 13) to measure the rigor and quality of students' high school course taking, measures the number of courses taken in academic subjects and their level—for example, advanced placement, general, remedial.
6. For reviews of career research see Katherine L. Hughes et al. (2001), David Stern et al. (2000), and Stern et al. (1992).
7. In this study, academy students could have been enrolled in one of twelve career academies in six comprehensive high schools in one district. The district's career-academy model included three years of academy-related course work, a summer internship after the junior year, and supplemental career exposure and college-planning activities, but the program model was not implemented uniformly across all of the academies.
8. For the purposes of the evaluation, each student's study assignment designation was retained throughout the research regardless of whether the academy students stayed in the academy or whether the control students eventually obtained an academy-like experience.
9. See Hughes et al. (2002) for the employer-research findings; and Orr (2005) for teacher findings.
10. This ranged from 55 to 100 percent among our schools, with most returning 70 percent or more.
11. To test the effect of eliminating these forty-eight surveys, we ran some of the analyses using the entire sample with a dummy variable

for observations that had missing information on race and gender, and then compared the results to the same analyses with the entire sample without using variables for race and gender as control variables. These changes did not influence the sign or significance of the coefficient for academy effects or any other variable.

12.   These instances are noted in the relevant text and tables.

13.   This process was established to ensure that parents and school personnel know about the educational decision that the student has made, to ensure that the student has some basic interest in the program, and to prevent students from being assigned as an administrative accommodation.

14.   In NAF academies that are part of the California Partnership Academy network, half of the students enrolled must meet "at-risk" criteria.

15.   We got similar results when we estimated a logistic regression with these same variables in which the dependent variable was whether or not the student was in an academy.

16.   Some NAF schools also have non-NAF academies. In some cases, these were started after the school staff judged that they had had a successful experience with the NAF academy. In other cases, schools have incorporated some NAF or other academy-like practices into their regular classes and programs.

17.   The majority of American high school students have jobs, but most of them have limited access to quality employment opportunities. School-provided internships, according to educational researchers, offer important advantages over the jobs students find on their own: more training, more interaction with adults at the workplace, and better connections between students' studies and their work experience (Hershey et al. 1999). School-sponsored work placements also give students access to more diverse workplaces than they would normally get on their own (Bailey et al. 2000; Hershey et al. 1999). Such is the case for these career-academy internships, as discussed later.

18.   Since four academies were honors or magnet programs and five were not, we also conducted a separate comparison of GPA differences between honors and magnet and nonhonors and nonmagnet academy seniors (not shown). We found insignificant differences between the two groups, initially and at the end of their senior year. Thus, being part of an honors or career magnet program had no influence on students GPAs independent of their academy status.

19.   The primary labor market consists of jobs with concrete careers and potential for long-range success. The secondary labor market consists primarily of low-pay, usually part-time or temporary jobs with little career advancement potential.

20. Students were asked to list the college that they were expecting to attend in the summer or fall. They were then asked to identify the type of institution. If they did so, we categorized them as planning to attend college in the summer or fall.

21. Students were asked to list the college they were going to attend. Those who stated that the college was a four-year school were categorized as planning to attend a four-year college. We repeated the analyses using as a variable whether the student was planning to attend a four-year college and had been accepted at college. There were no substantial changes in the results.

22. We repeated this analysis using only the finance academy students in the treatment group. The academy variable was positive and significant and all of the other variables had the same sign and significance as in the analysis using both types of academies.

23. Finally, as one more test, we did an analysis using all nine schools; in addition to demographic and course-taking variables, we inserted a control for each school. In this case we did not use the GPA. The school control approach is actually similar to our analysis using the GPA, since in this case all students in each school share the value of one variable (the individual school dummy variable). Therefore, this variable will pick up some of the influence of the difference in average GPAs in each school, as well as other school-related influences. This analysis did pick up significant individual school effects—students from some schools were much more likely to go to college than those from other schools. At the same time, the analysis showed the same positive finance academy effect. The other coefficients were similar; although the effects of parent's education and of moving recently were no longer significant, the coefficients did have the same signs.

REFERENCES

Adelman, Clifford. 1999. *Answers in the Tool Box: Academic Intensity, Attendance Patterns, and Bachelor's Degree Attainment.* Washington: U.S. Department of Education, Office of Educational Research and Improvement.

American Youth Policy Forum. 2000. *High Schools of the Millennium.* Washington, D.C.: American Youth Policy Forum.

Bailey, Thomas R., Katherine L. Hughes, and Tavis Barr. 2000. "Achieving Scale and Quality in School-to-Work Internships: Findings from Two Employer Surveys." *Educational Evaluation and Policy Analysis* 22(1): 41–64.

Balfanz, Robert, Will J. Jordan, and James M. McPartland. 2002. *Comprehensive Reform for Urban High Schools: A Talent Development Approach* (Sociology Education II). New York: Teachers College Press.

Bishop, John H., Ferran Mane, and S. Antonio Ruiz-Quintinella. 2000. "Who Participates in School-to-Work Programs? Initial Tabulations." Unpublished paper. Washington, D.C.: School-to-Work Office.

Bottoms, Gene. N.d. *Things That Matter Most in Improving Student Learning*. Atlanta: Southern Regional Educational Board.

Cannon, Debra G., and Benny Reed. 1999. "Career Academies: Teaming with a Focus." *Contemporary Education* 70(2): 48–51.

Carbrera, Alberto F., and Steven M. La Nasa. 2000. "Understanding the College Choice of Disadvantaged Students." *New Directions for Institutional Research* 107(Fall).

Castellano, Marisa, Samuel Stringfield, and James R. Stone. 2003. "Secondary Career and Technical Education and Comprehensive School Reform: Implications for Research and Practice." *Review of Educational Research* 73(2): 231–72.

Education Trust. 2001. "Youth at the Crossroads: Facing High School and Beyond." *Thinking K-16* 5(1): 1–19.

Elliott, Marc N., Lawrence M. Hanser, and Curtis L. Gilroy. 2000. *Evidence of Positive Student Outcomes in JROTC Career Academies*. Santa Monica, Calif.: RAND National Defense Research Institute.

Finn, Jeremy D. 1989. "Withdrawing from School." *Review of Educational Research* 59(2): 117–43.

Foothill Associates. 1997. *California Partnership Academies: 1995–96 Evaluation Report*. Nevada City, Calif.: Foothill Associates.

Hanser, Lawrence, and Cathleen Stasz. 1999. *The Effects of Enrollment in the Transportation Career Academy Program on Student Outcomes*. Paper presented at the meeting of the American Educational Research Association, Montreal (April 19–23).

Hershey, Alan M., Marsha K. Silverberg, Joshua Haimson, and Paula Hudis. 1999. *Expanding Options for Students: Report to Congress on the National Evaluation of School-to-Work Implementation*. Princeton, N.J.: Mathematica Policy Research, Inc.

Hughes, Katherine L., Thomas R. Bailey, and Melinda Mechur. 2001. *School-to-Work: Making a Difference in Education: A Research Report to America*. New York: Columbia University, Teachers College, Institute on Education and the Economy.

Hughes, Katherine L., Melinda M. Karp, and Margaret Terry Orr. 2002. " 'Business Partnerships for American Education': Employer Involvement in the National Academy Foundation's High School Career Academies." *Journal of Vocational Education and Training* 54(3): 365–94.

Jennings, Jack, and Diane S. Rentner. 1998. "Youth and School Reform: From the Forgotten Half to the Forgotten Third." In *The Forgotten Half Revisited: American Youth and Young Families, 1998–2008*, edited by Sam Halperin. Washington, D.C.: American Youth Policy Forum.

Kaufman, Philip, Denise Bradby, and Peter Teitelbaum. 2000. "High Schools That Work and Whole School Reform: Raising Academic Achievement of Vocational Completers Through the Reform of School Practice." Publication No. MDS-1295. Berkeley: University of California, National Center for Research in Vocational Education.

Kemple, James J. 1997. *Career Academies: Communities of Support for Students and Teachers: Emerging Findings from a 10-Site Evaluation.* New York: Manpower Demonstration Research Corporation.

———. 2001. *Career Academies: Impacts on Students' Initial Transitions to Post-Secondary Education and Employment.* New York: Manpower Demonstration Research Corporation.

Kemple, James J., Susan M. Poglinco, and Jason C. Snipes. 1999. *Career Academies: Building Career Awareness and Work-Based Learning Activities Through Employer Partnerships.* New York: Manpower Demonstration Research Corporation.

Kemple, James J., and JoAnn L. Rock. 1996. *Career Academies: Early Implementation Lessons from a 10-Site Evaluation.* New York: Manpower Demonstration Research Corporation.

Kemple, James J., and Jason D. Snipes. 2000. *Career Academies: Impacts on Students' Engagement and Performance in High School.* New York: Manpower Demonstration Research Corporation.

Kojaku, Lawrence, and Ann-Marie Nunez. 1998. *Descriptive Summary of 1995–96 Beginning Postsecondary Students, with Profiles of Students Entering 2- to 4-year Institutions.* Washington: U.S. Department of Education.

Lee, Valerie E., and Julia B. Smith. 1995. Effects of High School Restructuring and Size on Early Gains in Achievement and Engagement. *Sociology of Education* 68(00): 241–70.

Legters, Nettie. 1999. *Small Learning Communities Meet School-to-Work.* Baltimore: CRESPAR.

Legters, Nettie, Robert Balfanz, and James McPartland. 2002. *Solutions for Failing High Schools: Visions and Converging Promising Models.* Baltimore: Center for Social Organization of Schools.

Maxwell, Nan L. 2001. "Step to College: Moving from the High School Career Academy Through the Four-Year University." *Evaluation Review* 25(6): 619–54.

Maxwell, Nan L., and Victor Rubin. 2000. *High School Career Academies: A Pathway to Educational Reform in Urban School Districts?* Kalamazoo, Mich.: Upjohn Institute for Employment Research.

McPartland, James M., Robert Belfanz, Will Jordan, and Nettie Legters. 1998. "Improving Climate and Achievement in a Troubled Urban High School Through the Talent Development Model." *Journal of Education for Students Placed at Risk* 3(4): 337–61.

National Commission on Excellence in Education. 1983. *A Nation at Risk.* Washington: U.S. Department of Education.

National Commission on the High School Senior Year. 2001a. *The Lost Opportunity of Senior Year: Finding a Better Way.* Princeton, N.J.: Woodrow Wilson National Fellowship Foundation.

———. 2001b. *Raising Our Sights: No High School Senior Left Behind.* Princeton, N.J.: Woodrow Wilson National Fellowship Foundation.

Natriello, Gary, Edward L. McDill, and Aaron M. Pallas. 1990. *Schooling Disadvantaged Children.* New York: Teachers College Press.

Orr, Margaret Terry. 1990. *Employment and Educational Experiences of Academy of Finance Graduates: Final Report.* New York: Academy for Educational Development.

———. 2005. "Career Academies as a Professionally Engaging and Supportive Teaching Experience." *Education and Urban Society* 37(4): 453–89.

Orr, Margaret Terry, and Cheri Fanscali. 1995. *Academy of Travel and Tourism: 1993–94 Evaluation Report.* New York: Academy for Educational Development.

Orr, Margaret Terry, Norman Fruchter, Earl Thomas, and Lynne White. 1987. *Evaluation of the Academy of Finance: Impact and Effectiveness.* New York: Academy for Educational Development.

Oxley, Diane. 1997. "Theory and Practice of School Communities." *Educational Administration Quarterly* 33(Supplement): 624–43.

Reller, D. J. 1987. *A Longitudinal Study of the Graduates of the Peninsula Academies: Final Report.* Palo Alto, Calif.: American Institutes for Research in the Behavioral Sciences.

Stern, David, Charles Dayton, and Marylyn Raby. 2000. *Career Academies: Building Blocks for Reconstructing American High Schools.* Berkeley, Calif.: Career Academy Support Network.

Stern, David, Marylyn Raby, and Charles Dayton. 1992. *Career Academies: Partnerships for Reconstructing American High Schools.* San Francisco: Jossey-Bass.

U.S. Department of Education. 1998. *Digest of Education Statistics, 1997.* Washington: U.S. Department of Education.

Useem, Elizabeth, Ruth C. Neild, and William Morrison. 2001. *Philadelphia's Talent Development High Schools: Second-Year Results, 2000–01.* Philadelphia: Philadelphia Education Fund.

Wehlage, Gary G., Robert A. Rutter, Gregory A. Smith, Nancy Lesko, and Ricardo R. Fernandez. 1989. *Reducing the Risk.* London: Falmer Press.

Wirt, John, Susan Choy, Debra Gerald, Stephen Provasnik, Patrick Rooney, Satoshi Watanabe, Richard Tobin, and Mark Glander. 2001. *The Condition of Education 2001.* NCES Publication No. 2001-072. Washington: U.S. Department of Education.

Wirt, John, Patrick Rooney, Susan Choy, Stephen Provasnik, Anindita Sen, and Richard Tobin. 2004. *The Condition of Education 2004.* NCES Publication No. 2004-077. Washington: U.S. Government Printing Office.

Chapter 7

Labor-Market Linkages Among Two-Year College Faculty and Their Impact on Student Perceptions, Effort, and College Persistence

Ann E. Person and James E. Rosenbaum

SCHOOLS ARE THE main institutions preparing young people to enter productive roles in society. To support the assumption that schools respond to labor-market needs, many scholars refer to human-capital and functionalist theories. Even critics who disparage such responsiveness believe that it occurs (Bowles and Gintis 1976). Nonetheless, at the high school level research has produced little evidence to indicate how this correspondence might take place. Indeed, until recently the general observation has been that high schools and employers do not have much to do with each other (Lortie 1975; Useem 1986). Dan C. Lortie (1975) notes that the teaching role is characterized by its containment within individual classrooms, with no expectation of action outside the school. Studying high school staff and employers, Elizabeth Useem (1986) finds great suspicion of each toward the other, and a reluctance to trust each other or to interact. Moreover, many studies find that recent high school graduates with higher achievement do not get better jobs and pay than lower-achieving graduates, a circumstance implying that employers do not have much regard for high school achievement (Gamoran 1994; Griffin, Kalleberg, and Alexander 1981; Miller 1998; Murnane, Willett, and Levy 1995).

BACKGROUND

Recent national school-to-work legislation, particularly the Carl D. Perkins Vocational and Applied Technology Act of 1998 and the short-lived School-to-Work Opportunities Act (STWOA) of 1994, have prompted many reforms. In particular, both of these initiatives have yielded some exciting experiments in work-based learning around the nation; yet these are still small-scale efforts, and "work-based learning at the secondary school level has remained a marginal academic strategy" (Bailey, Hughes, and Moore 2004, 3). The 1997 National Employer Survey indicates that 39 percent of for-profit businesses with more than twenty employees report participating in some form of work-based learning (Cappelli, Shapiro, and Shumanis 1998). Whether these findings from the strong labor market of the late 1990s represent a serious enduring commitment by schools and employers or a transitory response to new reforms remains to be seen. Moreover, recent studies have described parents, teachers, and counselors as significant obstacles to improved work-based learning (Bailey, Hughes, and Moore 2004, 90; Hershey et al. 1999; Hughes 1998, 5), suggesting that even if employers are interested in school-to-work linkages, high school staff may not be responding.

Likewise, it is disappointing that such programs rarely help students get jobs after graduation. Many high school "career programs" focus on encouraging students to attend college (Stern et al. 1995) and do not emphasize direct entry into the job market or use employer contacts for job placement of recent graduates. For their part, employers may offer workplace learning for altruistic or public relations purposes rather than actually to recruit new employees (Rosenbaum 2001, chapter 5). Thus, it is not clear that efforts by either colleges or employers offer students much hope that they will be able to keep or move into good jobs with their employer or others (Bailey, Hughes, and Moore 2004; Mickelson and Walker 1997).

Unfortunately, systematic information about school-employer contacts can be difficult to obtain, as these linkages may rely on informal arrangements between individual teachers and employers (Brewer and Gray 1999). Moreover, many of the best national longitudinal studies of students (for example, National Education Longitudinal Survey [NELS], National Longitudinal Survey of Youth [NLSY], Panel Study of Income Dynamics [PSID]) and the best studies of employers (Neckerman and Kirschenman 1991; Holzer 1996; Moss and Tilly 2001) offer poor information about schools' job-placement assistance. However, analyses by James Rosenbaum (2001) of one national survey of students, the High School and Beyond 1982 cohort, found that among students with no college degrees, high school job placement led to earnings 17 percent higher ten years after high school graduation than those of students who applied directly to employers for work, and about twice the return of getting jobs through relatives (Rosenbaum 2001, chapter 9). Although school contacts that lead to job placement are rarely advocated or studied, they can have a powerful impact on students' careers.

If school or faculty contacts with employers can help students get good jobs, they might also have benefits for the motivation of students while they are still in school (Hamilton 1994; Hamilton and Hurrelman 1994). Studies find that many students believe that high school is irrelevant (Stinchcombe 1964; Steinberg 1996; Rosenbaum 2001), and reformers call for practices that enhance the relevance of education to employment. However, even policies to link curricula to work have rarely included employers. Many reforms integrate occupational content into the curriculum, without building linkages to employers (Grubb 1996; Perin 2001; Stern et al. 1995). Of the three central provisions of the STWOA—career development, curricular changes, and workplace experience—the goal of expanding student access to quality work experiences, which calls both explicitly and implicitly for links to employers, proved to be the most difficult and therefore the least-often implemented type of reform (Hershey et al. 1999). Indeed, a great deal of uncertainty remains about the specific behaviors and practices that support relationships between education and employers, much less how these contacts affect students.

Over 80 percent of high school graduates now enter postsecondary education in the eight years after high school (Adelman 2003), so the issues surrounding the school-to-work transition have moved up into colleges. For many reasons, community colleges are especially appropriate arenas for school-to-work and work-based learning programs. First, nearly half of all postsecondary students are enrolled at these institutions, and only a small minority of these students ever transfer to four-year colleges (Bailey 2003). Second, as local institutions community colleges are well positioned to collaborate with local employers and government, community, and labor organizations (Brewer and Gray 1999; Cross and Fideler 1989; Laanan 1995). Finally, with over thirteen hundred community colleges located in cities and towns across the nation, these institutions are one of the most readily available types of sites for skills training outside of universally available K-to-twelve education.

Accordingly, if there is a school-to-work "problem," it is also manifested in community colleges. Many community college students experience precisely the kinds of instability that the major school-to-work initiatives have sought to address. These students commonly move between schools or programs, they transition back and forth between school and jobs (Goldrick-Rab 2006), and they often fail to find work in the field they have studied (Grubb 1996). Yet such issues as they apply to the postsecondary level have received relatively little attention compared to the attention they get at the high school level. With the prominent exception of Tech Prep (which explicitly includes postsecondary institutions), few federal reforms have addressed the role of postsecondary education in school-to-work in any systematic way. Even STWOA-sponsored efforts, which were meant to bring comprehensive innovation to the school-to-work transition, might logically have included if not centered on community colleges; but very few actually did so (Hershey et al. 1999). Such omission may result to some extent from the tension between academic and vocational education that has been a central theme in the history of community colleges (Brint and Karabel 1989; Dougherty 1994). Community colleges' work-oriented programs already compete for resources with transfer programs, and the low status of vocational education, as well as the end of federal funding for STWOA, suggest that these schools are likely to face continuing difficulties in their efforts to smooth the college-to-work transition generally, as well as to foster college-employer linkages more specifically.

Still, there is a critical need for the kinds of technical preparation that community colleges can and do provide, and students in such programs could benefit from stronger links to jobs. W. Norton Grubb (1996) emphasizes the centrality of "mid-skilled" labor to the U.S. economy, noting that the sub-baccalaureate labor market (employment requiring less than a bachelor's degree) includes over three-fifths of all workers. Further, he notes that the highest job-growth rates are projected for sub-baccalaureate positions such as technicians and support staff, especially in areas such as health and information technology. As locuses of training for such jobs, two-year colleges play a significant role in the nation's workforce development, and they can provide a particularly rich source of information on education-employment connections. Yet it is not clear what education-employment connections exist, or how they are used by community colleges, and there are indications that community colleges are not well synchronized with employers' demands. Grubb (1996) notes that the benefits of sub-baccalaureate education for both employers and employees depend on graduates finding work in the field they have studied. This requires good information, which, Grubb asserts, is especially hard to get in the sub-baccalaureate labor market. Given such imperfect information, Grubb identifies colleges' institutional relationships with employers as a critical component in the labor-market success of their students. Yet he cites the "sluggish responsiveness of many educational institutions to shifting [labor-market] demand" (4) as a major hurdle that community colleges need to overcome in order to enhance their graduates' labor-market outcomes. Kevin Dougherty (1994) arrives at the same conclusion, arguing that "the community college indeed dances to the rhythms of the labor market, but it rarely keeps very good time" (67). The implication is that community colleges are, at least to some extent, missing the mark in linking with employers and supporting their students' chances for labor-market success.

Where Grubb's and Dougherty's analyses focus on the institution, Dominic J. Brewer and Maryann J. Gray (1999) examine college-employer relationships at the individual level with their study of labor-market-linkage activities by community college faculty. The authors' systematic analysis of the type and extent of employer linkages, however, yields anything but systematic results. On the contrary, Brewer and Gray conclude that linking activities "were often ad hoc and informal in nature" (415). Thomas Bailey, Noreen Badway, and Patricia J. Gumport (2002) echo this sentiment in their analysis of public and proprietary colleges, calling job placement at community colleges a "haphazard process . . . based on a case by case system of individual faculty or staff using employment relationships for the students in their programs" (34–35).

The studies by Grubb and by Brewer and Gray also identify institutional barriers to community colleges' links to labor markets. Among other obstacles, the authors point to a lack of resources and institutional support for linking activities, as well as departmental isolation within colleges that impedes the flow of information. Grubb optimistically asserts that linkages can be improved, yet Brewer and Gray note the general weakness of conceptual foundations and lack of empirical evidence for how linking can actually occur. This fact may underlie Grubb's insistence that "there is no substitute for individual community colleges examining the practices linking them to employers" (173). Although the authors correctly describe and diagnose many of the problems related to connections between two-year colleges and the labor market and offer some solutions, their analyses remain at the aggregate level. Even the studies by Brewer and Gray and by Bailey, Badway, and Gumport which use interviews and case studies as part of their analyses, present findings that reflect the average level of activity among colleges and instructors. This analytical approach is certainly useful, but it fails to shed light on the processes by which two-year-college faculty actually make and maintain labor-market connections, or the variation within the averages. We know very little about how or why some faculty members manage to overcome institutional barriers and attend to relationships with employers. Consequently, those linkages that do exist are inevitably viewed as random—the serendipitous result of particular individuals acting in specific contexts.

Several theoretical premises have guided thinking about faculty-employer relationships. Both human-capital and social-capital perspectives view school contacts with employers as serving the critical function of conveying information between employers and students (who are prospective employees). Signaling theory (Rosenbaum et al. 1990) provides the most direct discussion of the role of school staff in this process. Similarly, sociological theory (Meyer 1977) suggests that institutions can have recognized charters that enhance school staff's effectiveness in providing authoritative information about students. Indeed, institutions may use industry contacts to improve the correspondence between their curricula and the demands of the labor market (Rosenbaum et al. 1990) and possibly to build their own charters (Deil-Amen and Rosenbaum 2004). Recent research finds that high school faculty sometimes send employers trusted signals—authoritative information about the level of students' knowledge and skills necessary for employment (Rosenbaum 2001). Moreover, as noted above, students who get jobs through teachers' contacts have significantly higher earnings than those who get jobs through family contacts (Rosenbaum 2001).

However, beyond the actual job benefits of school-employer contacts—employment and wages—few scholars have considered the more immediate effects of such linkages on students who are still in school. David Stern and colleagues (1995) do focus on high school outcomes (for example, achievement, attendance, dropout rates) among students in academies combining academic and vocational curricula. But they do not point to the schools' or instructors' labor-market linkages as a potential factor influencing students' positive outcomes.

The present study uses qualitative data to examine two-year-college faculty members' connections with employers, and quantitative data to analyze the impact of these connections on students. First, through interviews with forty-one college instructors (who are also occupational-program chairs), we identify the behaviors and practices of two-year-college faculty in creating labor-market linkages. Whereas Bailey and his colleagues (2002) focus on averages, the current study seeks to determine which programs are marked by what processes, and how instructors capitalize on contextual supports or overcome obstacles to develop labor-market ties. In identifying the common characteristics of instructors, programs, and institutions that can be discerned as patterns in what might otherwise appear to be "haphazard" practices, this paper may also inform educators and policymakers as to what structures and practices promote successful labor-market linkages.

The second source of data, a survey of nearly 4,400 students at fourteen two-year colleges, allows us to examine students' perceptions of teacher and college contacts, and to examine whether these perceptions influence students' efforts and their consideration of dropping out of college. Combining qualitative and quantitative analyses, this study suggests that rather than focus solely on instructional activities, community colleges may also help students by fostering labor-market contacts.

RESEARCH DESIGN AND SAMPLE: TWO TYPES OF TWO-YEAR COLLEGE

This paper draws on a larger study on the school-to-work transition among two-year-college students in occupational programs. The broader study includes not only the program chair interviews and a large student survey (detailed and analyzed here), but also interviews with an additional fifty-five college administrators and staff, as well as nearly one hundred students. Prior articles drawing on the study have examined colleges' institutional prerequisites for and provision of cultural capital (Deil-Amen and Rosenbaum 2003), college information channels (Person, Rosenbaum, and Deil-Amen 2006), and institutional charters as a mechanism in the college-to-work transition (Deil-Amen and Rosenbaum 2004). This study explores teacher-employer contacts and the effects of these contacts on students.

Our sample includes seven public community colleges and seven private occupational colleges. Four of the seven occupational colleges are for-profit; the other three are nonprofit. All schools are located in a large Illinois city and its surrounding suburbs. The vast majority of two-year college students enroll at public community colleges, which have historically been oriented toward preparing students for transfer to four-year colleges. In contrast, private sub-baccalaureate institutions often focus specifically on career training and, therefore, might approach employer contacts very differently from the community colleges in our sample. Moreover, some of the larger private colleges emphasize job placement heavily in their advertising and recruiting materials, indicating a distinct focus on labor markets. Finally, the public-or-private debate surrounding high schools suggests that private colleges might also be more effective in some respects, as an older study by Wellford W. Wilms (1974) concludes.

In order to study comparable institutions, we chose a group of "occupational colleges," private colleges offering accredited associate's degrees of similar quality and in the same occupational fields as our community colleges. These occupational colleges are found in most large cities and are widely advertised in local media. Unlike the more common "trade schools," which offer occupational education but are not accredited to offer degrees beyond the certificate level, occupational colleges are accredited by national organizations, such as the North Central Association. Accreditation is granted to institutions or programs that meet or exceed educational standards set by the accrediting body, guaranteeing a certain level of quality with respect to faculty, facilities, and curricula. Nationally, only 4 percent of two-year-college enrollments are in private colleges, and only 6 percent of private colleges offer associate's degrees (Bailey, Badway, and Gumport 2002). Thus, as degree-granting institutions these occupational colleges are comparable to community colleges, but they are dissimilar to 94 percent of for-profit schools, which offer no degree above a certificate (Apling 1993). All fourteen schools in our study were systematically selected on the basis of the comparability of their occupational programs, including fields such as business, accounting, computer information systems and networking, computer-aided drafting, court reporting and paralegal, office technology, electronics, engineering, and a variety of health technician programs.

Of course, occupational colleges have some limitations. They are smaller than community colleges and offer fewer programs and a more limited general education curriculum. They are less devoted to the preparation of students as informed and cultured citizens because of their narrow focus on occupational preparation; and the faculty composition reflects this organizational mission, with a majority of the faculty composed of adjuncts or part-time faculty who have extensive professional experience in the fields they are teaching. In addition, these schools require students to declare their program at entry. Career exploration is severely limited and generally can take place only within the confines of an occupational field. Changes of major are possible but may lengthen the time it takes to complete a degree. Transfers to bachelor's degree programs are possible, but usually only to certain programs and colleges. Receiving no public subsidy, these private schools have much higher tuitions than do community colleges, but loans and grants make them affordable to low-income students, since the colleges are extremely proficient in helping students navigate the onerous financial aid process (Deil-Amen and Rosenbaum 2003). Because their students graduate more quickly and get skill-relevant jobs, one analyst concluded that these schools may be as cost-effective as low-tuition community colleges (Wilms 1974), but the issue has not been examined recently.

We do not infer that private colleges are better than public ones or that they should replace them (which is inconceivable, given their small number). We selected an unusual group of private colleges (ones that met the same accreditation standards as community colleges), and it should be noted that our topic does not illustrate some of the public colleges' strengths: low tuition, small classes, dedicated instructors, a variety of course offerings, flexibility of scheduling, and so forth. We are impressed with many aspects of community colleges, but in this chapter we consider a specific point, their handling of labor-market contacts in occupational programs— and this is a situation that raises some concerns.

Despite differences in sources of funding, levels of tuition, and size, the two types of colleges have many similarities. Compared to other colleges, both are regarded as relatively low-status institutions, have lower admissions requirements than four-year colleges, offer lower-status degrees, and have relatively few graduates who attain four-year degrees. Students enter both types of colleges seeking access to jobs in the primary labor market, and our survey of nearly 4,400 students in these colleges confirmed the findings of prior research (Dougherty 1994; Grubb 1996), that students in both types of college are from similar low social and economic backgrounds, have low high school achievement, and have similar goals.

Although they enroll similar students, analyses of national data show that for-profit degree-granting institutions enroll and graduate somewhat greater proportions of disadvantaged college students than their public counterparts (Bailey, Badway, and Gumport 2002), and data from our fourteen colleges also reflect this trend (Illinois Board of Higher Education 2004, chapter 6).

The two types of college in our sample differ in another important respect. The community colleges are, on average, much larger than the occupational colleges. The total fall 2003 enrollments for the community colleges in our sample range from about eight thousand to about fifteen thousand students, whereas the occupational colleges vary a great deal more, enrolling from about five hundred students at our smallest college to over five thousand at the largest. The difference is less stark when only full-time students are considered: the community colleges average about three thousand, and the privates enroll an average of just under eighteen hundred (Illinois Board of Higher Education 2004). We certainly recognize the potentially important influence of college size for the analyses discussed in this paper. Still, we feel that our qualitative focus may actually shed light on what aspects of size are important with respect to questions about linking between colleges and labor markets.

As with most qualitative studies, we cannot prove the typicality of our cases. In particular, doubts could be raised about the emphasis on transfer in our seven community colleges, especially given Stephen Brint and Jerome Karabel's (1989) finding that occupational goals predominate in the stated missions of community colleges. Yet our community colleges are similar to others on this key issue: 50 percent of the students in our community colleges are enrolled in transfer programs, and the average for the entire state is also 50 percent (Illinois Board of Higher Education 2004, table VI-2). Moreover, our findings are compatible with those of other studies (Brewer and Gray 1999; Cross and Fideler 1989) which found that community-college administrators and faculty are nearly evenly split in their ranking of transfer (general education) and workplace preparation as the top institutional priorities. Our community colleges seem typical on this key issue. In contrast, our occupational colleges are *not* typical. Rather than being a random sample, our occupational colleges offer some of the best programs in their respective occupational fields, and may be considered to represent an ideal type. Thus, these colleges provide a different perspective on how two-year colleges can operate than what one can observe in community colleges.

Although we have heard reports of a few exemplary community college programs that focus on occupational preparation and engage in practices similar to the occupational colleges studied here, these exemplary colleges do not seem to be typical in national surveys (Brewer and Gray 1999). Even Brint and Karabel's (1989) finding of emphasis on contacts with employers seems to be more about image than actual connections, because Brint notes "the curious lack of interest of 'career oriented' community colleges in developing ties with local employers or studying their skill needs" (Brint

2003, 25). As we see it, the value of comparing occupational programs at "typical" community colleges with similar programs at "ideal" occupational colleges is that the comparison can shed light on a few specific practices that might be implemented on a broader scale to improve outcomes among students seeking occupational preparation.

Although the public colleges in our sample offer a much greater variety of majors and courses than the private colleges (which concentrate strictly on occupational programs), this research focuses only on occupational programs at the two types of college. These programs are in the same fields and prepare students for the same kinds of jobs, so they are likely to offer the same skills and recruit students with similar goals and motivations.

QUALITATIVE METHODS AND ANALYSIS

As noted, this chapter presents results from two types of studies. The first study is qualitative. Over a two-year period, from 2000 to 2002, the research team interviewed forty-one instructors at the fourteen colleges in our sample. These individuals were selected from the colleges' well-established large-enrollment programs and some "specialty" programs. All of these instructors also served as chairs for their occupational programs. This focus permits comparability with past research, which has looked primarily at the role of instructors in creating and maintaining labor-market linkages. Chairs, as the individuals responsible for a given program, are apt to serve as a first point of contact for employers. Similarly, to the extent that programs must keep records or produce reports on their students' outcomes (especially in the labor market), this duty usually falls to the chair. Finally, program chairs are also likely to know a great deal about their program's history and continuing development, even as they have close contact with students through teaching. We cannot assess the extent to which these forty-one respondents are representative of two-year-college faculty or program chairs, but we do know that these respondents offer a particularly rich source of information on what faculty–employer contacts exist and what processes underlie them. Table 7.1 describes the program-chair interview sample.

TABLE 7.1   **Description of Program Chair Interview Sample**

Program	Total Interviews	Community College	Occupational College
Business and management	9	6	3
Health	7	5	2
Computer	7	5	2
Electronics and engineering technology	6	2	4
Design (CAD, architecture)	4	2	2
Accounting	3	3	0
Paralegal and court reporter	2	0	2
Office administration and secretarial	2	2	0
Environmental technology	1	1	0
Column total	41	26	15

Source: Authors' data.

Interviews were semistructured; all respondents were asked a core set of questions about their work. Broad themes included college and departmental organization, curricular development, student performance, and the job market for graduates. More specific areas important to the current analysis dealt with employer influence on the curriculum, formal and informal communication with industry representatives, job-placement activities, and instructor involvement in the field outside the classroom. The semistructured interviews also allowed for elaboration of particular points that an individual might raise. Through the interviews we were able to ascertain faculty actions and motivations and the institutional and organizational practices that might enhance or inhibit labor-market linking activity. Interviews lasted one to two hours and were taped and transcribed verbatim.

Personality characteristics may have some influence on instructors' choices to make and maintain labor-market linkages, but our study did not focus on such personal traits. Rather, our aim was to identify distinct practices at an institutional level that shape individual behaviors. For instance, every occupational college we studied made explicit promises to help students find jobs and collected systematic data on graduates' jobs, whereas none of the community colleges we studied systematically did so (Deil-Amen and

Rosenbaum 2004). Such institutional practices may have an impact on faculty actions, regardless of instructors' personalities. Moreover, from a policy perspective, institutional structures and practices are certainly a more appropriate target of policy intervention than individual traits.

When we coded transcript data, we began with deductive coding of responses to specific questions about labor-market-linkage activities, including questions about the instructors' own activities, institutional linking activities, and instructors' perceptions of students' typical ways of finding jobs. At the same time, we conducted open inductive coding of broad employment-related themes, such as labor-market influences on the curriculum, demand for employees in a given area, and so on. Later, we reanalyzed the data and coded more specifically for themes that had emerged as important across cases, including, for example, individual "calling," or personal motivation to help students, which provided some insight into the reasons why individual instructors create and maintain links with the labor market.

Levels of Linking Activity

Prior studies have, appropriately, emphasized faculty members' modest average involvement with employers. This study, however, examines the nature of linkages that are forged, with special focus on institutional contexts. We discovered that the program chairs in our sample differed in the amount and intensity of their linking activity and also their stance toward active versus passive linking activities. Their activities fell into three categories: high linking activity; moderate linking; and minimal linking. A brief explanation of each level follows, and a typical case is provided for each level. For the sake of consistency, all of the examples are from the same occupational field, computer information systems (CIS), and all are from community colleges.

Minimal linking activity. Taking as our example a program chair we call Mr. Jones, the only linking activity Mr. Jones describes in the interview is his personal interaction with colleagues in the CIS field, but he reports that he does not often use these contacts to get students jobs. He explains, "People who are looking for students usually go to the four-year schools first. If they don't find somebody there, they'll try to find somebody in-house who could be promoted into that. They don't often come here. Or if they do, they come here with unrealistic expectations." Asked about his department's advisory committee, an outside board whose purpose is advising departments on labor-market needs in their field, he states, "Had one a few years ago. I am now told that I will have one again. . . . An advisory council [would] just be five of my best friends. You know, director of programming here—that kind of thing—manager of software support. Just go, call five of my friends, and we'll have a lunch somewhere." Throughout the interview, Mr. Jones expresses some suspicion about the value of contacts with employers, and his reported actions reflect this ambiguity.

Moderate linking activity. Ms. Mendes is the CIS chair at a different community college. She describes her work with the department's advisory committee explicitly in terms of the committee members' usefulness as potential sources of jobs for students. She also notes that adjunct faculty in her department, who continue to work in the field, sometimes have job opportunities at their places of employment and that "they share that with me." She continues, "And I do get a lot of calls from companies in the district that they're looking for help-desk people, support people, whatever." Note that she engages in several different types of labor-market linking, but she most often receives information from contacts who approach her, rather than taking the initiative to foster contacts.

High linking activity. Like Ms. Mendes, Ms. Lenz speaks of adjunct faculty as an important source of information about jobs and the labor market. Rather than waiting for them to come to her, however, she reports making efforts to stay in constant communication with them. In addition to finding faculty with industry experience to teach courses, Ms. Lenz reports, "I see my job as not only hiring these people, but also going out to industry, and not just having a meeting yearly with the new advisory committee, [but] actively being out there and seeing what they want." In addition to working with adjunct faculty, the advisory committee, and people in industry, Ms. Lenz also conducts surveys of her program's graduates to see how they have fared in the labor market, as well as surveys of employers who have hired her students to assess whether or not they are meeting employer expectations.

FINDINGS

As the literature indicates, there is indeed an "ad hoc" element to faculty efforts to make labor-market connections, but faculty behaviors appear to be more patterned and more nuanced than surveys indicate.

Institutional Structures and Practices at Community and Occupational Colleges

Beyond a particular instructor and program, colleges themselves can play an important role in fostering as well as hindering faculty labor-market linkages via their own institutional structures and practices. Indeed, qualitative evidence reveals that certain institutional structures and practices—of the college itself and of professions with which programs are associated—may affect the level of faculty effort directed toward building and maintaining links with potential employers and some may turn out to be barriers.

Resource constraints. Perhaps the most commonly cited institutional barrier to instructors reaching out to employers is the lack of time reported as a resource constraint by so many instructors in our sample. Fiscal constraints do not appear to be as problematic. All but one of those faculty members who sought reimbursement for linking activities such as participating in professional meetings, invited talks, and so forth reported that funds were readily available. It is possible that some faculty would not seek financial support for linking activities because they believe it would be a fruitless endeavor. Perhaps more important, if more financial resources were available, more administrators and support staff could be hired and faculty would be less pressed for time. In fact, two of the activities mentioned most frequently by department chairs as taking up a lot of time were hiring faculty and handling administrative paperwork. Hiring faculty could be handled with the help of human resources administrators and administrative paperwork could be handled with the help of support staff.

Employment of adjunct and part-time faculty. Another institutional factor that we observed at most of the colleges in our sample is the trend away from hiring full-time, tenure-track faculty in favor of part-time and adjunct instructors—a trend that appears to support employer linkages on the one hand yet impede them on the other. Among computer-oriented programs in particular—computer information systems (CIS), information technology (IT), network-specialist programs—chairs frequently cited their own and other facultys' work in their field as a source of labor-market connections that could benefit entire programs and individual students alike. Program chairs explained how they may update program curricula based on input from faculty working in the field; and individual students sometimes get jobs directly through such connections. As one IT chair puts it, "Part-time faculty enhance the program because they're out there doing what it is that they're teaching." Still, not all program chairs view such involvement as beneficial. Another CIS chair laments, "The loss of four full-time teachers is a major loss to the department. . . . I can't improve my program with part-timers." Only two program chairs, both at community colleges, spoke in uniformly negative tones of part-timers and adjuncts. One instructor reported that high turnover among part-time and adjunct faculty resulted in curricular discontinuity. Both chairs felt that the time required for finding and hiring part-time faculty impinged upon their other activities, including making employer contacts.

Division of labor. A final category of institutional supports for and obstacles to linkages is bureaucratic in nature. The division of labor within the colleges often assigns contact with employers to a specific person or unit. In our broader sample of college staff, it was most common for representatives of career services offices to report making employer contacts as a contractual obligation. Similarly, department and program chairs often named a specific person— usually the coordinator of internship or externship programs—as the person formally charged with forging employer linkages. The benefit of this type of division of labor is that contacts are institutionalized and more likely to be sustained, despite staff turnover or changes in local job markets. It may also be easier for faculty to assist students who seek information about jobs when they can direct them to an individual who is formally responsible for such information.

A downside of this division of labor, however, is that bureaucratic structures tend to isolate departments and individuals with specific functions. In the presence of career services and internship coordination structures, faculty can easily dismiss their own potential role in connecting with the labor market, because such connections are formally defined as someone else's job. In fact, of the twelve instructors coded as low for linking activities, six suggested career services as the appropriate place for making connections with employers; four of these offered this information as a response when we asked them specifically to describe their *own* linking activities. Even among the instructors who referred us to career-services personnel, the level of faith in the career-services function varied widely. An office administration technology (OAT) chair was enthusiastic, reporting, "I always try to connect [students] with career services," while a CIS chair was more blasé, stating, "I assume that [students] will go to, at some time, the . . . job-placement office." We by no means interpret this evidence to mean that career services offices are not useful to institutions or students. Rather, we note only that the presence of such offices may discourage some faculty from considering development of employer linkages to be their own responsibility.

Differences in Institutional Structures and Practices Across Community and Occupational Colleges

Although the institutional issues identified up to this point applied more or less equally to both the community colleges and the occupational colleges in the sample, there were institutional factors that affected faculty linking activities differently in the two college types.

Interdepartmental communication. The most prominent difference between the community colleges and their occupational counterparts was the nature of faculty interactions with career services and advisory committees. The CIS chair cited above, who "assumes" students will eventually find their way to career services, is somewhat typical of community college faculty, in that he does not appear to know exactly what services are provided—although he referred to the office as "job placement," this service is not in fact offered—and he didn't consider it his business to know. At the occupational colleges in our sample, although a few program chairs cited career services or internship coordinators as the people in charge of making contacts with the job market, these individuals nevertheless were aware of precisely who could provide a student with information on jobs or internships, as well as the nature of the services these individuals or offices could provide. As we previously noted, college size may influence intra- and interdepartmental communication; still, it is noteworthy that faculty at one of the largest private colleges in our sample were among the very best informed about other divisions' labor-market connections.

Advisory committees. As noted previously, advisory committees consist of representatives from local labor markets who work with college officials to ensure that colleges (and especially occupational departments) are in tune with the demands of the field, from both the technical and the labor-demand perspectives. Most of the colleges in our sample have some formal requirement regarding advisory committees.

Community college program chairs report a wide range of involvement with respect to advisory committees: from the CIS chair cited earlier (who has no interaction with the group and who would be satisfied with a committee of "five friends having lunch") to a management chair who considers the committee her primary connection to the corporate world, meets with them frequently, and relies heavily on their input in devising the curriculum. In contrast, the program chairs from occupational colleges were more uniform in reporting frequent and meaningful involvement with their advisory committees. Indeed, in our occupational college sample, even the least active program chair meets with his advisory committee between two and four times each year.

Bureaucratic hurdles and curricular development. The process of applying the information garnered from advisory committees and other sources to enhance the curriculum is much more streamlined at the occupational colleges than at the community colleges in our sample, according to faculty reports. Community college faculty, on the other hand, describe cumbersome bureaucratic processes of curricular innovation, mandated by system and/or state regulations. "You gotta jump through a lot of hoops," says one business chair, in a statement typical of the community college faculty. A business chair at an occupational college describes a very different process, typical of his counterparts at the occupational schools: "We move so quickly—with almost no bureaucracy—that if I want to make a change, we make it."

Institutional history and mission. The two types of colleges have very different histories and mandates. Community colleges have traditionally emphasized general education and transfer to four-year colleges (although this has been changing recently), whereas occupational colleges have emphasized more specific workforce training. Indeed, our interview data show that the faculty at the two college types articulate very different institutional missions. Community college faculty discuss their mission as broad and holistic, using terms like "developmental" and "life-long learning." As one community college department chair explained, "With our mission, really, you've got to serve everybody's needs. That's the function of a community college, [to] deal with all the different needs." In contrast, occupational college faculty see their school's mission as more narrow: career preparation and facilitation of entry into suitable skilled jobs. They use terms like "applied learning" and "career-oriented" to describe their missions. As one chair succinctly put it, "Our mission is to serve students, so that they [have] an opportunity to be successful in a career."

The different institutional factors influencing the community and occupational colleges suggest that instructors at the private colleges might be more apt to engage in higher levels of linking activity. Table 7.2 offers some support for that contention, although the difference is not overwhelming. Less than half (46 percent) of community college instructors were coded as engaging in high levels of linking activity, and about a third were coded as engaging in only minimal linking. At the occupational colleges, 60 percent of instructors were found to engage in high levels of linking, and just 20 percent were at the low end. (Note that coding was conducted without

TABLE 7.2   **Level of Linking Activity, by College Type**

Level of Linking	Community College	Occupational College
Minimal	35%	20%
	(9)	(3)
Moderate	19%	20%
	(5)	(3)
High	46%	60%
	(12)	(9)
Total N	26	15

Source: Authors' data.
Note: Actual N appears in parentheses.

explicit information on the respondent's department or college, although this information was often revealed in the transcript.)

The four factors cited above as shaping linking activities differently at the two college types (interdepartmental relations, advisory committee interactions, bureaucratic responsiveness, institutional missions) suggest that community college instructors will tend to have weaker contacts with employers. Yet this outcome is not inevitable. Indeed, one could easily imagine community college reforms that would alter any of these four factors, and this could lead to greater faculty-employer linkages. Indeed, community colleges relying on federal Perkins funding are required to be responsive to labor markets. In our sample, however, we saw these distinctions clearly between the two college types. Moreover, by describing the contextual factors that appear to influence labor-market linking the most, we offer some insight into the barriers and supports that faculty at both types of colleges might face.

External Factors—Professional Associations

Whether a college is public or private is not the sole determinant of outcomes. Although the community college faculty in our sample report less high-level linking and more minimal linking with employers, it is noteworthy that twelve of twenty-six occupational program chairs in community colleges (almost half) engage in a high level of linkage activity. From what we can tell, this activity was not encouraged structurally by the institution. Instead, some faculty members engaged in linking activity because they felt it contributed to their program and benefited students.

Our data also show that linking activity may be supported by institutional structures outside the college, namely the professional associations affiliated with some of the instructors' fields.

In sociology, professions are defined as exclusive fields that both create abstract knowledge and apply it to particular cases (Abbott 1988; Perlstadt 1998). Classic examples of traditional professions include medicine and law. Their "exclusivity" is a result of both high educational qualifications and endorsement requirements that are stipulated and controlled by a governing body, usually a professional association (Perlstadt 1998). Such regulation of membership leads to shared knowledge and activities, which could be considered a shared professional culture, and may encourage a sense of "calling" among members. Accordingly, faculty reports suggest that the characteristics of professions that are especially pertinent to faculty labor-market linkages include the rules and regulations governing membership and established professional networks.

In many occupations, professional associations are highly active, with numerous committees and regular meetings that provide opportunities for members of the profession to interact. The chair of the program for training physical therapy assistants at a community college in our sample explains: "As faculty, we're responsible for maintaining currency in our field. . . . You read the publications, you read the journals, go to professional development course work. We attend state and international meetings. . . . And so we keep up with those kinds of things." Professional associations foster both social and work-related interactions among members. The response of an architecture instructor who was asked how students get jobs hints at the importance of such organizations: "Well, you tie into the *network,* the architectural *community*" (our emphasis). Echoing this view, the chair of the occupational therapy (OT) program at one community college notes that employers prefer to deal with the department directly rather than contacting the college's career services office, because members of the profession know each other. She notes, "They would call the program. The OT community is not that large."

Although state licensing may require a certain degree of involvement with professional associations in some fields (this is the case of many health technician programs), we see the same kind of activities for paralegal and accounting programs, where active professional associations provide program legitimacy and employer contacts. Interestingly, the implications of college program association with a profession are important for instructors in both an individual sense and a structural sense. For an individual instructor, membership in a professional organization leads to personal identification with that profession; simultaneously, membership fosters networking activity with colleagues in the profession. The chair of the paralegal program at a private college offers a rich explanation of the relationship:

> I do a lot of networking. I'm very involved in the [county] bar association . . . I go to some [city] bar association committee meetings. I try and network with attorneys whenever I can. . . . Those are employers for paralegals. I'm on the publications board for the [county] bar association . . . I'm

on the Labor and Employment Committee for [the bar association]; I'm also on [several bar association committees] . . . so I try and meet as many lawyers as I can, consistent with my academic load.

Asked whether such activities are part of his job description, this program chair hesitates: "I don't know how to answer that question. . . . It's something I feel I need to do if I'm going to publicize the program." This instructor seems to be motivated by a personal sense of responsibility to the program in his charge. Moreover, he clearly identifies himself as a member of the legal profession. Asked about adapting the paralegal curriculum to suit the needs of the legal profession, he states, "I know how lawyers work. I've been one; I am one." This program chair's personal identification with the legal profession is bolstered by professional structures that encourage collegiality and enforce membership rules. Both personal and structural aspects foster and sustain the instructor's links to potential employers for his students.

An accounting instructor who is also chair of the business department at a community college offers a similar example. He reports being "intimately involved" with accounting firms in the city. "I keep an active communication with managers and partners because we're members of the American Accounting Association." Asked if this is part of his formal job description, he responds, "I consider that my responsibility, however, I don't think that that is part of my formal responsibilities in terms of my contract." Still, he also notes that "the goal is to prepare people to take the CPA exam," so participation in the formal professional association (which determines exam content) is reinforced beyond personal identification with the broader profession.

Instructors in fields that lack a distinct professional association also feel compelled to stay abreast of developments in their occupational areas. Yet in the absence of formal associations, shared culture, or professional requirements, these instructors' energies may yield fewer concrete linkages with employers than the efforts of instructors in fields with a distinct professional association. For example, instructors in CIS, business, and secretarial report reading trade publications to stay abreast of developments in their respective fields. Such endeavors almost certainly ensure that instructors have some appropriate information on labor markets to share with their students, but information is only one useful aspect of linkages. Reading industry publications would not normally translate into actual contact with potential employers.

Of course, it is possible that some of the observed findings might be explained by personality characteristics rather than the apparent professional association influences. Yet it is noteworthy that at our community colleges (where, as we have discussed, college structures do not promote linking), half (six of twelve) of the program chairs who engaged in high-level linking activity were from programs associated with a profession, whereas less than a quarter (two of nine) of those coded as engaging in minimal linking were from programs associated with a profession.

Given the small size of the faculty interview sample, it is difficult to detect distinct patterning of labor-market linking by program. Even when combined into groups of related departments, our sample often includes less than five respondents in most fields. Table 7.3 displays data from the four programs with the most respondents: business; computers; electronics engineering; and health. As table 7.3 shows, chairs of health programs—which are marked by relatively strict state-mandated rules for employment, including certification—show overwhelmingly high levels of linking activity (86 percent were coded as high linkers, and none were coded as minimal linkers). Instructors in business and computer fields, which are not governed by professional associations, show relatively low levels of linking (only about 30 percent coded high in linking, and over 40 percent coded minimal in each case). The role of professional

TABLE 7.3   Level of Linking Activity, by Program Type

Level of Linking	Business	Computer	Electronics or Engineering	Health Programs	Others
Minimal	44%	43%	33%	0	25%
	(4)	(3)	(2)		(3)
Moderate	22%	29%	17%	14%	25%
	(2)	(2)	(1)	(1)	(3)
High	33%	29%	50%	86%	50%
	(3)	(2)	(3)	(6)	(6)
Total N	9	7	6	7	12

Source: Authors' data.
Note: Actual N appears in parentheses.

associations in electronics and engineering programs is more difficult to assess. Some of the programs in our sample emphasize engineering, which is certainly governed by professional regulations, whereas others emphasize electronics, which is not.

STUDENTS' PERCEPTIONS OF CONTACTS

Most studies of college-employer contacts have centered on their usefulness in developing job-relevant curricula and in securing employment for students. This study examines whether college-employer contacts might influence students' motivation and persistence (re-enrollment) while they are still in school. Lawrence Steinberg (1996) emphasizes that motivation may be enhanced by students' perceptions of curriculum relevance, but he does not consider what institutional actions might stimulate those perceptions and he has nothing to say about employer contacts. Vincent Tinto (1993) suggests that students' persistence is influenced by extracurricular activities and living on campus (neither of which are common in nonresidential two-year colleges), but he does not examine labor-market contacts. Even some reforms that consider the motivating influence of career activities in course work do not look at the role of labor-market contacts in program effectiveness. For instance, career academies assume that by injecting career content into the curriculum, students' motivation is increased; but labor-market contacts are not a necessary feature of academies (Stern, Raby, and Dayton 1992). Stephen F. Hamilton and Klaus Hurrelman (1994) suggest that motivation may be increased by transparency of connections between school and the labor market, and they describe the ways that connections fostered by apprenticeships motivate German students.

Motivation and persistence are clearly problematic issues for these institutions: community colleges' five-year degree completion rates are 26 percent, and only 11 percent for African Americans (Bailey, Badway, and Gumport 2002). Degree completion rates in private two-year colleges tend to be better (Brint 2003). Unfortunately, systematic national analyses of these institutions are uncommon, and we have records of degree completion rates at just one of our occupational colleges: 65 percent overall, and 57 percent for African Americans. The present analyses examine how students vary in their perceptions of the extent to which their teachers or college can help them get good jobs, and whether positive perceptions may lead to improved effort in college and to fewer doubts about college persistence.

STUDENT SURVEY METHODS AND ANALYSIS

We administered a survey to 4,365 students in comparable core occupational classes in the fourteen colleges in our sample. Classes were selected to maximize the number of students in occupational programs (over 90 percent of survey respondents report an occupational major), as well as to include variation with respect to beginning and advanced students. All students in a sampled course were asked to complete the survey, and nearly all complied. Although the student body of these colleges is extremely diverse, by focusing only on students in comparable programs preparing for similar occupations, we were likely to be studying students with similar goals in the two types of colleges. Indeed, our analyses indicate that students in our sample in the two types of college were very similar in gender, age, and high school achievement. Despite higher tuition in the private colleges, these students were somewhat more likely than those in community colleges to have parents with low income and less than high school education (Person and Rosenbaum 2006). Finally, we did not find that students differed systematically across the two college types in terms of external obligations that might impede their college progress, such as jobs, children, and so forth. For example, although community college students report working slightly more hours per week, occupational college students were more likely to have dependent children.

The survey touched on a wide range of topics, many of which are reported in other papers (Deil-Amen and Rosenbaum 2003, 2004; Person, Rosenbaum, and Deil-Amen 2005; Person and Rosenbaum 2006), including students' family background, education and work history, current college experiences, and their goals and aspirations for the future. Regrettably, we did not anticipate the professional association finding reported above, so neither students or program heads were surveyed on this topic.

We asked students for their perceptions of the benefits of college and teacher contacts with employers. The present analyses focus on two key independent variables, which show the potential influence of students' responses to two items: (1) "My teachers' contacts could help me get a good job"; and (2) "My college's contacts could help me get a good job." Student responses were on a five-point Likert-type scale (1 = "strongly disagree" to 5 = "strongly agree"). Using OLS regression, we examined two outcomes: (1) changes in student effort as compared to effort in high school; and (2) the extent to which the student had considered dropping out of college. Since students in our sample are clustered within classrooms in schools, it is necessary to adjust for potential correlation in the data. Toward this end, we employed Huber-White statistical techniques (using the robust cluster commands available with Stata software) and report the resulting robust standard errors in table 7.4. The Huber-White adjustment does not affect the regression coefficients, but adjusts standard errors to account for potential non-independence of observations.

For our first analysis, we examined changes in student effort since high school. Students were asked, "Compared to when I was in high school, my effort now is . . ." with responses ranging from 1 ("much lower") to 5 ("much higher"). In table 7.4, the first two columns (models 1 and 2) report the influence of a host of variables on changes in student effort since high school. Following the lead of prior research on students' college completion, we control for several independent variables: gender, race, age (and age-squared to capture nonlinear effects), high school achievement, and parent education. Given the patterns identified in our qualitative analyses, we also control for college type (public community college or private occupational college).

Gender predicts the outcome, with females showing significantly greater increases in effort since high school than males (model 1). African American and Latino students also experience greater positive changes in effort than their white counterparts (the reference category). Age, too, is a significant predictor of improved effort, though the relationship is curvilinear (indicated by the positive direction of age and the negative direction of age-squared), with the positive effect dropping off between about thirty-eight and forty years in the two models, well beyond the age range of most of the

TABLE 7.4   **OLS Regression of Student Outcomes on Individual and Institutional Variables (Unstandardized Coefficients)**

	College Effort Versus High School Effort		Considered Dropout	
	b		b	
	(Robust SE)		(Robust SE)	
Variable	Model 1	Model 2	Model 3	Model 4
Male	−.080**	−.080**	−.016	−.016
	(.026)	(.026)	(.022)	(.022)
African American	.109**	.098**	.030	.035
	(.035)	(.035)	(.031)	(.031)
Latino	.089*	.095**	.017	.015
	(.036)	(.035)	(.030)	(.030)
Asian or Asian American	−.013	−.019	−.013	−.010
	(.047)	(.046)	(.035)	(.034)
Other (nonwhite)	.268	.250	.182	.191
	(.201)	(.191)	(.193)	(.188)
Age	.053***	.057***	.019**	.017*
	(.010)	(.010)	(.007)	(.007)
Age-squared	−.0007***	−.0007***	−.0003**	−.0003*
	(.0001)	(.0001)	(.0001)	(.0001)
High school grades	−.264***	−.260***	−.037*	−.039*
	(.019)	(.019)	(.016)	(.016)
Parent education	−.002	−.003	−.014	−.013
	(.010)	(.010)	(.008)	(.008)
Occupational college	.139***	.082**	−.128***	−.098***
	(.027)	(.028)	(.023)	(.024)
Teacher contacts		.053***		.035**
		(.016)		(.013)
College contacts		.081***		.037**
		(.017)		(.014)
Constant	4.042	3.547	1.343	1.606
R^2	.082	.100	.012	.021

Source: Authors' data.
Note: N = 4,150
*p ≤ .05; **p ≤ .01; ***p ≤ .001.

observations. High school grades are negatively associated with increased effort, which makes sense, given that students with high achievement in the past are likely to have exerted a great deal of effort during high school. Parent education shows no significant influence. Finally, private colleges are associated with significant increases in effort since high school. As model 2 shows, however, this private college influence is partly explained by students' perceptions of college and teacher contacts, both of which are strong and significant, and which reduce the coefficient on private school by over 40 percent of its prior magnitude (model 2 versus model 1).

Next, students were asked, "In the past year, have you ever considered dropping out of college?" Responses were given on a scale ranging from 1 ("not at all") to 4 ("very seriously"). Gender, race, and parent education show no significant influence on consideration of dropping out (model 3). Age again shows a significant curvilinear relationship with the outcome, with increased thoughts of dropping out peaking between the ages of twenty-eight and thirty-one in models 3 and 4. Better high school grades are associated with less consideration of dropping out. And finally, private colleges are associated with a strong and significant reduction in students' thoughts of dropping out. In model 4 we find that college and teacher contacts again have an impact in reducing thoughts of dropping out, and they again reduce the magnitude of the coefficient for private schools.

As these analyses indicate, students' perceptions of college and teacher contacts are potentially important influences, and are associated with improved student effort since high school and fewer thoughts of dropping out of college. What is more, the perceived benefits of contacts partly account for the positive influences of private colleges.

Of course, many students in two-year colleges aspire to transfer to four-year colleges, including many of the students in our sample. It is commonly assumed that labor-market contacts may be unimportant for the motivation of students with plans to obtain a bachelor's degree. However, from interviews with students (part of the larger study, but not treated systematically in the current analyses), it was our impression that many students with plans to obtain a bachelor's were concerned about the potential job payoffs of their two-year degrees, either because of an interest in getting a better job while pursuing the bachelor's or because of uncertainty about whether they will succeed in completing the bachelor's.

We repeated the above analyses, restricting the sample solely to students with plans for a bachelor's or higher degree. These analyses (not reported here) yielded virtually the same pattern of influences. Even for students with bachelor's plans, the perceived usefulness of labor-market contacts in securing a job is linked to positive changes in student effort and reduced doubts about college persistence.

We must caution that it is possible that students who seek out teachers or colleges with job contacts may differ in unmeasured ways from those who do not, or that their positive perceptions of contacts are endogenous to their positive outcomes. However, we have conducted extensive analyses and have been unable to detect prior differences (Person and Rosenbaum 2006). Moreover, the dependent variable for effort represents behavioral changes that have occurred over time, since the student's prior schooling experiences, supporting inferences that changes are related to college attributes. What we have found are some teachers and colleges with strong contacts with employers, which can help graduates get jobs. Our interviews and surveys indicate that students see these contacts, and they report that these contacts give them confidence that their efforts will pay off in better jobs. The present analyses indicate that students respond with greater efforts to attain these benefits. Unmeasured student differences may conceivably explain some portion of these effects; nevertheless we would be surprised if college–labor market contacts had no impact. Indeed, anyone hearing students' statements would have difficulty doubting the impact contacts have on some students. For example, one IT major at an occupational college in our sample stated:

> If you're ever feeling down, I mean, there have been times when I've been kinda depressed between my job, the economy's so horrible, we're spending all this money for school, and actually had an instructor say, "Come here," take us into a lab, go to a website and say, "What's your specialty?" type it in, and on the website it's showing the baseline salary and the requirements they need for it. He's like, "This is what you're working for." You know, that makes you feel good! [Laughs.] So, it's nice. . . . By the time that you graduate, you'll have a very full working knowledge of exactly what the industry's looking for, because they [the teachers] are coming from the industry . . . so they know exactly what, you know, the jobs they're looking for. That is so helpful. It really is.

CONCLUSIONS AND DIRECTIONS OF FUTURE RESEARCH

In this chapter we have examined the role of college-employer linkages at two different levels—department chairs' linkage activities and students' perceptions of the benefits of contacts. Department chairs report several institutional factors that influence whether and how they try to forge employer linkages, and we find that occupational colleges both tend to have more structural practices that encourage linkages than do community colleges and have more program chairs who initiate and maintain such linkages than do community colleges. Department chairs also report ways that professional associations facilitate such linkages, and we find that instructors in occupational fields with such associations are more likely to have such linkages.

We have also discovered that students' perceptions of the potential benefits of college and teacher linkages significantly predict students' increased efforts at school and reduce thoughts of dropping out. Students' perceptions of linkages account for part of the statistical influence of private colleges, even for students with plans to get a bachelor's degree. We lack information as to how many of these students ultimately complete a degree, but we suspect it may be related to the indicators we have analyzed. In any case, for these students, many of whom had poor high school achievement and little family exposure to college, if linkages improve their efforts in college and reduce their doubts about completion, those are real accomplishments.

In the present analyses we have ignored several processes. First, we have not looked at more centralized traditional contacts, for instance, through the career services office (for discussion of these services, see Deil-Amen and Rosenbaum 2004 and Person and Rosenbaum 2006). Finally, our students report their perceptions of likely benefits from contacts, but we have no data on students' actual use of contacts, much less whether or not using them turns out to be beneficial. These issues require further examination. More detailed student interviews, surveys with data on institutional practices, and longitudinal data on student outcomes would greatly advance our understanding of these questions.

These results suggest the potential for improving program effectiveness at community colleges. Our qualitative findings may be useful if programs seek to increase faculty-employer linkages. For instance, our interview data suggest that the benefits of adjunct faculty may be more mixed than is usually considered, and the isolation of career services encourages some faculty members to conclude that labor-market links are not something with which they should be concerned. In all of the community colleges, top administrators have emphasized occupational preparation, much like the top administrators in prior studies (Brint and Karabel 1989). However, our analyses have found many examples where the enthusiastic words of community college presidents are not accompanied by corresponding actions of their occupational program chairs. Colleges may need to make special efforts in fields where professional associations do not exist. Finally, in addition to the efforts colleges often make to improve student motivation and persistence through instructional techniques and special services, our findings suggest that college and faculty contacts with employers may also be powerful influences.

Some of our findings may also be applicable to high school settings, the locus of the vast majority of school-to-work reforms. In particular, some of the "best practices" that support college-employer links identified in our occupational colleges could also be implemented in high schools. The integration of career development—which, incidentally, was identified as the most successful aspect of STWOA (Hershey et al. 1999)—with regular classroom activities could include not only curricular innovations but also invitations to school counseling staff and area employers to come into the classroom. Of course, this presupposes that counseling staff be given better preparation to address career-services issues than some studies have suggested they normally receive (Rosenbaum 2001). Bringing employers into high schools could also be systematized if schools developed advisory committees like those observed in our occupational colleges, where members' input was taken seriously by the schools. As in the college setting, such committees could advise school administrators about the skill needs of local economies, even as they could make students aware of jobs in their community and potentially provide quality job placements.

One important hurdle to implementing school-to-work activities in high schools is suggested by our findings on college history and mission: contemporary high schools' "college-for-all" mission. Since the 1980s high schools have adopted a mission of college preparation for all students (coinciding with the rise of the community college), with the unfortunate result that many school-to-work activities have either been abandoned or are stigmatized (Rosenbaum 2001; Hershey et al. 1999). The "college-for-all" mission of American high schools has done much to expand college enrollment, yet it appears to have done little to change student behaviors that would actually prepare students for college-level work; consequently, the number of actual graduations from college has not increased commensurately (Rosenbaum, Deil-Amen, and Person 2006).

Our quantitative findings suggest a way to overcome the hurdle posed by the college-for-all mission of American high schools: clarification of the steps from school to work at the postsecondary as well as the college level. When high school advising includes clear messages about the payoffs of effort in school, student engagement may improve here just as effort was shown to improve in our college student survey. Some high school programs, including Tech Prep and career academies, have already provided models for clarifying school-to-work pathways. Our study suggests that even these programs could benefit from added attention to the role of school structures in supporting such clear pathways to work.

If our results are replicated by subsequent research, it would suggest several implications for policy. Our findings suggest, first, that school structures and professional associations can influence faculty members' labor-market contacts. Policymakers often assume that labor markets operate on their own, but our findings suggest that distinct procedures can be utilized to assist graduates in obtaining jobs appropriate to their training. Second, our findings suggest that school-employer contacts can clarify the steps in the school-to-work transition and increase students' perceptions of and confidence in payoffs, which in turn may improve students' effort in school and reduce their thoughts of dropping out. Indeed, the statement of these findings tempts one to say that they are just common sense.

Thus it is remarkable that these commonsense observations are rarely noted. With degree attainment rates in many colleges substantially below 50 percent, reform organizations such as the Education Trust have put degree completion on the national agenda. Similarly, the persistent problem of lack of engagement among high school students has been noted by researchers and advocacy organizations. Reformers' calls for improved guidance, curricula, and financial aid may have benefits if these measures are implemented, but it is not certain that such reforms will be sufficient if students have doubts about the ultimate payoff of their education. Reformers do not appear to have considered the problems of perceived incentives or the potential of employer contacts to have a positive effect on students' efforts and attainment. This study suggests that students' awareness of faculty and school contacts with the labor market may lead them to experience positive outcomes that will improve their educational success. Even in the presence of high schools' and colleges' focus on academic rather than vocational preparation, linkages to work and students' perception of incentives should be considered as potentially important influences on student outcomes.

REFERENCES

Abbott, Andrew. 1988. *The System of Professions: An Essay on the Division of Expert Labor*. Chicago: University of Chicago Press.

Adelman, Clifford. 2003. "Principal Indicators of Student Academic Histories in Postsecondary Education, 1970–2000." Washington: U.S. Department of Education, Institute of Education Sciences.

Apling, Richard N. 1993. "Proprietary Schools and Their Students." *Journal of Higher Education* 64: 379–416.

Bailey, Thomas. 2003. "Community Colleges in the 21st Century: Challenges and Opportunities." CCRC Brief. New York: Columbia University, Community College Research Center, available at Community College Research Center website: http://www.tc.columbia.edu/centers/iee/CCRC/PAPERS/Briefs/brief15.pdf (accessed July 24, 2006).

Bailey, Thomas, N. Badway, and P. J. Gumport. 2002. "For-Profit Higher Education and Community Colleges." Publication of the National Center for Postsecondary Improvement. Available at the NCPI website: http://www.stanford.edu/group/ncpi/documents/pdfs/forprofitandcc.pdf (accessed July 24, 2002).

Bailey, Thomas, Katherine Hughes, and David Moore. 2004. *Working Knowledge: Work Based Learning and Educational Reform*. New York: Rutledge Falmer.

Bowles, Samuel, and Herbert Gintis. 1976. *Schooling in Capitalist America*. London: Routledge.

Brewer, D. J., and M. J. Gray. 1999. "Do Faculty Connect School to Work? Evidence from Community Colleges." *Educational Evaluation and Policy Analysis* 21(4): 405–16.

Brint, Stephen. 2003. "Few Remaining Dreams: Community Colleges Since 1985." *Annals of the American Academy of Political and Social Sciences* 586(1): 16–37.

Brint, Stephen, and Jerome Karabel. 1989. *The Diverted Dream: Community College and the Promise of Educational Opportunity in America.* New York: Oxford University Press.

Cappelli, P., D. Shapiro, and N. Shumanis. 1998. "Employer Participation in School to Work Programs." *Annals of the American Academy of Political Science* 559(1): 109–24.

Cross, Patricia K., and Elizabeth F. Fideler. 1989. "Community College Missions: Priorities in the Mid-1980's." *Journal of Higher Education* 60(2): 209–16.

Deil-Amen, Regina, and J. Rosenbaum. 2003. "The Social Prerequisites of Success: Can College Structure Reduce the Need for Social Know-How?" *Community College at a Crossroads: Emerging Issues. Annals of the American Academy of Political and Social Science* 586(March): 120–43.

———. 2004. "Charter Building at Low Status Colleges." *Sociology of Education* 77(3): 245–65.

Dougherty, K. 1994. *The Contradictory College: The Conflicting Origins, Impacts, and Futures of the Community College.* Albany: State University of New York Press.

Gamoran, Adam. 1998. "The Impact of Academic Preparation on Labor Market Outcomes for Youth Who Do Not Attend College: A Research Review." In *The Quality of Vocational Education: Background Papers from the Vocational Education,* edited by Adam Gamoran. Washington: U.S. Department of Education.

Goldrick-Rab, Sara. 2006. "Following Their Every Move: An Investigation of Social-Class Differences in College Pathways." *Sociology of Education* 79(1): 61–79.

Griffin, Larry J., Arne L. Kalleberg, and Karl L. Alexander. 1981. "Determinants of Early Labor Market Entry and Attainment: A Study of Labor Market Segmentation." *Sociology of Education* 54(3): 206–21.

Grubb, W. Norton. 1996. *Working in the Middle: Strengthening Education and Training for the Mid-Skilled Labor Force.* San Francisco: Jossey-Bass.

Hamilton, Stephen F. 1990. *Apprenticeship for Adulthood: Preparing Youth for the Future.* New York: Free Press.

———. 1994. "Employment Prospects as Motivation for School Achievement: Links and Gaps Between School and Work in Seven Countries." In *Adolescence in Context: The Interplay of Family, School, Peers, and Work in Adjustment,* edited by F. K. Silbereisen and E. Todt. New York: Springer.

Hamilton, Stephen F., and Klaus Hurrelman. 1994. "The School-to-Career Transition in Germany and the United States." *Teachers College Record* 96(2): 329–44.

Hershey, Alan M., Marsha K. Silverberg, Joshua Haimson, Paula Hudis, and Russell Jackson. 1999. *Expanding Options for Students: Report to Congress on the National Evaluation of School-to-Work Implementation.* Princeton, N.J.: Mathematica Policy Research, Inc.

Holzer, Harry. 1996. *What Employers Want.* New York: Russell Sage Foundation.

Hughes, Katherine. 1998. "Employer Recruitment Is Not the Problem." IEE Working Paper No. 5. New York: Columbia University, Teachers College, Institute on Education and the Economy (June).

Illinois Board of Higher Education 2004. 2004 Data Books. Available at Illinois Board of Higher Education website: http://www.ibhe.state.il.us/Data%20Bank/DataBook/2004/Table%20VI-13.pdf.

Laanan, F. S. 1995. "Community Colleges as Facilitators of School-to-Work." ERIC Clearinghouse for Community Colleges. ERIC Identifier ED383360. Available on-line at ERIC Digests website: http://www.ericdigests.org/1996-1/work.htm (accessed November 28, 2005).

Lortie, D. C. 1975. *Schoolteacher: A Sociological Study.* Chicago: University of Chicago Press.

Meyer, J. W. 1977. "The Effects of Education as an Institution." *American Journal of Sociology* 83(1): 55–77.

Mickelson, Roslyn, and Matthew R. Walker. 1997. "Will Reforming School to Work Education Resolve Employer Dissatisfaction with Entry-Level Workers?" Paper presented at the annual meeting of the American Sociological Association, Toronto (August 8–12).

Miller, Shazia R. 1998. "Shortcut: High School Grades as a Signal of Human Capital." *Educational Evaluation and Policy Analysis* 20(4): 299–311.

Moss, Philip, and Chris Tilly 2001. *Stories Employers Tell.* New York: Russell Sage Foundation.

Murnane, Richard J., John B. Willett, and Frank Levy. 1995. "The Growing Importance of Cognitive Skills in Wage Determination." *Review of Economics and Statistics* 77(2): 251–66.

Neckerman, Kathryn, and Joleen Kirschenman 1991. "Hiring Strategies, Racial Bias, and Inner City Workers." *Social Problems* 38(4): 801–15.

Perin, Dolores. 2001. "Academic-Occupational Integration as a Reform Strategy for the Community College: Classroom Perspectives." *Teachers College Record* 103(2): 303–35.

Perlstadt, H. 1998. "Accreditation of Sociology Programs: A Bridge to a Broader Audience." *Canadian Journal of Sociology* 23(1): 195–207.

Person, Ann E., and James E. Rosenbaum. 2006. "Educational Outcomes of Labor-Market Linking and Job Placement for Students at Public and Private 2-year Colleges." *Economics of Education Review* 25(4): 412–29.

Person, Ann E., James E. Rosenbaum, and Regina Deil-Amen. 2005. "The Structure of the Life Course in Modern Society: Colleges, Careers, and the Institutional Structuring of the Transition to Adulthood." In *Advances in Life Course Research: Individualized? Standardized? Differentiated?*, edited by R. Macmillan. Greenwich, Conn.: Elsevier.

———. 2006. "Student Information Problems in Different College Structures." *Teachers College Record* 108(3): 374–96.

Rosenbaum, James E. 2001. *Beyond College for All: Career Paths for the Forgotten Half*. New York: Russell Sage Foundation.

Rosenbaum, James E., Regina Deil-Amen, and Ann E. Person. 2006. *After Admission: From College Access to College Success*. New York: Russell Sage Foundation.

Rosenbaum, James E., T. Kariya, R. Settersten, and T. Maier. 1990. "Network and Market Theories of the Transition from High School to Work: Their Application to Industrialized Societies." *Annual Review of Sociology* 16(00): 263–99.

Steinberg, Lawrence. 1996. *Beyond the Classroom*. New York: Simon & Schuster.

Stern, David, Neal Finkelstein, J. Stone, J. Latting, and C. Dornsife. 1995. *School to Work: Research on Programs in the United States*. Washington, D.C., and London: Falmer.

Stern, David, Marilyn Raby, and Charles Dayton. 1992. *Career Academies: Partnerships for Reconstructing American High Schools*. San Francisco: Jossey-Bass.

Stinchcombe, Arthur. 1964. *Rebellion in a High School*. Chicago: Quadrangle Books.

Tinto, V. 1993. *Leaving College*. Chicago: University of Chicago Press.

Useem, E. 1986. *Low-Tech Education in a High-Tech World: Corporations and Classrooms in the New Information Society*. New York: Free Press.

Wilms, Wellford W. 1974. *Public and Proprietary Vocational Training: A Study of Effectiveness*. Berkeley: University of California, Berkeley, Center for Research and Development in Higher Education.

Chapter 8

Smoothing the Transition from School to Work: Building Job Skills for a Local Labor Market

Nan L. Maxwell

MOVING FROM SCHOOL into the labor market is often a difficult transition for youths. Even though many high school students work for pay while still in school, they often spend the years after leaving school moving from one job to another. The long-term effect of this churning is indeterminate. Some research argues that early unstable labor-market experience per se either is unrelated to labor-market outcomes as an adult (Gardecki and Neumark 1998) or is beneficial (Becker and Hills 1980, 1983), if appropriate skill matches ensue (Osterman 1980). Other research points to harmful long-term results from this sort of floundering, finding that youth unemployment or job churning reduces subsequent wages (D'Amico and Maxwell 1990; Lynch 1989; Ellwood 1982; Meyer and Wise 1982), and that employment stability increases adult wages (Neumark 2002). In any event, programs and policies that produce a quicker matching of youths' skills with those required by employers can produce efficiency gains, as demonstrated by the success of programs in European high schools that build students' job skills to connect with local employers' needs (Vickers 1995). This finding was the impetus for the 1994 School-to-Work Opportunities Act (STWOA) of 1994. If school-to-work programs and institutions could build labor-market skills that are in demand in the local labor market, high school students entering the labor market could presumably make a smoother transition into the workplace.

Implicit in the STWOA and many school-to-work programs and institutions is the assumption that building academic and workplace skills used in the local labor market will increase employment and wages for youths whose formal education ends in high school. The STWOA states as its purpose "to improve the knowledge and skills of youth" (section 3a, number 9). To this end, states were directed to use funds to encourage local partnerships of education, government, and employers and to "[develop] a system for labor market analysis and strategic planning for local targeting of industry sectors or broad occupational clusters that can provide students with placements in high-skill workplaces" (section 205, number 15).

It stands to reason that if skills are needed in the labor market, more-skilled youths will have an increased probability of employment and higher wages than lesser-skilled youths as they move from school into the workplace. This general advice may provide little useful guidance to school-to-work practitioners, however, if skills demanded by employers are heterogeneous and successful school-to-work transitions depend on acquiring particular skills that are in demand by firms. When skill demands are specific to local labor markets, school-to-work programs and institutions may be more successful when they provide students with skills in demand in the market they will enter. Thus, successful school-to-work efforts may require identifying skills in high demand in the jobs available to youths. These skills may or may not be those used once the youth gains labor market experience or those used as the foundation upon which to build skills for career progression. They are, however, the skills that boost employment and wages early in one's career and, as a result, allow youths to gain a foothold in the labor market. For youths whose education ends in high school, that foothold is in relatively low-skilled entry-level positions, operationalized in this study as jobs available to individuals with no more than a high school education and no more than one year of work experience.

We suggest that the role a skill plays in a youth's transition into the workplace depends on its relative scarcity in the local labor market. If individuals competing for low-skilled, entry-level jobs possess a skill that many job seekers have, and thus firms have no difficulty in filling in existing positions, possessing the skill would neither facilitate employment nor increase wages. In fact, firms may find they can attract individuals at a lower wage if an excess supply of workers with the needed skill exists. But if firms have difficulty finding enough workers with the required skill, wages would increase in positions using the skill and youths possessing the skill would find employment easily. Thus, being equipped with skills for which there is high relative demand in a labor market will increase wages and the probability of employment for youths as they enter the labor market.

If possession of skills that are relatively scarce boosts youth employment and wages, school-to-work programs and institutions would likely be more successful if they could determine which skills are scarce in the labor market and build programs that provide youths with those skills. So far, however, the link between skills and successful school-to-work transitions has not been established empirically, in part because existing data sets generally do not include detailed information on skills demanded and supplied in the same labor market. The Bay Area Longitudinal Surveys (BALS) do contain such information,[1] and thus they allow us to assess how acquisition of certain skills might increase youth employment and bring higher wages to labor-market entrants with no more than a high school education. More specifically, the BALS afford the opportunity to use a local labor market to examine the relationship among skills, employment, and wages for youths who do not continue education past high school, and instead enter low-skilled entry-level jobs. Furthermore, by identifying variation in skill demands in different industries, the BALS also provide information on how important it might be for school-to-work programs and institutions to target skill building geared to specific industries. If differences in the types of skills used in different industries are slight, then programs may serve students best by simply building a general set of skills. Analyzing the BALS therefore provides some information on the potential value of school-to-work programs trying to build skills in demand in the labor markets that students will enter. More generally, the analysis adds to the literature on the skills needed in the jobs available to youths who truncate their education in high school. Of course, since this analysis focuses on a single labor market, it has more of the flavor of a case study, and so should be generalized to other labor markets quite cautiously.

DATA

The BALS research project was designed to study the skills required by employers in low-skilled entry-level jobs in three counties in the San Francisco Bay Area, and the skills that individuals supply in the same labor market. The jobs covered in the BALS data—requiring no more than a high school education and no more than one year of experience—are ideal for studying the role of skills in youth transitions from high school to the labor market.[2] The BALS collected information about fifty-three different skills that local employers require in low-skilled entry-level jobs, and also contain information about the skills supplied by youths (aged eighteen to twenty-five) and other low-skilled individuals in the same local labor market. Comparing employers' demands and individuals' skills permits us to construct measures of relative demand for specific skills in the local labor market, and then to study whether individuals possessing skills with a high relative demand face an easier transition from school to work.

The BALS data come from 405 "employer surveys" administered on-site to firms that were hiring for a specific low-skilled entry-level position,[3] and 766 "household surveys" administered face-to-face to randomly selected individuals in one zip code in the BALS counties, the 94544 zip code in Hayward, California, in Alameda County.[4] Employer surveys were administered from June 1998 to October 2002, and household surveys from March 2002 to January 2003.[5] Because of its central location, employers in the three-county BALS area rely heavily on Hayward for workers. Twenty-five percent of all workers in the BALS counties reside in Alameda County and 63.9 percent of the workers living in Alameda county work in the BALS local labor market.[6]

At the core of the BALS data collection on both employers and individuals is a series of questions about skills. For each employer in the survey, the BALS selected one low-skilled entry-level position that the employer was hiring for,[7] and asked a battery of questions about the characteristics of the job (such as average wage at entry) and another battery of questions about whether workers in the position were required to perform certain skill-based tasks. Fifty-three skills associated with the tasks were grouped into six areas: reading and writing in English (eight specific skills); math (nine specific skills); communication (eight specific skills); problem solving (eleven specific skills); use of equipment (seven specific skills); and use of computer software (ten specific skills). Each specific skill (and each grouping) that was included in the data collection was generated from discussions with employers in focus groups that revealed their use in low-skilled entry-level positions in the Bay Area. These skills were translated into survey language for the household survey through a series of informal focus groups with individuals from the population under study.

The skills surveyed in the BALS correspond closely to skills identified by the National Center for Research on Evaluation, Standards, and Student Testing as those needed in low-skilled jobs (O'Neil and Allred 1996). This research found that academic skills, higher-order thinking skills (problem solving), and interpersonal and teamwork (communication) skills frequently serve as a foundation on which to build vocational skills used in the workplace.[8] The BALS skills also correspond closely to those uncovered by Richard J. Murnane and Frank Levy (1996) using case studies of management practices at Diamond-Star Motors, Northwestern Mutual, and Honda. This research showed that jobs for low-wage workers require the general skills of timeliness, hard work, and a positive attitude, as well as the "new basic skills" of reading, math, problem solving, communication skills, and computer ability. Surveys of employers of low-wage workers in Atlanta, Boston, Detroit, and Los Angeles confirmed the use of these new basic skills in entry-level jobs (Holzer 1996). Over half required daily reading of at least a paragraph, about half required the use of computers and arithmetic, and nearly half required writing. Motivation, personality, and the ability to get along with others were also highly valued by entry-level employers, particularly retail firms (Moss and Tilly 2000).

We apply the distinction between academic and new basic skills drawn by Harold F. O'Neil and Keith Allred (1996) to the definitions of new basic skills in Murnane and Levy (1996) to classify the BALS skills. "Academic skills" include reading and writing (in English) and math skills. "New basic skills" include communication, problem solving, and ability to use computer software. "Workplace skills" reflect what might be considered more traditional blue-collar (production) and pink-collar (office) skills used in low-skilled positions. In our scheme, "workplace skills" is a residual category and comprises skills in the BALS that do not fall into skill categories designated by O'Neil and Allred (1996) or Murnane and Levy (1996).

A factor analysis of each of the six BALS skill groupings in the employer survey identified fifteen skill sets used in low-skilled entry-level jobs. Factor analysis assumes the existence of a system of underlying constructs in our measures of skills and uses the correlations between the measured skills to uncover the underlying patterns in the skill groupings. The factors were then interpreted as identifying the main types of skills required in low-skilled entry-level jobs in the BALS local labor market by identifying the most highly correlated skills loading onto each factor.[9]

"Academic skill sets" include two skill sets pertaining to reading and writing in English (simple and complex) and three math skill sets (algebra, applied math, and measurement). "New basic skill sets" include two communication skill sets (communication with customers and with coworkers), three problem-solving skill sets (prioritizing, evaluating, and leading), and three computer software skill sets (productivity enhancers, multimedia, and financial). "Workplace skill sets" include two equipment skill sets (office and production).[10]

We constructed supply-side measures of an individual's skill set by mapping the responses to skill questions in the employer survey to those in the household survey, a relatively straightforward process since skill tasks in the employer survey mapped one-to-one to those for households, except in the area of English. Once individuals' skill sets were mapped to skill sets from the employer survey, we linked the measure of each skill in the household survey to the comparable skill in the skill set developed from data from the employer survey. Our supply-side measure of an individual's skill set was created by summing the number of skills that an individual possessed within a given skill set.[11]

Comparing the parallel constructs for the skills employers need in low-skilled entry-level jobs with those possessed by workers filling those jobs lets us approximate the relative demand for each skill. Specifically, we compare the percentage of jobs (j) using a specific skill with the percentage of individuals with only a high school education or short-term work experience who state that they possess the skill to approximate the level of relative demand for each skill (sk).[12] We use t-tests to compare the percentage of jobs requiring a particular skill (d_j^{sk}) to the percentage of the low-skilled individuals (and medium-skilled individuals, for comparison) with the skill (s_i^{sk}). Statistically significant differences ($p = .05$) between d_j^{sk} and s_i^{sk} suggest that a high relative demand ($d_j^{sk} > s_i^{sk}$ or $hd^{sk} = 1$ and 0 otherwise) or low relative demand ($d_j^{sk} < s_i^{sk}$ or $ld^{sk} = 1$ and 0 otherwise) exists *for a particular skill*. Skills with no significant difference in the proportions may be closer to in balance in the local labor market ($d_j^{sk} = s_i^{sk}$ or $e^{sk} = 1$ and 0 otherwise).

Clearly, few individuals enter the market with only one skill and few jobs require only one skill. Instead, jobs require a set of skills and individuals bring an array of skills to the labor market. We therefore capture the relative demand for each skill set and classify each, on the basis of relative demand for the skills in the set, into nonoverlapping categories: high relative demand, low relative demand, and mixed (more balanced) demand, as follows, where n is the number of individual skills in a particular skill set:

(1a)   High D = 1 if $\dfrac{\displaystyle\sum_1^n hd^{sk}}{\displaystyle\sum_1^n ld^{sk} + \sum_1^n e^{sk}} \geq 1$, High D = 0 otherwise,

(1b)   Low D = 1 if $\dfrac{\displaystyle\sum_1^n ld^{sk}}{\displaystyle\sum_1^n hd^{sk} + \sum_1^n e^{sk}} \geq 1$, Low D = 0 otherwise,

(1c)   Mixed D = 1 if High D = 0 and Low D = 0,

       Mixed D = 0 otherwise.

The BALS also contain other information that is essential for this research. The employer survey provides detailed information about jobs, including wages, and the household survey provides demographic and labor-force information. Because 125 of the individuals in the household survey are youths aged eighteen to twenty-five, the BALS allow us to examine employment during the school-to-work transition years as it relates to skills, for those entering the labor market after high school.

EMPIRICAL METHODS

We examine the relationship between skills demanded and supplied, and employment and wages during the school-to-work transition period as youths who are not planning to continue their education leave high school and enter low-skilled entry-level jobs. We proceed in three steps. First, we describe the types of skills used in these jobs. Next, we study industry differences in skill requirements, using the percentage of low-skilled entry-level jobs requiring each skill and comparing the average factor scores (that is, measure of skill set intensity) in local industries that provide the majority of low-skilled entry-level employment opportunities.

Finally, we estimate the relationship between the skills, the relative demand for skills, and employment and wages. First, we use information from the BALS household survey to examine how the skills that youths possess affect their employment probabilities, using a logit estimation that models employment as determined by the skill sets held by out-of-school youths aged eighteen to twenty-five with only a high school level of education:[13]

$$(2) \qquad \text{Emp}_y = \kappa + \text{AC}_y \alpha_{ac} + \text{NB}_y \alpha_{nb} + \text{WP}_y \alpha_{wp} + X_y \gamma + \epsilon_y,$$

where:

Emp = a binary variable measuring the employment of a youth (y), with 1 indicating an employed youth
AC = a vector of academic skill sets
NB = a vector of new basic skill sets
WP = a vector of workplace skill sets
X = a vector of control variables, including demographics and work experience

In this analysis, skill sets (AC, NB, WP) reflect skills possessed by youths. If skills raise the probability of youth employment, coefficients will be positive and significant ($\alpha > 0$). If possessing skill sets with a high relative demand does more to facilitate employment, those coefficients on skill sets with a higher relative demand will tend to be the ones that are positive and significant.

We use information from the BALS employer survey to examine the potential for skills to increase wages in jobs available to youths as they move into the labor market by estimating the determinants of a variety of measures of wages on the job:

$$(3) \qquad W_j = \kappa_0 + AC_j\beta_{ac} + NB_j\beta_{nb} + WP_j\beta_{wp} + C_j\psi + \omega LM + \epsilon_j$$

where

> W = a measure of the wage in the low-skilled, entry-level job (j);
> C = a vector of control variables describing the firm and its entry-level position, including size, industrial sector, and unionization in the low-skilled entry-level position; and
> LM = a measure of labor market activity (the county's unemployment rate) during the month of surveying.

In this analysis, skill sets (AC, NB, WP) reflect skills required in low-skilled entry-level positions. We expect wages to be higher in jobs using skill sets with a high relative demand as firms bid up wages in their competition for needed skills. This process would be indicated by larger positive estimated coefficients on skill sets for which relative demand is high ($\beta > 0$).

Higher wages could be manifested in the current wage or in future earnings that increase the present value of earnings but not the entry-level wage (or both). To capture each of these possibilities, we estimate equation 3 with three different wage-related measures: the log of the hourly wage (logW), which measures wages at the point of entry into the low-skilled position; whether or not an opportunity exists to advance from the entry-level position; and whether or not the wage in the entry-level job can ever reach fifteen dollars an hour. We use OLS to estimate the equation for the hourly wage, and logit analysis for the other dependent variables.

RESULTS

What kinds of jobs are available to youths that enter the labor market after high school? We answer this question using both national and local databases, and all tell a similar story (table 8.1). Jobs for youths are concentrated in six occupational categories: food preparation and serving; building and grounds cleaning and maintenance; sales; office and administrative support; production; and

TABLE 8.1 Percentage of Workers and Jobs in Typical Low-Skilled Occupations

(1)	All Jobs, U.S. National Data, 2001	Low-Skilled, Entry-Level		
		U.S. Population With a High School Education or Less	O*NET Job Zone 1 Jobs	BALS Employer Survey
	(2)	(3)	(4)	(5)
Occupational category				
Food preparation and serving	2.1	8.7	6.7	8.2
Building and grounds cleaning and maintenance	1.2	6.5	2.2	8.4
Sales and related	2.7	11.9	4.4	12.1
Office and administrative support	7.3	14.8	14.8	33.1
Production	14.5	13.9	34.1	12.1
Transportation and materials moving	6.8	10.2	13.3	10.6
Percentage of total employment opportunities	34.6	66.0	75.5	84.5
N	—	74,741,962	135	405

Source: Data on the distribution of occupations in 2001 (column 2) is taken from Occupational Employment Statistics (OES) data (survey of establishments) (U.S. Department of Labor, Bureau of Labor Statistics 2002) and is based on the number of occupations, not employment, within a firm, consistent with O*NET and BALS data. Data on U.S. population with a high school education or less (column 3) are from the U.S. Census 2000 Public Use Microdata Sample (PUMS), the 1 percent sample (U.S. Bureau of Census 2003). O*NET job zone 1 information (column 4) is taken from the Occupational Information Network (O*NET) database (www.onetcenter.org).

Notes: Numbers represent the percentage of workers (column 3) or jobs (columns 2, 4, and 5) in each occupational category. Occupations were included in the table if they had more than 5 percent employment in at least two of the three databases of low-skilled, entry-level workers or jobs.

transportation and materials moving. At least two-thirds of all jobs available to youths fall into these occupational categories, although they make up only about one-third of all jobs in the United States.

The BALS data suggest that jobs available to youths require a relatively large number and variety of academic and new basic skills (table 8.2), consistent with the description of similar jobs in other labor markets (Holzer 1996; Murnane and Levy 1996; O'Neil and Allred 1996).[14] Virtually all the BALS jobs require youths to have academic skills. About three-quarters require the worker to read written instructions, safety warnings, labels, invoices and work orders, logs, or journals; to write simple sentences; to fill out forms or logs; and to read manuals, computer printouts, and contracts or agreements. About two-thirds require reading forms, memos, and letters, and over 70 percent require math (addition and subtraction).

Virtually all jobs also require communication and problem-solving skills—two of the three new basic skills. Over 80 percent require interacting with others to accomplish a task, acting appropriately at work, or being perceptive of others. Over 60 percent require dealing with customers, problem-solving collaboratively, identifying work-related problems, prioritizing tasks, or gathering information. Computer software skills, also considered a new basic skill, are used in relatively few low-skilled entry-level BALS jobs. Although 16 to 27 percent of the positions require the use of productivity-enhancing software, less than 5 percent require more specialized computer software. With the exception of using telephone systems, no one particular workplace skill is required in half of the jobs.

Because the factor score computed from our factor analysis quantifies, in relative terms, the importance of each skill set in each job, we use it to measure how much a particular job requires the skills contained in a particular skill set. The factor score is computed as a linear combination of the original skill variables (1 = job requires a skill, 0 = not) times a weight derived from the factor loading. Factor scores are standardized with a mean of zero, and about two-thirds of the values lying between +1.0 and −1.0 (with a range of approximately +3.0 to −3.0). A relatively high and positive factor score for a particular skill set means that the job requires many of the skills in the skill set. A relatively large negative score indicates that the job requires skills that are not part of the skill set.

TABLE 8.2   **Skills Used in Low-Skilled Entry-Level Jobs in the BALS Local Labor Market**

Type of Skill	Skill Task	Percentage of Jobs Using
NB[a]	Interact with coworkers to accomplish a task	90.8
NB	Choose words and manner of expression appropriate at work	85.3
NB	Be perceptive of verbal and nonverbal cues from others	81.5
AC[b]	Read written instructions, safety warnings, labels (product or shipping), invoices/work orders, logs, and journals	78.3
AC	Write simple sentences, short notes, and simple memos	77.6
AC	Fill out forms; record data or time into log or chart	74.1
AC	Read manuals, computer printouts, contracts, and agreements	73.8
NB	Identify work-related problems	70.3
NB	Prioritize tasks	68.8
AC	Read forms, memos, and letters	67.6
NB	Deal with customers	64.6
WP	Use telephone systems	63.6
NB	Problem-solve collaboratively or in teams	63.3
NB	Gather information	62.6
NB	Identify potential solutions to problems	52.9
WP[c]	Make and receive business phone calls	49.4
AC	Sort and categorize information	48.1
NB	Explain products and services	47.6
NB	Handle complaints	47.4
WP	Use copiers	44.9
WP	Use measurement instruments such as ruler, scale	44.9
NB	Identify barriers to solutions	44.1
WP	Use equipment (calculator, cash register, business machine)	43.9
WP	Use fax machines	42.1
AC	Perform simple measurements (lengths, volumes)	41.6
WP	Use answering machines	37.9
NB	Make decisions independently	35.2
NB	Use Windows- or DOS-based computers	34.2
AC	Solve simple equations	34.2
AC	Estimate or round off numbers	32.7
NB	Implement solutions	31.7

(continued)

TABLE 8.2   *Continued*

Type of Skill	Skill Task	Percentage of Jobs Using
AC	Make change	30.7
NB	Sell a product or service to a customer	28.4
NB	Use word-processing programs	27.4
AC	Use ratios, fractions, decimals, or percents	27.4
NB	Evaluate results	26.9
AC	Write letters using correct structure and sentence style	24.2
AC	Proofread	23.4
NB	Use e-mail	23.2
AC	Organize information into a brief written report	22.9
NB	Use spreadsheet programs	20.4
NB	Use database software	17.2
AC	Compute discounts, markups, or selling price	17.2
NB	Use Internet browsers	16.0
WP	Use production machinery	15.2
NB	Problem-solve in a leadership role	14.5
AC	Interpret data from graph, tables, or charts	13.5
WP	Use heavy equipment	12.0
NB	Use financial-inventory software	3.0
NB	Use graphics software	2.5
NB	Use webpage design and authoring	1.7
NB	Use desktop-publishing programs	1.5
NB	Use multimedia authoring and editing software	1.0
	N	402

Source: Data are from the BALS employer survey.
Notes: The table includes only the fifty-three skills used in the analysis in this paper. Seven additional skills were excluded from our analysis because they were not discriminating in the factor analysis used to build skill sets: (1) perform addition and subtraction (72.3 percent); (2) give spoken instructions in the workplace (56.4 percent); (3) take telephone messages accurately (54.6 percent); (4) perform multiplication and division (49.6 percent); (5) read telephone book (47.2 percent); (6) read maps (35.2 percent); and (7) use Macintosh or Apple computers (4.5 percent).
[a]New basic skills
[b]Academic skills
[c]Workplace skills

One way in which we use the factor scores is to assess whether or not there are important differences across industries in the skills used in low-skilled entry-level positions (table 8.3).[15] If skill sets are used equally in each industry, the average factor score for jobs in each industry will be close to the aggregate mean of zero. Phrased somewhat differently, if an industry has a factor score close to zero, it suggests an average level of use of skills in the skill set. In this analysis we focus on the industrial sectors where the majority of low-skilled entry-level positions are to be found.

In the BALS local labor market, three-quarters of the jobs available to youths fall into three industrial sectors—services, manufacturing, and retail trade—with each sector requiring different types of skills (table 8.3). The service sector requires the highest level of skills. Medical- and education-service establishments have positive and relatively high factor scores in eleven of the fifteen skill sets, indicating that this sector uses simple and complex English, algebra and measurement, communication with customers and coworkers, prioritizing tasks and leadership, productivity-enhancing and multimedia software, and office equipment skills. Service-sector jobs other than business, medical, and education have positive and relatively high factor scores in ten of the fifteen skill sets: simple and complex English, applied math and measurement, communication with customers and coworkers, prioritizing tasks, evaluating and leadership, and office equipment use. The only skill sets not used in this sector are computer software and production equipment. The business-service sector has positive and relatively high factor scores in ten of the fifteen skill sets: simple and complex English, communication with customers and coworkers, evaluation and prioritizing problem-solving skills, productivity-enhancing and multimedia and financial software skills, and office equipment use.[16] The retail-trade sector has few positive and relatively high factor scores; exceptions are communication with customers and coworkers and applied math skills. The manufacturing sector has a positive and relatively high factor score in production equipment skills.[17]

The demand for skills is one half of the story; the supply of skills is the other. When youths leave high school, they compete for entry-level jobs with other youths. In addition, though, individuals hired into entry-level jobs in the BALS labor market frequently have some college or more than one year of work experience

(Maxwell 2006). Consequently, youths leaving school also compete with low-skilled adults. Hence, the potential supply of skills among the workforce for this labor market extends to all individuals who might apply for low-skilled entry-level positions, and not just youths leaving high school. We therefore extend our measure of skills supplied to include individuals with either a high school education or no more than one year of work experience. We might call the latter midlevel competitors for these jobs. We test for significant differences between the skills held by adults (aged twenty-six or more) and youths (eighteen to twenty-five), between employed and nonemployed youths, and between aggregate demand and supply.[18]

We see from table 8.4 that few significant differences exist between the percentage of low-skilled adults twenty-six and over and of youths eighteen to twenty-five reporting an ability to execute entry-level tasks "very well," suggesting that youths might be competitive with adults when applying for many low-skilled entry-level jobs. There are some exceptions, however. On the one hand, youths report less ability to compute discounts and markups and to read manuals, computer printouts, and contracts and agreements, skills required in nearly three-quarters of the jobs. On the other hand, youths claim a better ability to use Internet browsers, webpage design and authoring software, and desktop publishing programs. But few low-skilled entry-level positions require these skills (table 8.2).

Striking differences appear between the reported levels of skills of employed and nonemployed youths (table 8.4), with the nonemployed reporting lower levels of skills in 65 percent of the measured skills. The largest differences fall in areas of high demand: academic and communication skills. Nonemployed youths report lower levels of skills in 90 percent of the reading and writing English skills, 90 percent of the math skills, and 88.8 percent of the communication skills. Although fewer differences exist in other skills, nonemployed youths report lower levels of skills in 62.5 percent of the equipment-use skills, 30 percent of the computer software skills, and 28 percent of the problem-solving skills.

Table 8.5 shows that the high number of skills reported held by entry-level and midlevel workers produces a low relative demand for most skills required in surveyed jobs in the BALS local labor

TABLE 8.3 Industrial Differences in Skill Requirements in the BALS Local Labor Market, by Industry

| | Services | | | | | |
Skills	Business Services	Education and Medical	Other Services	Manufacturing	Retail Trade	Other Industries
Academic skill sets						
English reading and writing						
Simple English	0.121	0.286	0.025	−0.400	−0.138	0.118
Complex English	0.249	0.137	0.117	−0.408	−0.236	0.160
Math						
Algebra	−0.062	0.066	−0.113	−0.118	−0.081	0.216
Applied math	−0.182	−0.094	0.114	−0.440	0.421	−0.097
Measurement	−0.244	0.267	0.107	0.018	−0.179	0.077
New basic skill sets						
Communication						
Customers	0.135	0.058	0.141	−0.867	0.402	−0.112
Coworkers	0.134	0.158	0.176	−0.201	0.038	−0.199

Problem solving						
Prioritize	0.224	0.276	0.096	-0.350	-0.140	-0.003
Evaluate	0.167	-0.031	0.201	-0.077	-0.210	0.028
Exert leadership	-0.288	0.066	0.225	-0.246	-0.015	0.107
Software						
Productivity enhancers	0.220	0.369	-0.163	-0.337	-0.276	0.251
Multimedia	0.458	0.138	-0.149	-0.136	-0.086	-0.052
Financial	0.063	-0.083	-0.003	0.007	-0.021	0.026
Workplace skill sets						
Equipment						
Use office equipment	0.286	0.382	0.073	-0.608	-0.281	0.197
Use production equipment	-0.057	-0.281	-0.203	0.768	-0.311	0.194
Percentage of employment	12.5	12.0	16.5	12.7	22.4	23.9
N	50	48	66	51	90	96

Source: Data are from the BALS employer surveys.
Notes: Numbers represent the average factor score in each industry. The boxed text highlights factor scores exceeding .05.

TABLE 8.4 Local Labor Market Supply of Skills in Low-Skilled Entry-Level Jobs

Skills	Age Stratification		Youth Employment Stratification	
	Aged 26 and Older	Aged 18 to 25	Employed Youths	Not Employed Youths
Frequently used skills[a]				
Interact with coworkers to accomplish a task	72.9	65.6	69.8	61.3
Choose words and manner of expression appropriate at work	61.5	61.6	73.0	50.0**
Be perceptive of verbal and nonverbal cues from others	63.4	64.8	73.0	56.5**
Read written instructions, safety warnings, product or shipping labels, invoices and work orders, logs and journals	77.0	75.2	81.0	69.4**
Write simple sentences, short notes, and simple memos	52.1	45.6	55.6	35.5**
Fill out forms; record data into a log or chart	60.3	59.2	65.1	53.2**
Read manuals, computer printouts, contracts, and agreements	59.6	48.8**	47.6	50.0
Identify work-related problems	66.9	68.0	77.8	58.1**
Prioritize tasks	66.5	65.6	69.8	61.3
Read forms, memos, and letters	77.3	74.4	79.4	69.4**
Deal with customers	64.5	66.4	76.2	56.5**
Use telephone systems	56.3	64.8	68.3	61.3
Problem-solve collaboratively or in teams	82.6	77.6	81.0	74.2
Gather information	68.9	66.4	63.5	69.4
Identify potential solutions to problems	61.8	60.0	61.9	58.1
Less-used academic skills				
English reading and writing				
Write letters using correct structure and sentence style	50.3	42.4	52.4	32.3**
Proofread	51.4	48.8	57.1	40.3**
Organize information into a brief written report	41.9	41.6	47.6	35.5**

264

Math				
Use ratios, fractions, decimals, or percents	45.9	36.8	41.3	32.3
Estimate or round off numbers	65.1	66.4	73.0	59.7**
Solve simple equations	50.5	57.3	68.3	45.9**
Make change	87.8	86.4	93.7	79.0**
Compute discounts, markups, or selling price	61.8	46.4**	55.6	37.1**
Interpret data from graph, tables, or charts	46.9	50.4	57.1	43.5**
Perform simple measurements (lengths, volumes)	74.5	72.8	77.8	67.7**
Use measurement instruments (ruler, scale)	75.3	71.2	81.0	61.3**
Use equipment such as a calculator, cash register, business machine	73.7	76.8	87.3	66.1**
Less-used new basic skills				
Communication				
Make and receive business phone calls	65.2	69.6	77.8	61.3**
Explain products and services	59.5	60.0	66.7	53.2**
Handle complaints	55.7	53.6	61.9	45.2**
Sell a product or service to a customer	48.4	54.4	61.9	46.8**
Problem solving				
Sort and categorize information	64.9	65.6	69.8	61.3
Identify barriers to solutions	57.2	59.2	63.5	54.8
Implement solutions	64.9	67.2	71.4	62.9
Evaluate results	63.1	60.8	66.7	54.8**
Make decisions independently	80.3	84.0	84.1	83.9
Problem-solve in a leadership role	69.1	66.4	73.0	59.8**
Computer software				
Use word-processing programs	37.8	46.4	46.0	46.8
Use spreadsheet programs	27.8	31.2	31.7	30.6
Use database software	23.0	25.6	23.8	27.4

(continued)

TABLE 8.4 *Continued*

Skills	Age Stratification		Youth Employment Stratification	
	Aged 26 and Older	Aged 18 to 25	Employed Youths	Not Employed Youths
Use e-mail	50.5	58.4	66.7	50.0**
Use Internet browsers	44.4	61.6**	66.7	56.5**
Use webpage design and authoring	10.8	18.4**	19.0	17.7
Use multimedia authoring and editing software	8.0	13.6	15.9	11.3
Use graphics software	11.7	16.8	15.9	17.7
Use desktop-publishing programs	12.4	24.0**	30.2	17.7**
Use financial-inventory software	11.2	13.6	15.9	11.3
Less-used workplace skills				
Equipment				
Use answering machines	70.0	76.8	82.5	71.0**
Use copiers	69.8	74.4	87.3	61.3**
Use fax machines	58.3	53.6	58.7	48.4**
Use Windows-, or DOS-based computers	40.8	49.6	60.3	38.7**
Use production machinery	28.5	22.4	23.8	21.0
Use heavy equipment	22.3	22.4	27.0	17.7**
N	547	125	63	62

Source: Data are from the BALS household surveys.

[a]Frequently used skills are those used in 50 percent or more of the low-skilled entry-level jobs, as seen in table 8.2. The survey question generally reads, "How well can you . . ."; the figures represent the percentage who say they can execute the skill "very well." Item-specific nonresponse sometimes lowered the N to 545 for the twenty-six and older subpopulation.

**Significant ($p \leq .05$) difference between youths and individuals twenty-six and older or employed and not employed youths.

market, including complex English, algebra, applied math, measurement, leadership, production equipment, and multimedia and financial software. Conversely, simple English, ability to interact with coworkers, and prioritizing tasks are in relatively high demand. Four skill sets (customer service, evaluation, productivity software, and office equipment) have some skills with high relative demand, some with low relative demand, and some skills in relative balance.

Finally, we expect possession of skills that are in relatively high demand to help youths to move more easily into the labor market. Our results suggest that out-of-school youths with relatively higher levels of academic skills have an increased probability of employment during the school-to-work transition period (table 8.6). Youths reporting higher levels of simple English and applied-math skills have a significantly higher probability of employment than youths with lower levels of these skills, a finding somewhat inconsistent with our framework, since applied math has a low relative demand in the BALS labor market.[19] The most obvious explanation for this association, which is not testable with this data set, is that employers use these somewhat observable and widely used skills as a way of discerning generally more-skilled youths.

We also expect employed youths with skills in relatively higher demand to earn higher wages. Analysis of wages in the BALS labor market suggests this might be the case (table 8.6). Possession of simple English, productivity enhancers, and office-equipment skill sets, all of which have a high or mixed demand, increase starting wages. In addition, jobs requiring tasks in the priority and productivity-enhancing skill sets—which are in high or mixed demand—have a higher probability of generating wages that reach fifteen dollars an hour (presumably if the worker demonstrates possession of the required skills). Simple English and task prioritization, two of the three skill sets with a high relative demand, increase the probability of a promotional opportunity above entry level, while use of financial software, which is in relatively low demand, lowers this probability. Thus, the BALS presents limited evidence that youths possessing skills in high relative demand in the local labor market earn (or will earn) higher wages.

One reason why skills in short supply might not significantly increase wages is that they are not observable prior to employment. If firms cannot determine whether an applicant has the desired

TABLE 8.5   **Percentage of Employers Reporting Demand for Various Skills in the BALS Local Labor Market**

	Demand (Percentage of Jobs Needing)	Supply (Percentage of Entry and Midlevel Workers with)
Academic skills		
English reading and writing skills		
Simple		
Read written instructions	78.3	66.2**
Read forms, memos and letters	67.6	66.7
Read manuals, computer printouts, contracts and agreements	73.8	46.8**
Write simple sentences, short notes, and simple memos	77.6	35.2**
Fill out forms; record data or time into log or chart	74.1	44.8**
Complex		
Write letters using correct structure and sentence style	24.2	34.1**
Proofread	23.4	38.7**
Organize information into a brief written report	22.9	28.2
Math		
Algebra		
Use ratios, fractions, decimals, or percents	27.4	32.8
Estimate or round off numbers	32.7	51.1**
Solve simple equations	34.2	41.7**
Interpret data from graph, tables, or charts	13.5	33.6**
Applied		
Make change	30.7	81.7**
Compute discounts, markups, or selling price	17.2	47.3**
Use equipment (calculator, cash register, business machine)	43.9	64.4**
Measurement		
Perform simple measurements (lengths, volumes)	41.6	67.2**
Use measurement instruments (ruler, scale)	44.9	67.9**

(continued)

TABLE 8.5 *Continued*

	Demand (Percentage of Jobs Needing)	Supply (Percentage of Entry and Midlevel Workers with)
New basic skills		
Communication		
With customers		
Make and receive business phone calls	49.4	53.6
Deal with customers	64.6	55.4**
Explain products and services	47.6	49.5
Handle complaints	47.4	45.7
Sell a product or service to a customer	28.4	42.1**
With coworkers		
Choose appropriate work words and manner of expression	85.3	50.3**
Be perceptive of verbal and nonverbal cues from others	81.5	52.8**
Interact with coworkers to accomplish a task	90.8	60.5**
Problem solving		
Prioritize		
Prioritize tasks	68.8	61.1**
Gather information	62.6	60.1
Sort and categorize information	48.1	56.0**
Identify work-related problems	70.3	58.3**
Evaluate		
Identify potential solutions to problems	52.9	52.2
Identify barriers to solutions	44.1	41.1
Evaluate results	26.9	53.7**
Leadership		
Problem-solve collaboratively or in teams	63.3	76.8**
Make decisions independently	35.2	75.3**
Problem-solve in a leadership role	14.5	61.1**
Implement solutions	31.7	57.3**
Computer software		
Productivity enhancers		
Use word-processing programs	27.4	26.0
Use spreadsheet programs	20.4	18.3

(*continued*)

TABLE 8.5 *Continued*

	Demand (Percentage of Jobs Needing)	Supply (Percentage of Entry and Midlevel Workers with)
Use database software	17.2	15.0
Use e-mail	23.2	36.1**
Use Internet browsers	16.0	34.9**
Multimedia		
Use webpage editing and authoring software	1.7	9.4**
Use multimedia authoring and editing software	1.0	7.1**
Use graphics software	2.5	8.1**
Use desktop-publishing programs	1.5	10.4**
Financial		
Use financial-inventory software	3.0	6.9**
Workplace skills		
Office		
Use telephone systems (multiple lines)	63.6	51.1**
Use answering machines	37.9	63.9**
Use copiers	44.9	62.1**
Use fax machines	42.1	44.5
Use Windows- or DOS-based computers	34.2	28.8
Production		
Use production machinery	15.2	24.2**
Use heavy equipment	12.0	22.4**
N	402	393

Source: BALS employer (Demand) and household (Supply) surveys.

Numbers represent the percentage of employers stating that the skill is needed in the low-skilled entry-level job (Demand) or the percentage of low-skilled and mid-skilled individuals saying they can execute the skill very well. Low-skilled individuals have no more than a high school education and no more than one year of work experience and mid-skilled individuals have no more than a high school education *or* no more than one year of work experience.

**Significant (p = .05) differences

skill, it might be reticent to offer increased wages in order to get it. Although we cannot use the BALS data to test this proposition directly, we note that skills in relatively high demand that bring increased wages are relatively easy for employers to determine prior to hiring (simple English, use of productivity-enhancing software, and office-equipment use), whereas those that do not bring increased wages are relatively difficult to observe (leadership, evaluation, and working with co-workers).

The relationship with wages of two skill sets—use of production equipment and customer service—is seemingly inconsistent with the notion that possessing skills with a high relative demand in the local labor market increases youths' wages. This suggests that other non-skill factors may come into play in determining wages in low-skilled entry-level jobs. For example, industries using production equipment carry a higher risk of nonfatal injury (U.S. Department of Labor, Bureau of Labor Statistics 2002a). If using production equipment increases risk of injury on the job, the positive relationship of this skill to wages (current or future) may reflect higher wages compensating for risk.

SUMMARY AND DISCUSSION

Using a unique data source, the Bay Area Longitudinal Surveys (BALS), we study the jobs that youths enter after leaving high school in a particular labor market. These jobs, in which stated required education and requirements for work experience are low, are concentrated in six occupational categories: food preparation and serving; building and grounds cleaning and maintenance; sales; office and administrative support; production; and transportation and materials moving. Low education and work requirements could be interpreted to mean that skill requirements in jobs available to youths leaving high school are modest and lie in a fairly narrow range, implying further that it should be relatively easy for school-to-work programs to identify and provide the skills necessary for a successful school-to-work transition—or perhaps even that it is not so important to provide workplace skills.

The data suggest, however, that this inference may be incorrect. Virtually all jobs in the BALS labor market require the acade-

TABLE 8.6 Jobs for Youths in the BALS Local Labor Market, by Skill

	Level of Demand	Youth Employment (Log Odds)	Log Wage (Coefficients)	Wage Reaches $15 per Hour (Log Odds)	Promotion Possible (Log Odds)
Academic skill sets					
Simple English	High	3.360**	.042***	1.225	1.419**
Complex English	Low	1.167	.020	.814	1.261
Applied math	Low	9.373**	−.028*	.905	.925
Algebra	Low	0.570	.006	.957	1.057
Measurement	Low	0.143*	.004	1.062	.992
New basic skill sets					
Customers	Mixed	1.693	−.042**	.879	.844
Coworkers	High	0.343	.016	1.129	1.202
Prioritize	High	0.168*	.016	1.422**	1.476**
Evaluate	Mixed	5.383	−.001	1.189	.795
Leadership	Low	0.761	−.004	.800	.791
Productivity enhancers	Mixed	2.253	.052***	1.501**	1.091
Multimedia software	Low	0.272*	.003	1.102	1.366
Financial software	Low	0.397	−.004	.960	.777**

mic skills of reading, writing, and math, and the new basic skills of communication and problem solving, suggesting that schools need to build a broad foundation of academic and new basic skills to help youths transition into the labor market from high school. This conclusion draws support from other research showing the wide-spread use of these skills in relatively low-skilled jobs in other labor markets. For example, Nan L. Maxwell (2006) uses data from the national Occupational Information Network (O*NET) database to examine 109 different knowledge areas, skills, and abilities needed in jobs requiring little education and no work experience, and finds that mathematics, reading comprehension, writing, oral and writ-ten comprehension and expression, and deductive reasoning are each used in at least 50 percent of low-skilled jobs (see also Holzer 1996 for similar evidence). This research suggests a need for schools to teach academic (reading, writing, and math), communi-cation, and problem-solving skills if they are to provide adequate labor-market preparation even to students who plan to enter the labor market right after leaving high school.

The need to build academic skills in high school is undisputed; there is less consensus around the need for schools to teach com-munication and problem-solving skills. In California—the state that sets graduation requirements for the youths in the BALS study—stu-dents are required to take courses that build academic skills[20] and to pass a high school exit exam consisting of English language arts and mathematics. Communication and problem-solving skills are addressed less explicitly in the state's graduation requirements, if they are targeted at all. Arguably, problem-solving skills might be addressed via the research and technology and mathematical rea-soning requirements in the exit exam, and communication skills might be covered in the California Content Standards for English-Language Arts.[21] The contrast between the explicit focus on aca-demic skills and the less-than-explicit focus on communication and problem-solving skills suggests that California educational policies might not be grounded in building skills that youths entering the labor force after high school will need in the workplace.

The evidence from this study also suggests that schools might want to tackle the challenge of creating programs that provide stu-dents with needed labor-market skills. In 65 percent of the skills used in low-skilled entry-level jobs covered in the data, nonemployed youths in the BALS labor-market report lower levels than employed youths. Perhaps most problematic is the fact that non-employed youths report lower levels of about 90 percent of the academic and communication skills—skills used extensively in low-skilled entry-level jobs in the BALS labor market. Skills may also underlie youths' wages once employed, as some skill sets with a high relative demand in the BALS labor market raise wages in entry-level positions or increase the likelihood of future wage increases.

Data limitations precluded the exploration by this study of the need for schools to build the "softer" skills such as dependability, work ethic, honesty, motivation, time management, and adaptability. Other studies (for example, Rosenbaum 2001) argue that employers seek these skills as actively as they seek academic ones. Because such evidence suggests that the decision to hire or retain youths in a job depends on their soft skills, discussions between policymakers, educators, and businesspeople frequently center on the need for schools to teach the soft skills to high school students. Of course, for schools to help students learn the skills in high demand in the labor market—be they academic, labor-market oriented, or soft—they need to be able to identify these skills, and, when necessary, tailor these skills to the workplace. For example, in the BALS labor market, more low-skill entry-level jobs use targeted workplace-specific reading and writing skills (for example, writing simple sentences, filling out forms or logs, and reading written instructions, manuals, computer printouts, contracts and agreements, forms, memos, and letters), than use general reading and writing skills (for example, proofreading; using correct spelling, grammar, and style in writing; and writing complex or creative materials or reports). If students learn primarily general reading and writing skills divorced from their workplace applications (for example, using literary response and analysis, one of California's content standards for English Language Arts), they might not be able to transfer their skills to reading and writing more technical workplace material.

One way school-to-work and career and technical education programs try to enhance the transfer of skills learned in school to the labor market is by teaching skills in a workplace context. But findings in this chapter suggest that this, too, poses a danger, if the work-related context becomes too narrow. In particular, the evidence points to differing skill requirements by industry. This in turn suggests that difficulties might arise if there are industrial shifts in the local labor market, or if youths move away from the local labor market, for which skills were tailored. School-to-work programs that use the workplace to motivate students to learn skills that can be transferred to a wide variety of workplace settings may be more successful than programs that provide students with more narrowly focused skills.

Regardless of how this challenge is to be met, this discussion of balance between depth and breadth in building skills for the workplace assumes that the schools can identify the skills needed in the labor market in the first place. This study was able to identify the skills needed in jobs available to youths in one particular labor market only by virtue of having access to a unique source of data. Schools and programs generally do not have access to BALS-type data. Even if they did, they might not have the time or capacity to effectively analyze them. Instead, schools and programs are likely to rely more on ad hoc and instructor-dependent linkages to labor markets as sources of labor-market information, as exemplified by the labor-market linkages in community colleges described by Ann E. Person and James E. Rosenbaum in chapter 7 of this volume. Other examples of labor-market linkages used by school-to-work and career-education programs include advisory boards, internship placements, mentorship programs, job fairs, and job shadowing. These informal contacts with employers may provide valuable insights as to how skills are applied in some workplaces, but they seem unlikely to reliably uncover broad patterns and trends in needed workplace skills.

One way to obtain BALS-like labor-market information and to link it explicitly to school-to-work and career and technical education programs is to partner local researchers with school districts in data collection. Indeed, the BALS was launched from such a partnership, albeit in the welfare-to-work arena. As welfare-to-work programs geared up for their increased caseload with changes in welfare legislation, agencies began to recognize the need to learn more about skills needed for jobs available to low-skilled workers, as well as to make linkages with employers for job placements. In the area covered by the BALS, many welfare-to-work program staff had little experience with or knowledge of the workplace, having never worked in the private sector.[22] As a result, initial program development was often grounded in nationally distributed welfare-to-work curricula, and job search and placement often centered on reading newspaper ads. Program heads realized that clients were not being served as well as they might be and partnered with a local university to gather information about skill needs in the local labor market and to provide program staff with linkages to employers.

The result was the BALS data collection program, which provided a means, by conducting the survey, to contact employers about their entry-level jobs, and gave an opportunity to researchers to gather labor-market information while forging linkages between employers and programs. Surveyors located employers that were hiring in low-skilled entry-level jobs through an initial screening process. If firms were hiring entry-level workers, a time was set for the surveyor and program staff to visit the work site to collect information from employers about the knowledge and skills needed in entry-level jobs. Researchers conducted the survey at the work site, and when the interview was complete the program staff asked specific questions about how the firm might make links with the program. In many cases a two-way pipeline was built with information flowing from firms to the program, and job placements flowing from the program to the firm. Research data were formally fed back to the program in the form of a report and informally in terms of relationship building between firms and program staff.

Programs benefited from the partnership in ways that might also be useful for schools wanting to build stronger links between their programs and the labor market. Staff who had never worked in the private sector gained insight into the culture of business and in many cases altered their curriculum to include examples or activities suggested by employers during their postsurvey discussions. A few employers became involved in the programs as speakers or internship hosts (paying for welfare-to-work participants). Job placements were numerous.

Two major difficulties occurred in this process, both of which are also reported in chapter 7 of this volume with regard to community colleges. These areas of difficulty need to be anticipated by school-to-work practitioners seeking to strengthen labor-market linkages. The first problem was a time constraint. Limited program funding meant staff were overstretched and frequently were doing more than one job. Taking a couple of hours out of a day to meet with employers was often difficult. Second, high turnover rates among program staff meant that the labor-market linkages were short-lived. Contacts built with employers were broken because not one of the program staff passed on information about labor-market linkages to his or her successor.

These difficulties suggest that efforts to more systematically link schools to employers and the local labor market must be ongoing and may require a shift in schools' institutional orientations, particularly at the district level, because economies of scale may be present in coordinating partnerships. District offices may be able to coordinate and sustain research efforts, ensure that knowledge gained from the research is fed back into the curriculum, and offer incentives for teachers to engage in professional development that increases their knowledge about the workplace. Such a philosophical reorientation might ensure that resources can be directed toward the proactive gathering and use of labor-market information to build programs that help students make a smooth transition into the workplace.

The author wishes to thank Marigee Bacolod, Ronald D'Amico, Barry Hirsch, and David Neumark and an anonymous referee for comments, Aude Sanchez for heroic efforts at data collection, and Yu Liu and Atanas Maximov for research assistance. This research was partially funded by the U.S. Department of Housing and Urban Development, the Rockefeller Foundation, the San Francisco Department of Human Services, and the W. E. Upjohn Institute for Employment Research. Although numerous individuals made this study possible, the author assumes full responsibility for any errors.

NOTES

1. For more information about BALS see (www.hire.csueastbay.edu/Hire/bals.htm).
2. Over half do not require a high school degree and nearly 60 percent require no work experience (Maxwell 2006).
3. Surveys for employers were fielded in San Francisco, Alameda, and San Joaquin counties; the response rate was 21.4 percent. A descrip-

tion of the survey methods, including a comparison of firms in the BALS data set with those in the three-county area, is available at www.hire.csueastbay.edu/hire/discpap/abstracts/D04-06-04.pdf. This report shows that jobs used in this study represent a smaller proportion of construction jobs than in the three-county area, consistent with the BALS restriction that jobs be available through an open application process.

4. There was a 37.3 percent response rate. For a description of the community see www.hire.csueastbay.edu/hire/discpap/abstracts/F04-01-01.pdf or www.hire.csueastbay.edu/hire/discpap/abstracts/D03-11-08.pdf. A description of the survey methods—including a comparison of the household survey group's demographics and other characteristics (such as whether they were renters, their level of education) to census data—is available at www.hire.csueastbay.edu/hire/discpap/abstracts/D04-06-04.pdf.

5. Only partial overlap exists between the fielding of the two surveys: 19.3 percent of the employer surveys were undertaken in the field at the same time as the household surveys; 66.2 percent were fielded a year prior to the household surveys; and 14.6 percent were fielded about 3.5 years prior to the household surveys.

6. Numbers are the author's computations based on the U.S. Census 2000 Public Use Microdata Five-Percent Sample (PUMS) (U.S. Bureau of the Census 2003).

7. Firms that were hiring in one low-skilled, entry-level position were asked questions about that position. If they were hiring in more than one position, a position for surveying was selected using the criterion of maximizing the variability of jobs in the sample. The report available at www.hire.csueastbay.edu/hire/discpap/abstracts/D04-06-04.pdf shows the representativeness of the sample.

8. A fourth category identified as important that is not skill based (and is not studied in this chapter) is personal characteristics and attitudes.

9. Because we had no a priori expectation of the number of underlying skill constructs in any of the original skill groups, we allowed the factor analysis to determine the number of factors that accounted for the observed covariation in each skill construct. We used the criterion of .5 as a significant loading to identify skills in each set. Although a typical rule of thumb for identifying patterns in the factors is a loading greater than .3, we chose the more stringent criterion so as to bundle only the most closely related skills. We specified an oblique factor solution, which produces correlated extracted factors, since it seemed reasonable to assume correlation between the skills in each grouping. We identified only factors with eigenvalues exceeding one.

A description of the methods used to build the fifteen skill sets is available at www.hire.csueastbay.edu/hire/discpap/abstracts/D04-06-07.pdf. The factor analysis used to construct the skill sets shows that each of the constructs explains between 61.3 (communication) and 70.3 percent (equipment) of the variation in the entry-level skill requirements.

10. The specific skills needed in each skill set are mapped in table 8.5.

11. If individuals stated that they could execute a task using the skill very well, they were said to possess the skill.

12. Although information on job vacancies and applicant flows from firms is typically used to measure excess demand and supply in a labor market, it might be of limited use in this study, even if it were available. Our interest is in the relative demand for specific skills, which may or may not overlap with the number of workers available for hiring.

13. We analyze employment for out-of-school youths because we are interested in the ability of school-to-work programs to facilitate employment and increase wages for individuals who are not continuing their formal education.

14. These findings also are confirmed using national ONET data (Maxwell 2006).

15. Tables available from the author provide detailed information on the variables available in the BALS, including the individual skill measures used in the factor analysis.

16. Of note is the fact that the business-service sector does not have relatively high and positive factor scores in math or leadership, perhaps because jobs are entry-level (Maxwell 2006).

17. Jobs outside the three industries hiring the majority of low-skilled, entry-level workers require skill sets of simple and complex English, algebra, measurement, leadership, productivity-enhancing software, and office and production equipment.

18. Individuals could misstate their level of skills. If misstatement varied systematically—if, say, unemployed respondents overstated their skills by a greater degree than did employed respondents—our results would be biased. Our analysis assumes that the type and magnitude of misstatements are similar across groups and skill categories.

19. Other skills with a high relative demand have an insignificant (p = .05) association with employment. Youths without work experience are less likely to be employed in the school-to-work transition period, and being white is negatively correlated with employment in the BALS sample, perhaps an artifact of the restriction to out-of-school youths with no more than a high school education. Whites

not continuing their education are a more negatively selected group than are Latinos and blacks.

20. California requires year-long courses in English (three courses), math (two), science (two), social studies (three), visual or performing arts or foreign language (one), and physical education (two). See www.cde.ca.gov/ci/gs/hs/hsgrmin.asp for more specifics on course requirements.

21. See www.cde.ca.gov/ci/gs/hs/ for information about the high school exit exam in California, and www.cde.ca.gov/be/st/ss/ for information about content standards. The content standards set explicit standards in written and oral English language conventions, listening and speaking strategies, and speaking applications.

22. This discussion is based on welfare-to-work departments in two different counties and three different community-based organizations, all of whom partnered in portions of the BALS data collection.

REFERENCES

Becker, Brian, and Stephen Hills. 1980. "Teenage Unemployment: Some Evidence of the Long-Run Effects on Wages." *Journal of Human Resources* 15(Summer): 295–312.

———. 1983. "The Long Run Effects of Job Changes and Unemployment among Male Teenagers." *Journal of Human Resources* 17(Spring): 197–211.

D'Amico, Ronald, and Nan L. Maxwell. 1990. "The Impact of Post-School Joblessness on Male Black-White Wage Differentials." *Industrial Relations* 33(2): 184–205.

Ellwood, David. 1982. "Teenage Unemployment: Permanent Scars or Temporary Blemishes?" In *The Youth Labor Market Problem: Its Nature, Causes, and Consequences,* edited by Richard B. Freeman and David A. Wise. Chicago: University of Chicago Press.

Gardecki, Rosella, and David Neumark. 1998. "Order from Chaos? The Effects of Early Labor Market Experiences on Adult Labor Market Outcomes." *Industrial and Labor Relations Review* 51(2): 299–321.

Holzer, Harry J. 1996. *What Employers Want: Job Prospects for Less-Educated Workers.* New York: Russell Sage Foundation.

Lynch, Lisa M. 1989. "The Youth Labor Market in the Eighties: Determinants of Reemployment Probabilities for Young Men and Women." *Review of Economics and Statistics* 71 (February): 37–45.

Maxwell, Nan L. 2006. *The Working Life: The Labor Market for Workers in Low-Skilled Jobs.* Kalamazoo, Mich.: Upjohn Institute for Employment Research.

Meyer, Robert H., and David. A. Wise. 1982. "High School Preparation and Early Labor Force Experience." In *The Youth Labor Market Problem,* edited by Richard B. Freeman and David A. Wise. Chicago: University of Chicago Press.

Moss, Philip, and Chris Tilly. 2000. *Stories Employers Tell: Race, Skill, and Hiring in America.* New York: Russell Sage Foundation.

Murnane, Richard J., and Frank Levy. 1996. *Teaching the New Basic Skills.* New York: Free Press.

Neumark, David. 2002. "Youth Labor Markets in the U.S.: Shopping Around vs. Staying Put." *Review of Economics and Statistics* 84(3): 462–82.

O'Neil, Harold F., and Keith Allred. 1996. "Review of Workforce Readiness—Theoretical Frameworks." *Work and Occupations* 23(3): 252–76.

Osterman, Paul. 1980. *Getting Started.* Cambridge, Mass.: MIT Press.

Rosenbaum, James E. 2001. *Beyond College for All: Career Paths for the Forgotten Half.* New York: Russell Sage Foundation.

U.S. Bureau of the Census. 2003. *Census 2000 Public Use Microdata Sample (PUMS), Census of the Population and Housing,* available at http://www.census.gov/population/www/cen2000/pums.html.

U.S. Department of Labor, Bureau of Labor Statistics. 2002a. *Industry Injury and Illness Data, 2002* (SWR01), available at http://www.bls. gov/iif/oshsum.htm (last accessed June 26, 2006).

———. 2002b. "Occupational Employment and Wages, 2001." Press release, November 6. Available at ftp://ftp.bls.gov/pub/news.release/ history/ocwage.11062002.news.

Vickers, Margaret. 1995. "Employer Participation in School-to-Work Programs: The Changing Situation in Europe." In *Learning to Work: Employer Involvement in School-to-Work Transition Programs,* edited by Thomas R. Bailey. Washington, D.C.: Brookings Institution.

Index

Boldface numbers refer to figures and tables.